Black Voices in the Halls of Power

In *Black Voices in the Halls of Power*, authors Jennifer R. Garcia, Christopher T. Stout, and Katherine Tate explore how US lawmakers use racial rhetoric to elevate the voice of Black communities, influence policy, and shape voter trust. Through a combination of data-driven research and accessible storytelling, the book uncovers the strategic ways politicians speak about race, revealing how rhetoric impacts policymaking and representation and offering fresh insights into race and power in American politics. The book explores how politicians craft messages to appeal to diverse audiences and use political communication to advance legislative priorities. It also examines how legislators' engagement in racial outreach affects voter attitudes. Given the increasingly important role of race on the national political stage in the US, the book provides a critical yet engaging examination of race, rhetoric, and representation in Congress.

Jennifer R. Garcia is an Associate Professor in the Politics Department at Oberlin College. Her work has been published in several journals, including Political Communications, Legislative Studies Quarterly, and Political Research Quarterly.

Christopher T. Stout is a Professor of Political Science at the University of California, San Diego. He researches how US voters respond to race-based political messages. His previous work has earned multiple awards, including Best Book in US Electoral Politics (APSA) and the W.E.B. DuBois Best Book Award (NCOBPS), along with appearing in dozens of peer-reviewed journals.

Katherine Tate is a Professor of Political Science at Brown University. She is the author of several books, including the award-winning *Black Faces in the Mirror: African Americans and Their Representatives in the US Congress* (2004).

Cambridge Studies in American Legislatures

General Editors

Laurel Harbridge-Yong, *Northwestern University*
Jeff Harden, *University of Notre Dame*
Justin Kirkland, *University of Virginia*

Associate Editors

Sarah Anzia, *University of California, Berkeley*
Dan Butler, *Washington University in St. Louis*
Jason Casellas, *University of Houston*
Chris Clark, *University of North Carolina, Chapel Hill*
David Fortunato, *University of California, San Diego*
Tracy Osborn, *University of Iowa*
Kathryn Pearson, *University of Minnesota*
Tracy Sulkin, *University of Illinois Urbana-Champaign*
Chris Warshaw, *George Washington University*
Alan Wiseman, *Vanderbilt University*

Cambridge Studies in American Legislatures publishes research that confronts major questions affecting the study of legislative politics and political representation in the United States. The series advances problem-driven work that significantly advances theoretical understanding of legislative processes at the national, state, and local levels, as well as scholarship that compares the US to deliberative institutions around the world. It is comprised of studies that employ a diverse set of methodological tools that help researchers develop original insights into legislatures' role in American democracy.

Other Books in the Series
Michael P. Olson, *Stolen Representation: Black Disfranchisement and State Legislative Politics in the American South*

Black Voices in the Halls of Power

Race and Rhetorical Representation in Congress

JENNIFER R. GARCIA
Oberlin College, Ohio

CHRISTOPHER T. STOUT
University of California, San Diego

KATHERINE TATE
Brown University, Rhode Island

Shaftesbury Road, Cambridge CB2 8EA, United Kingdom

One Liberty Plaza, 20th Floor, New York, NY 10006, USA

477 Williamstown Road, Port Melbourne, VIC 3207, Australia

314–321, 3rd Floor, Plot 3, Splendor Forum, Jasola District Centre,
New Delhi – 110025, India

103 Penang Road, #05-06/07, Visioncrest Commercial, Singapore 238467

Cambridge University Press is part of Cambridge University Press & Assessment,
a department of the University of Cambridge.

We share the University's mission to contribute to society through the pursuit of
education, learning, and research at the highest international levels of excellence.

www.cambridge.org
Information on this title: www.cambridge.org/9781009681476
DOI: 10.1017/9781009681469

© Jennifer R. Garcia, Christopher T. Stout, and Katherine Tate 2026

This publication is in copyright. Subject to statutory exceptions and to the provisions
of relevant collective licensing agreements, no reproduction of any part may take
place without the written permission of Cambridge University Press & Assessment.

When citing this work, please include a reference to the DOI 10.1017/9781009681469

First published 2026

Cover image: MirageC / Moment / Getty Images

A catalogue record for this publication is available from the British Library.

*A Cataloging-in-Publication data record for this book is available from the Library
of Congress*

ISBN 978-1-009-68147-6 Hardback
ISBN 978-1-009-68143-8 Paperback

Cambridge University Press & Assessment has no responsibility for the persistence
or accuracy of URLs for external or third-party internet websites referred to in this
publication and does not guarantee that any content on such websites is, or will
remain, accurate or appropriate.

For EU product safety concerns, contact us at Calle de José Abascal,
56, 1°, 28003 Madrid, Spain, or email eugpsr@cambridge.org.

Contents

List of Figures		*page* vii
List of Tables		ix
Acknowledgments		xi
1	Introduction: Echo in the Halls: Racial Rhetorical Representation in the Modern Era	1
2	Pushing the Agenda or Reacting to the Moment: Why Communication Directors Engage in Rhetorical Outreach	28
3	Who Racializes? Exploring the Demographic Factors of Members of Congress Who Provide Racial Rhetorical Representation through an Intersectional Perspective	50
4	The Highs and the Lows: Predicting Racial Rhetorical Representation around High- and Low-Profile Racial Events	70
5	Crystal Clear: Rhetorical Representation and Defining Novel Racial Issues	92
6	Depth and Breadth: Exploring the Breadth of Racial Topics Members of Congress Speak About When They Engage in Racial Rhetorical Representation	109
7	Not All Talk Is Cheap: The Link between Different Forms of Rhetorical Representation and Legislative Activity in Congress	131
8	Can Racial Rhetorical Representation Improve Approval Ratings?	149

9 What If It Fails? Is Rhetorical Representation without Legislation Valuable in the Eyes of the Constituents	171
10 Conclusion: Is Racial Advocacy Enough?	187
Data and Methods Appendix	207
Appendix	229
Bibliography	253
Index	275

Figures

1.1	Outline of the Plan of the Book	*page* 24
3.1	Average Levels of Racial Rhetorical Representation in Press Releases (2015–2021) and Tweets (2019–2021) Across Racial/Ethnic Groups and Congressional Session	62
4.1	Percent of High-Profile Racial Appeals among Only Racial Appeals for Elected Officials of Different Racial/Ethnic Groups	82
4.2	Google Trends Search Scores for Black Lives Matter from 2015–2021	86
4.3	Percent of BLM Topics Mentions in Press Releases Monthly By Race of the Elected Officials and Google Trend Search Scores (2015–2021)	87
5.1	The Percent of Press Releases from the 114th, 115th, and 116th Congresses Which Include Mentions of Uncrystallized Black Issues by the Race of the Representative.	102
5.2	The Percent of COVID-related Press Releases in the First Six Months of the Pandemic Which Include Racialized Outreach	107
5.3	The Percent of COVID-related Tweets in the First Six Months of the Pandemic Which Include Racialized Outreach	108
6.1	Average Number of Racial Topics Discussed in Press Releases and Tweets by Race/Ethnicity of Member of Congress	127

8.1	Websites of Hypothetical U.S. House Representative by Treatment Type	158
8.2	Average Approval Rates for Hypothetical Politician by Treatment Type for Black Respondents	160
8.3	Average Approval Rates for Hypothetical Politician by Treatment Type for White Liberal Respondents	162
8.4	Average Approval Rates for Hypothetical Politician by Treatment Type for White Moderate/Conservative Respondents	163
9.1	Change in African American Support for Hypothetical Candidate When Bill They Advocated for Became Law/Failed to Become Law by Treatment Type	178
9.2	Change in White Support for Hypothetical Candidate When Bill They Advocated for Became Law/Failed to Become Law by Treatment Type	180

Tables

1.1	Difference in Demographic Partisanship among Representatives Whose Press Releases We Could Access and Those We Could Not Access in Each Congress. Comparison data is drawn from the Daily KOS Congressional Demographic Profile	page 20
3.1	Percent of Racial Outreach in Press Releases (2015–2021) and Tweets (2019–2021) for Black, White, Latino, and Asian American Members of Congress.	65
4.1	List of High-Profile Topics	80
6.1	Common Topics in Press Releases and Tweets and Highest Probability Words in Each Category	117
6.2	Proportion of Black-Centered Press Releases in Each Topic for White, Black, Latino/a, and AAPI Members of Congress	119
6.3	Proportion of Black-Centered Tweets in Each Topic for White, Black, Latino/a, and AAPI Members of Congress	124
7.1	Correlation Plot between Different Forms of Legislative Activity and Racial Rhetorical Representation as Measured Through Press Releases	144
7.2	Correlation Plot between Different Forms of Legislative Activity and Racial Rhetorical Representation as Measured Through Tweets	145
7.3	Correlation Plot between Different Forms of Legislative Activity and Racial Rhetorical Representation as Measured Through Tweets	146

8.1	Average Responses in Four Categories Detailing Approval for Hypothetical Elected Official by Race and Issue Type	166
9.1	Percent of Mentions of Whether Information about Bill Fate Shapes Approval of Hypothetical	183

Acknowledgments

This book was only possible because of the generous support of our colleagues, family, and friends. We were fortunate to cross paths with so many wonderful social scientists who were kind enough to give us the space to speak about this project and provide advice to improve this manuscript. While this is far from an exhaustive list, we are grateful for Marisa Abrajano, Maneesh Arora, Kristen Barber, David Bernell, Katherine Bolzendahl, Louis DeSipio, Lorrie Frasure, LaGina Gause, Alison Johnston, Danielle Lemi, Gregory John Leslie, Natalie Masuoka, Jock Mills, Dwaine Plaza, Leah Ruppanner, Tye Rush, Elizabeth Schroeder, Rorie Solberg, Michael Tesler, Michael Trevathan, Andrew Valls, Mike Parkin, and Adam Howat who in some capacity provided feedback on this research.

One of the main joys of being a professor is being able to work with so many incredible undergraduate and graduate students. Through teaching and discussions with our students, we gained valuable insight into our research project. While there are too many to name, we would like to highlight a few who offered research assistance and played a large role in the development of our coding around Black racial outreach. We are forever indebted to Katarina Bosworth, Ivy Chase, Erik Chi, Karina Mondragon, and Mohammed Shakibnia for their research assistance. We are also fortunate to have several students who have entered into the political communication side of politics. Speaking with them played a very important role in the development of our theory. We are thankful to Ashley Kuenzi, Emileni Lopez, Esther Mathews, Tabitha Pitzer, Metzin Rodriguez, Gabriel Shepherd, and Claire Waggoner for being willing to share their insights into public-facing politics.

Our theory and the contributions of this book would be significantly less rich without the willingness of many communications directors in the U.S. House of Representatives who generously shared their insights with us. Communications directors' important work helps build trust in our institutions and, as detailed in this book, ensures that all people in our diverse country know that congressional offices are listening to them and amplifying their voices.

We would also like to thank our friends and family who keep us sane and on track during turbulent times. While this list is not exhaustive, we would like to thank Alfred Flores, Kenn Ghaffarian, Emily and Dan Faltesek, Dante Jackson, David Jackson, Dana Jackson, Holly Jackson, Nick Jackson, Jon Stoll, Miguel Sanchez, Emily and Nick Sass, Becky Wilson, Manuel, Rachel and Elliott Garcia, Ilana and Evan Kresch, Cortney Smith, and Tracy Tucker for being a source of positivity in our lives.

We would like to thank the Cambridge Studies in American Legislatures Series Editors and, in particular, Justin Kirkland, who was our main editor for this project. Justin was very responsive, thoughtful, and extremely helpful in guiding us in this project. He also selected amazing reviewers whom we do not know, but are eternally grateful for. The book improved immensely because of their guidance and their pushing us to think more deeply about the contributions of the book. Review processes are often difficult, but the constructive and timely feedback from the editors and reviewers made this, dare we say, an enjoyable experience.

Jennifer Garcia is grateful to the following people:

> I started my academic career at UC Irvine, where I was fortunate to work with and be mentored by Matt Beckman, Louis DeSipio, Bernard Grofman, and Michael Tesler. I am particularly indebted to Matt, who, as my advisor, helped me figure out what kind of scholar I wanted to become. He spent hours and hours talking to me about my dissertation and helped me completely revise my job talk at the pub after my first practice talk. UC Irvine is also where I met Katherine Tate and Chris Stout. I am deeply grateful to both of them. Katherine helped pave the way for scholars like me to do this kind of work. I pinch myself now, thinking that we have just written a book together. In Chris, I found a lifelong collaborator. He is the best kind of scholar – supportive, creative, and intelligent. It has been a joy working with these two generous and brilliant scholars. Beyond the

world of UC Irvine, I'm also endlessly grateful for the support of Sophia Jordán Wallace, Nadia Brown, and LaGina Gause. They have boosted me up and made me feel like there is a place for me in political science.

I'd also like to acknowledge my family. First, my parents, Manuel and Maggie Garcia. If there's one thing I have always known, it is that their love for me is boundless and unconditional. Their persistent support and advocacy have led me to where I am today. It's undoubtedly true that this project would not have been possible without them (and the babysitting services my mom provides).

Second, my husband, David Forrest. On our wedding day, I accidentally fell into a creek in my dress before the ceremony. Before the tears could come, he jumped in after me. From that moment on, we've jumped into everything together. Every step of the way in this book project, David was right there with me – talking over ideas, helping solve problems, keeping my spirits up when writing proved challenging, picking up more of the slack at home when I needed a little more time to work. Him by my side is the reason I'm able to do any of this. All of my accomplishments are his, too.

Lastly, my kiddos, Ben and Madeline Forrest. They are my everything. They are smart and inquisitive, caring and joyful, hilarious and delightfully themselves. They've taught me more than I could have ever imagined. Not a day goes by that they don't put a smile on my face and remind me of what's truly important. Everything I am and everything I do is so much better because of them.

Christopher Stout is grateful to the following people:

My parents have sacrificed so much for me, and their continued support made this project possible. My mother and father have been the best parents and grandparents a person could have. They have served as a model for how I parent and how I want to parent/grandparent in the future. While younger, I always looked up to my sister Vanessa Stout, who is also an academic. I work hard to emulate her work, her teaching, and her efforts to make this world a better place to live.

I truly do not know where I would be without my wife, Kelsy Kretschmer. I am more certain of every decision I made in life because it led me to her. In many ways, she could be a co-author in everything I write, including this book. She has solved countless research problems for me, and our discussions make me a better person and scholar.

My children are an endless source of motivation. They inspire everything that I do. Calvin Stout is consistent, smart, and determined. I learn so much from how Calvin reacts to any challenge. He embodies the growth mindset, and when I am struggling, I think about his resilience. Parker Stout is so intelligent, outgoing, and hardworking. I try to channel her focus and work ethic whenever I am writing. She makes me smile every day.

I will conclude by acknowledging how fortunate I have been in my education journey. At each step, I have worked with dedicated mentors who made my life better. At UC Irvine, I was fortunate to work with Louis DeSipio, Bernard Grofman, and Carole Uhlaner, who helped mold me into the scholar that I am. Looking back, I am not sure I would have been successful in another program. I would also like to thank my advisor and co-author on this project, Katherine Tate. Katherine was the epitome of what a good advisor should be. She was patient and encouraging. She continues to give me advice to this day. Her research was my motivation to attend graduate school, and I am grateful that I have been able to write with her over the course of my career.

UC Irvine is also where I met Jenny Garcia, who was my office mate in her early years. Over the past decade, we have had the opportunity to work on several projects together. Through these collaborations, I have learned so much and have become a better scholar. I feel privileged to have collaborated with her for many years and look forward to working together more in the future.

Finally, I want to thank my undergraduate advisor, Martin Johnson, who passed away in 2020. I was not the greatest undergraduate student, but Martin made me feel like I could do well in graduate school. He encouraged me to apply to Bunche, he read my statement of purpose for graduate school more than one should, he gave me my first research experience, and when I was struggling during my first year of grad school, he offered some important words of encouragement. I try to live by his example every day. Without a doubt, Martin Johnson changed my life and showed me how impactful a good educator can be in uplifting others.

Katherine Tate is grateful to the following people:

I thank Chris Stout for inviting me to collaborate. He and Jenny Garcia made working on this project pleasant and enjoyable. I would work with them again in a heartbeat. They are truly remarkable scholars.

Eva Kozlowski, an undergraduate at Brown, worked on the book project, creating Excel files when all we had were data points. Brown University was supportive of this project. Specifically, I thank Janet A. Blume, Deputy Provost, for Brown's financial support. My adult children and my son's spouse deserve a shout-out. Thank you, Luke, Aldea, and Sophie. I also dedicate this book to my grandsons, Jean and Adam.

I

Introduction

Echo in the Halls: Racial Rhetorical Representation in the Modern Era

Members of Congress engage in numerous activities to care for their constituents on Capitol Hill. From introducing legislation to answering and following through on requests for services to voting on bills on the floor of Congress, legislators work to ensure that their constituents are well represented in government. Members of Congress also speak out publicly about issues that concern their constituents to ensure that they have a voice in the halls of power. This rhetorical form of representation is particularly important for members of underrepresented groups whose concerns have traditionally been ignored.

In fact, many elected officials identify the opportunity to provide a voice to groups who have been overlooked as an important part of their mission in government. In detailing his motivation to run for elected office, Yussef Salaam, one of the wrongly convicted Central Park Five, spoke about the importance of amplifying Black voices. In a July 2023 interview with the PBS Newshour Salaam proclaimed, "when others are marching in the streets, they need someone in the halls of power that can echo their voice, that can lift them up, that can carry them into those spaces, and be an advocate for them in the most powerful way."[1] Yussef Salaam is not alone in this regard. Andrea Jenkins, a Black transwoman who served in the Minneapolis City Council spoke about the importance of giving Black people a voice in government. "It's a mission…I really believe in the statement that representation matters. And then we need

---

[1] https://ga.video.cdn.pbs.org/captions/newshour/d091ac5f-8304-4607-95d2-50c304ba11fe/captions/LoF1rh_caption_en.txt

Black voices..."[2] Others, like Black Florida Congresswoman Sheila Cherfilus McCormick, have been explicit that one of their goals in Congress is to ensure that those outside of the seats of power have an opportunity to have their voices heard. In her biography page, she "vows to be a voice for the voiceless."[3]

A growing literature in political science is recognizing the importance of elected officials speaking out and amplifying the voices of marginalized groups in government (Gamble 2011, Evans and Clark 2016, Gillion 2016, Gervais and Wilson 2017, Haines et al. 2019, Arora and Kim 2020, Bonilla and Tillery 2020, Hargrave and Langengen 2021, Russell 2021, Dietrich and Hayes 2023, Vishwanath 2024). Much of this work has highlighted that descriptive representatives are more likely to advocate for their identity groups in their speech (Canon 1999, Gershon 2008, Gamble 2011, Gervais and Wilson 2017). Other work has shown that the tenor and intensity with which descriptive representatives speak about issues pertaining to their identity are significantly different from non-descriptive representatives. (Dietrich et al. 2019, Hargrave and Langengen 2021, Hargrave and Blumenau 2022).

Research on this form of representation, which has been labeled rhetorical representation, is in its nascent stages (Gillion 2016, Cormack 2018, Haines et al. 2019, Hargrave and Langengen 2021, Wäckerle and Silva 2023). This form of representation is becoming a more important part of legislators' jobs as political polarization, filibusters, and divided government make it difficult for Congress to pass legislation. Rhetorical representation is likely even more significant for African Americans who not only encounter these hurdles in the legislative process but also face systematic racial barriers in Congress (Hawkesworth 2003, Grose 2011, Tyson 2016, Minta 2021).

We are interested in how members of the U.S. House engage in Black rhetorical representation and whether this matters, especially now in the post-Obama age, where Black political power has continued to increase (Tate 2010, 2014). Scholars once called this period of expansion of Black political power, "post-racial" (Gillespie 2010, McIlwain and Caliendo 2011, Harris 2012, Lewis et al. 2013). Barack Obama and other Black politicians seeking White support were to win their elections by downplaying racial concerns in their public outreach (Hamilton 1977, Gillespie

---

[2] www.pbs.org/newshour/politics/i-represent-more-than-myself-black-politicians-reflect-on-their-historic-firsts
[3] https://cherfilus-mccormick.house.gov/about

2010). While this deracialized approach increased Black representation in public office, it meant that Black people had few government officials speaking out on their behalf (Gillion 2016).

However, others recently contend that Obama's election in 2008 triggered a racial backlash and George Floyd's murder led to a national racial reckoning (Tesler 2016, Bunyasi and Smith 2019, Stout 2020). This racial reckoning has polarized public opinion on racial issues. These divisions have created a sense of urgency for elected officials to speak out about Black political interests in a context where Black people are seeing a retrenchment in their political rights and prominent politicians work to combat what they see as a "woke" political agenda. Instead of avoiding racial topics, we argue that today's politicians' use of racial rhetorical outreach is central in combating systemic racial inequality.

While this increase in advocacy for Black political interests is certainly important to African Americans (Dietrich and Hayes 2023), it is likely equally as important *how* members speak out about racial issues. We draw an important and unexplored distinction in racial rhetorical outreach by disaggregating what we label as proactive racial rhetorical representation and reactive rhetorical representation. The latter is most likely a reaction to an event, high-profile news story or crises and frequently highlights traditional racial topics which are already in the public eye. This outreach may help elected officials build connections with their constituents (Eulau and Karp 1977, Chapman Sinclair 2002). In contrast, proactive racial rhetorical representation uses the elected official's public platform to raise new racial issues, keep less salient racial topics on the agenda, and highlight the achievements of lesser-known African Americans in ways that are driven less by immediate public pressures. Proactive racial rhetorical representation may have the benefit of not only building trust with constituents but also potentially altering the policy landscape to be more inclusive of the interests of marginalized groups.

In this book, we engage in a deep dive into Black-oriented rhetorical representation by exploring U.S. House Representatives' racial communication between 2015 and 2021. We use a wealth of data, including interviews with communications directors in Congress, hundreds of thousands of press releases and tweets, legislative activity including bill sponsorship, co-sponsorship, and committee hearing transcripts, survey data, and experimental analyses, to understand several important questions around racial rhetorical representation.

In particular, we explore the motivations of members of Congress to speak about Black political interests in government. We also delve into how elected officials may use rhetorical representation to alter the legislative landscape by speaking about lower salience topics, ensuring racial interests are accounted for in uncrystallized issues, and speaking to the diversity of interests within the Black community. Beyond exploring the policy impact of rhetorical representation, we also explore whether different types of racial public outreach can help build connections between elected officials and their constituents.

We consider this in two primary areas. First, can legislators build trust with their constituents by following through on their rhetoric with tangible legislative activity, such as bill sponsorship or co-sponsorship? Second, we explore which type of racial messaging matters to voters and why using experimental analysis, which includes both quantitative and qualitative responses. Through looking at racial rhetorical representation from different angles, circumstances, and through the lenses of both congressional offices and the voters, we hope to provide a complete analysis of the benefits of this form of representation.

WHAT IS RHETORICAL REPRESENTATION?

In her seminal book, *The Concept of Representation*, Pitkin (1967) outlines four forms of political representation: formal, descriptive, substantive, and symbolic representation. While formal representation focuses on the norms and procedures that govern how representatives are selected, Pitkin (1967) distinguishes the other forms of representation as "standing for" (descriptive and symbolic representation) and "acting for" (substantive representation).

According to Pitkin, descriptive and symbolic representation are both described as "standing for." In terms of descriptive representation, it occurs when representatives mirror, in some way, the people they represent. Broadly defined, this can include a legislator and constituents sharing a profession, or what Schwindt-Bayer and Mishler (2005: 408) refer to as functional representation. For instance, Montana U.S. Senator Jon Tester, a self-proclaimed third-generation farmer, descriptively represents farmers across his state. However, descriptive representation is most commonly used to describe the sharing of immutable characteristics, like race, ethnicity, and gender. For the purposes of our study, an African American who is represented by an African American legislator is descriptively represented.

Symbolic representation, according to Pitkin, occurs when representatives serve as symbols who "evoke feelings and attitudes" among the represented. "Symbolic representation is concerned not with who the representatives are or what they do, but how they are *perceived and evaluated* by those they represent" (Schwindt-Bayer and Mishler 2005: 409). Many have interpreted Pitkin's depiction of descriptive and symbolic representation as not requiring any action to be taken by the representative in order to be present.[4]

In contrast, substantive representation occurs when representatives act "in the interests of the represented in a manner responsive to them" (Pitkin 1967: 209). Often, we think of this in terms of policy responsiveness (Miller and Stokes 1963), measured as the congruence between constituent interests and legislative actions, like voting and sponsoring legislation. For example, a legislator who votes for a restrictive abortion bill is taking action to substantively represent a pro-life constituent. However, others have argued for a more expansive understanding of substantive representation (Eulau and Karps 1977, Minta 2011, Schulze 2013, Gamble 2011, Lowande et al. 2019).

Eulau and Karp (1977) argue that substantive representation can be broken down into four subcategories, which indicate some actions being taken on behalf of the constituents. In addition to policy responsiveness, they also consider substantive representation to include service responsiveness, allocation responsiveness, and symbolic responsiveness. Service responsiveness is centered on the ability of legislators to provide responsiveness to their constituents' requests. Allocation responsiveness is tied to representatives bringing resources back to their district. Symbolic responsiveness, which is the most relevant to our focus, occurs when legislators make "public gestures of a sort that create a sense of trust

---

[4] However, recent work in women's political representation has urged a more expansive understanding of Pitkin's conception of descriptive representation to include talking functions (Shogan 2001, Piscopo 2011, Hinojosa et al. 2018). Piscopo (2011) encourages a "re-conceptualization of descriptive representation, wherein legislators resemble their constituents not through passively sharing phenotypes, but through actively making claims" (449). Piscopo (2011) and Shogan (2001) consider all speeches given by women representatives, about women as evidence of the talking function of descriptive representation. Shogan asserts, "When a legislator provides relevant information about a represented population, he or she engages in one type of descriptive representation" (2001: 130). However, Hinojosa et al. (2018) push back on this by urging a distinction between "speaking for" women and "speaking as" women (410). They argue that both men and women can "speak for" women as a form of substantive representation. In contrast, only women are able to "speak as" women, thus making it a form of descriptive representation. To provide descriptive representation through a talking function, according to Hinojosa et al. (2018) requires female legislators to "invoke their own gender" in their statements (408). They deem this descriptive presentation.

and support in the relationship between representative and represented" (Eulau and Karps 1977: 241).

Symbolic responsiveness includes a variety of "public gestures" which entail actions like mirroring the attire of the constituents (Fenno 1977), posing with objects like a flag or bible (Callahan and Ledgerwood 2016), or actions like kneeling during the national anthem (Towler et al. 2020). The public understands political issues and electoral choices, Edelman (1964) contends, through political symbols (see also Sinclair Chapman 2018, Tate 2003). Symbols help simplify issues, garner emotional support, and resonate with cultural values and beliefs. For Edelman (1964), the use of symbols also gives the impression that the government is working on pressing issues of the day.

Speech is an important form of symbolic responsiveness (Dietrich and Hayes 2023). When this speech is centered on advancing the politics of a particular group, Haines et al. (2019) label it as rhetorical representation. For our purposes, politicians provide rhetorical representation to African Americans when they discuss issues, legislation, and/or policies directly impacting Black communities, recognize African Americans, highlight their intentions to address problems faced by Black people, and/or outline their work on behalf of this group via a public forum. We argue that rhetorical representation is an especially significant subset of substantive representation.

Members of Congress have free rein to speak about whatever issues or topics they want. This allows for a greater variety of topics to be discussed via rhetorical representation. The ease with which legislators can put out a tweet or draft a press release means that elected officials can engage in rhetorical representation much more often than they can in bill introduction and in a less institutionally constrained way than with voting (Davidson et al. 2019).

Elected officials can also move more quickly in their public outreach than they can in the legislative process. This leads rhetorical representation to be more flexible in response to moments of crises and allows legislators to immediately let their constituents know that they are thinking about them.

There is an important and growing body of work focused on studying Black-related speech, one form of symbolic responsiveness. Here, studies have looked at how representatives can use rhetoric to signal symbolic meaning to constituents. Of note is the work of Dietrich and Hayes (2023), who convincingly show that legislators can be more effective advocates for different policies and build strong relationships with their constituents through the use of symbols in their rhetorical outreach. They find that Black House members are more likely than White House members to "use symbols of the African American struggle for civil rights when speaking on the House floor and that the correct application of these symbols can convey meaning to Black constituents" (Dietrich and Hayes 2023: 1369).

Much like Dietrich and Hayes (2023), we too are interested in better understanding the differences in rhetorical strategies used by descriptive and non-descriptive representatives. However, we deviate from them in that we focus less on the use of symbols[5] as the key divide between Black and non-Black legislators. Instead, we are more interested in the differences in motivations to speak out as distinguishing descriptive and non-descriptive representatives. We contend that legislators who view race as a key part of their legislative identity will be more proactive in their outreach. In doing so, they will speak about a broader set of topics, expend more effort to keep issues on the agenda, and ensure that race is considered in new policies. This proactive outreach not only helps connect legislators to their constituents, but we argue it also has important policy implications. In contrast, legislators who want to appeal to Black voters but do not see race as a core part of their identity will speak about race differently. These elected officials will frequently speak about well-known racial issues and speak on racial topics when there is public pressure to do so. This different motivation to speak out should lead to different policy implications, as well as provide a lesser ability to connect with constituents.

Proactive and Reactive Racial Representation

An important contribution of our research is moving beyond the dichotomy of racial substantive outreach and focusing on how the different motivations to engage in racial rhetorical representation lead to different types of responsiveness. Those who see addressing racial inequality as a

---

[5] Moreover, we do not explicitly focus on symbols in rhetorical outreach. Rather, we focus on the variety of ways legislators speak on race in their outreach. We contend that when legislators are proactive in their racial rhetorical outreach, i.e., they raise low-salience racial issues, identify uncrystallized interests, and continuously speak out on racial issues, Black constituents will feel greater connection to those legislators. While this may provide a similar effect as using symbols in speeches on racial issues, our work is more focused on the effects of a legislator's proactive approach to racial rhetorical outreach than whether or not symbols are present.

primary part of their legislative identity are more intentional in their engagement around race in their public outreach. This intentionality is tied to proactive rhetorical representation. Elected officials engage in proactive rhetorical representation when they use their public platform to actively broaden the boundaries of racial discussions, keep racial issues on the agenda when they are no longer topical, and speak about racial issues in an unprompted manner which are not driven by immediate public pressures. We believe that this type of rhetorical representation has the greatest ability to both advance the policy interests of African Americans and improve voters' trust and approval for elected officials.

In contrast, elected officials who want to target key constituencies but do not see issues pertaining to race as being a core part of their legislative brand may engage in reactive rhetorical representation. Reactive rhetorical representation occurs when elected officials speak about race using topics that are already in the public discourse and generally in response to immediate external pressures. While this form of outreach supports marginalized groups by reinforcing existing demands, it does less than proactive racial rhetorical representation to actively change the public discourse around race. As a result, this type of rhetorical representation may be effective in building connections between elected officials and the targeted groups, but is less likely to substantively alter the policy environment.

There are many characteristics that distinguish proactive and reactive outreach. In this section, we discuss key areas where these two forms of targeted outreach may differ. The first way that elected officials engage in proactive rhetorical representation is by broadening the scope of racial topics in American political discourse. This can occur in two ways. Elected officials can highlight racial concerns in new areas that are not traditionally tied to race. These issues can be longstanding or novel. For example, U.S. House Representative Ayanna Pressley (D-MA) engaged in proactive rhetorical representation when she put out several tweets[6] and press releases[7] highlighting the role of public transportation access to communities of color. Similarly, U.S. House Representatives Lauren Underwood (D-IL) and Alma Adams (D-NC) engaged in this form of outreach when they used their public platform to highlight racial

---

[6] https://twitter.com/RepPressley/status/1293275449947283456
[7] https://pressley.house.gov/2023/04/24/rep-pressley-and-sen-markey-announce-fare-free-transit-legislation-freedom-to-move-act/

discrimination in the maternal care of Black women.[8] In both of these examples, rhetorical representation is used to highlight the many different ways that race intersects with everyday activities to limit opportunities for people of color. In doing so, elected officials who engage in proactive racial rhetorical representation help broaden the racial discourse by addressing previously overlooked forms of racial inequality. They also highlight a problem which could potentially mobilize legislative solutions.

Along the same lines, elected officials engage in proactive racial rhetorical representation when they speak about lower-profile racial topics. Despite the lack of public attention on the issue, members of Congress highlight it in the hope of raising awareness and expanding the public agenda. Legislators feel little pressure to speak on these issues because if they said nothing, the public would likely not notice their absence. These could be topics which are well established as being tied to racial inequality, but because of their controversial nature or their perceived lack of broad interest, are generally not discussed by elected officials. Examples of this may be discussions of topics around reparations for slavery,[9] Black hair care,[10] or lesser-known Black public figures.[11]

When speaking to communications directors in Black House offices, many explicitly discussed how a primary aim of theirs is to continually speak on issues important to the Black community that regularly go unheard and unrecognized. Given that these issues are rarely in the public eye, speaking out about them requires intentional effort by the legislators to continue to shed light on these topics.

This intentionality is also present in legislators' willingness to continue to talk about high-profile racial topics even when they fade from popular discourse. This is another hallmark of proactive rhetorical representation. For example, in April of 2014, a group of Black girls was kidnapped from the Government Girls Secondary School in the Borno State of Nigeria by Boko Haram, a United States-designated terrorist group. This event led to a viral hashtag #Bringbackourgirls which was tweeted from several high-profile figures like Michelle Obama, Mary J. Blige, and Anne Hathaway (Parkinson and Hinshaw 2021). Multiple members of Congress used the hashtag in their Tweets. #Bringbackourgirls was one of the top ten most

---

[8] https://blackmaternalhealthcaucus-underwood.house.gov/about
[9] https://twitter.com/RepJeffries/status/1382520052730232832?lang=en
[10] https://shontelbrown.house.gov/media/press-releases/after-brown-pressley-inquiry-fda-proposes-ban-harmful-chemicals-hair-relaxers
[11] https://clyburn.house.gov/press-release/clyburn-statement-reverend-shuttlesworth

popular hashtags of 2014. However, by 2015, interest in the issue largely faded.[12] Although the girls who were kidnapped by Boko Haram were not brought home, the public had shifted its attention to other issues.

One member of Congress, Democratic Congresswoman Frederica Wilson (FL-24), engaged in proactive rhetorical representation when she continued to speak about the issue even when it was no longer a high-profile topic. She continued to give speeches about the topic on the floor of the U.S. House of Representatives, she tweeted the hashtag daily for multiple years, and she organized "wear something red Wednesdays" to bring attention to the plight of the girls kidnapped by Boko Haram. In a speech on the floor of Congress, she noted months after the hashtag went viral, "While talking about the girls *may no longer be trendy*, it is more important than ever to bring them home…the time is now to keep pressure on the Nigerian government. We must tweet with the fervent passion that *extends beyond the glamour of a breaking news story*. We cannot slow down, we cannot lose momentum, we cannot rest until our girls are home."[13] Representative Wilson used proactive rhetorical advocacy to fight for funding for combating Boko Haram and for marshaling more resources to bring the girls of the school in Chibok home. This action to keep talking about a once high-profile racial topic when public interest has faded requires attentiveness and a personal dedication to the issue, which is consistent with proactive rhetorical representation.

As a result, legislators engage in proactive rhetorical outreach when they speak out on an issue regularly, even when there is no external event prompting the discussion, like a mass shooting or political party leaders providing rhetorical support through pre-written statements. These unprompted discussions signal to the electorate that the topic, in this case Black-oriented issues, is always top of mind to the elected official. Elected officials who engage in proactive rhetorical representation do not need an occasion or headline to speak out in support of African Americans; they do so on a regular basis, regardless of the external circumstances. Overall, proactive racial rhetorical outreach expands the racial issue agenda, not only in the kinds of issues that are raised but also by the continual and persistent outreach on the issue. This has the potential to both expand substantive representation in terms of advancing policy interests and symbolic responsiveness in terms of creating a sense of trust between the elected official and the constituent.

---

[12] www.pbs.org/newshour/show/many-lose-interest-bring-back-girls-vow-forget
[13] www.youtube.com/watch?v=ExTVQlx25J8

While the above examples highlight forms of proactive rhetorical representation, reactive rhetorical representation will likely be the most common form of racial outreach. We suspect that key events, protests, or holidays will prompt more elected officials to engage in Black-related rhetorical representation because silence in these areas may be more costly than putting out a statement. For example, many elected officials will put out statements in recognition of Black History Month or condemnations of White Supremacy following the Unite the Right Rally in Charlottesville in 2017. The former is nationally recognized, and it would be expected that attentive elected officials would highlight some aspect of Black history during the month of February. Such outreach would not be that risky, nor would it take incredible foresight to speak out, yet it would demonstrate an attentiveness to Black voters, which could be electorally beneficial and demonstrate symbolic responsiveness. The latter, too, would be both reactive and common. In large part, because there are few electoral costs to condemn White supremacy, given Americans' disdain for overt racism (Wetts and Willer 2022). Moreover, the rally of White supremacists and President Trump's ensuing comments about good people being on both sides would push elected officials to take a stand to show they are paying attention and to disassociate from such politically unpopular rhetoric. In both cases, elected officials engage in reactive rhetorical representation because their racially centered outreach was prompted by external circumstances.

Responsiveness to high-profile issues is a trademark of reactive rhetorical representation. We define high-profile issues as those that are clearly on the public's agenda and getting regular public and media attention. If the legislator never spoke out on the issue, it would still be salient in the public realm. Moreover, in some cases, if a legislator does not speak out on a high-profile issue, they may face negative electoral consequences (Milita et al. 2014, Gillion 2016, Gause 2022). During our interviews with communications directors, many said that when it became clear that their constituents cared about something or were being impacted by something, they felt compelled to issue a public statement. A safe way that elected officials can periodically shore up support from key constituencies is to speak about high-profile racial topics. Issues like voting rights, condemning White Supremacy, and, more recently, criminal justice reform are issues that have a profound and disproportionate impact on African Americans. The implications of discussing these issues are well known. As a result, legislators can appeal to African Americans using these topics and be less concerned about an unexpected backlash.[14]

Moreover, consistent examples of these forms of discrimination are often covered by the media, which cries out for some form of action from elected officials who want to demonstrate their value to Black voters. The perpetual nature of these social problems and the high level of coverage they receive make discussions about these topics a common form of race-based outreach. Elected officials who engage in reactive rhetorical representation still work to appeal and advance the goals of Black people; they just do so in a narrower manner, which is consistent with a well-known racial script. Overall, reactive rhetorical outreach reiterates the racial issue agenda by echoing traditional and salient issues and does so most when circumstances prompt their discussion. While reactive rhetorical representation can put additional pressure on existing policy solutions to be enacted and build connections with constituents, it is less likely to have the broader impacts of proactive rhetorical representation.

The Link Between Descriptive Representation and Proactive Racial Rhetorical Representation

We anticipate that Black legislators will be more likely than non-Black legislators to engage in proactive racial rhetorical representation for three primary reasons. First, Black legislators hold distinct electoral incentives that may encourage them to speak out on Black issues more than other legislators. Black constituents have been and continue to be a uniquely important sub-constituency for Black legislators' reelection efforts. Whether from a majority-Black district or, as is increasingly the case, from a non-majority–minority district, Black legislators uniquely rely on Black constituents for their reelection. For instance, Grose (2011) shows that Black Democratic members of Congress from districts in which African Americans make up 25 to 50 percent of the total population are more likely to rely on Black voters for reelection than White Democratic voters. Black elected officials' unique reliance on the Black population to win reelection may motivate them to continuously find ways to speak out for the political interests of their co-racial constituents.

Second, Black legislators may engage in more proactive racial rhetorical outreach than others due to their identity. As Black members of

---

[14] https://fivethirtyeight.com/features/what-americans-think-about-reparations-and-other-race-related-questions/

society, Black legislators have direct experience with racism and marginalization. Scholars have argued that Black legislators bring these distinct perspectives to Congress, shaping deliberations and the issues considered within the institution (Cannon 1999, Gamble 2011, Minta 2011). Mansbridge (1999: 647) argues that Black legislators have a "particular sensibility, created by experience," that enables them to identify Black interests on "uncrystallized issues," or issues where Black interests have not yet been fully formed and publicly recognized.

In addition to their personal experiences, the personal connections Black legislators have with the Black community enable them to better identify important issues facing Black people, which are overlooked by others. As members of the Black community themselves, their everyday interactions with Black family members, fellow parishioners at Black churches, fellow students and alumni of Historically Black Colleges and Universities, and even their Facebook feeds, provide them a greater connectedness to other Black people. Moreover, Grose (2011) shows that upon being elected to Congress, Black legislators are more likely to hire Black staffers and place their district offices closer to heavily populated Black areas. These relationships should provide a greater connectedness to the Black community, thus shaping their understanding of Black issues that are outside of the mainstream media. This greater awareness, in combination with stronger personal ties, should lead to stronger levels of advocacy for a greater variety of Black-related issues.

Black legislators also likely have a strong sense of group identity with the broader Black community. Due to their shared history and experiences with racism and oppression, some have argued that Black Americans hold a strong sense of linked fate, the belief that one's fate is intrinsically connected to the fate of the entire community (Tate 1994, Dawson 1995). For Black legislators, linked fate produces a feeling of added responsibility to represent Black Americans nationwide. As Rep. Louis Stokes said, "In addition to representing our individual districts, we had to assume the onerous burden of acting as congressman-at-large for unrepresented people around America" (Fenno 2003: 62). Studies have pointed to linked fate as at least part of the explanation as to why Black legislators are distinct in their representation of Black Americans (Tate 2003, Gamble 2011, Minta 2011, Broockman 2013). Others, however, have demonstrated that social pressure is also at play (White and Laird 2020). While Black Americans hold an array of policy opinions and ideological perspectives, they maintain a fairly strong political unity. White and Laird (2020) show that an important reason for this unity is the norm of group solidarity, which is prioritized by Black Americans. As such, whether it be group identity or the norm of group solidarity, Black legislators' belonging to the larger Black community may enhance their intentionality to engage in rhetorical outreach to Black Americans.

Lastly, Black legislators may rely more on proactive racial rhetorical outreach than other legislators due to the distinct barriers they face within Congress. While it's difficult to get much of anything done in Congress these days, this is particularly true for Black legislators. In addition to the forces of polarization and insecure majorities (Lee 2016), Black legislators face additional racialized barriers. Though the number of Black legislators has grown significantly over the last few decades, they remain minorities within Congress. In an institution governed by majority-rules, this can place significant constraints on their influence. However, even when the Democratic Party is in the majority, Black legislators still find their influence stymied. Studies have shown that despite the growing concordance between the CBC and the Democratic Party (Tate 2014), the Democratic Party has been hesitant to include racialized issues on their agenda (Frymer 2014). Moreover, policies associated with Black politicians are often viewed as "ideologically radical" (Peay 2021) and have the potential to be racialized (Tesler 2016), further inhibiting their advancement.

Black legislators also face racial prejudice and discrimination within Congress (Polsby 1968, Hawkesworth 2003, King and Smith 2005, Tyson 2016). For instance, in 1993, U.S. Senator Carol Moseley-Braun (D-IL), the only Black legislator in the United States Senate at the time, recalled an interaction with Sen. Jesse Helms (R-NC). Upon entering the elevator she was standing in, he began singing "Dixie." He then turned to Sen. Orrin Hatch (R-UT) and said, "I'm going to make her cry. I'm going to sing 'Dixie' until she cries."[15] Rep. Barbara Lee[16] and Sen. Tim Scott[17] have both recounted individual experiences of being denied access to certain members-only areas in the Capitol. In the summer of 2023, GOP Rep. Eli Crane referred to Black people as "colored people" during a speech on the House floor.[18] In fact, in early 2024, the New York Times published an article outlining the frequency at which Republican

---

[15] www.latimes.com/archives/la-xpm-1993-08-06-mn-20952-story.html
[16] www.cnn.com/videos/politics/2024/01/19/barbara-lee-personal-racism-capitol-vpx.cnn
[17] https://www.politico.com/story/2016/07/tim-scott-capitol-racism-senate-225507
[18] www.nbcnews.com/politics/congress/rep-eli-crane-refers-black-americans-colored-people-house-floor-rcna94200

members of the House and Senate were engaging in "bigoted attacks" on people of color, including legislators like Rep. Cori Bush.[19]

Beyond these individual acts of prejudice, scholars have pointed to institutionalized marginalization within Congress. For instance, studies have shown that Black legislators have been put on less prestigious committees than White legislators (Tate 2003, Griffin and Keane 2011, Rocca et al. 2011) and committees whose jurisdictions do not overlap with their personal or constituents' interests.[20] Additionally, Hawkesworth (2003) shows that congresswomen of color are systematically silenced and dismissed within Congress. Moreover, Peay (2021) shows that Black sponsored bills are disproportionately winnowed in congressional committees. As such, traditional avenues of policy influence are not always available to Black lawmakers. This forces them to rely on unique strategies to overcome these distinct barriers (Hawkesworth 2003, Tyson 2016).

One way Black legislators can circumvent some of these constraints, while still trying to attain influence in policymaking, is through proactive racial rhetorical outreach. Black legislators, like all legislators, have a great deal of discretion in the statements they make to the public. When they are unable to gain traction on a policy priority within the normal legislative process, they can turn to rhetorical outreach in an effort to advance their priorities. One way they can do this is by continuously issuing public statements on an issue to try to get it more attention so that it becomes difficult for Congress to ignore it.

Racial rhetorical outreach by Black legislators can also alter the way an issue gets discussed. For instance, during the COVID-19 pandemic, Black legislators regularly brought up inequality in access to health care and the disparate impact of the pandemic on Black and Brown communities. This added perspective shapes the way the issue gets discussed in the future. Moreover, Black legislators are able to use their communications as a way to signal to key players, like party leaders, interest groups and advocacy organizations, and other legislators, that they are ready and willing to work on their policy priorities. Repeatedly issuing statements on a particular policy may help better position that legislator to be included in the

---

[19] www.nytimes.com/2024/02/13/us/politics/republicans-racist-language.html
[20] Upon entering Congress, Rep. Shirley Chisholm was assigned to the Agriculture committee. Representing Brooklyn, NY, Rep. Chisholm said "All I'm asking for is something more relevant than Agriculture." https://history.house.gov/Blog/2019/January/1-3-Chisholm/

legislative process when the opportunity arises to advance legislation in that policy area. Issuing statements can also signal to other legislators and organizations that you're ready and willing to work on policy in this area. This may help build policy coalitions and improve the legislative effectiveness of the politician.

Why Racial Rhetorical Representation is Important for American Politics

While there are unique reasons for descriptive representatives to engage in proactive racial rhetorical outreach, it is important to discuss the value that such outreach produces in the legislative process and in connecting members of Congress with their constituents. The American federal legislative process is slow and often filled with what seems like insurmountable hurdles (Sinclair 2016). A casual political observer may look at elected officials and believe that they are doing little to address the most pressing problems in society. This disconnect between social problems and public policy has the potential to have a demoralizing effect on the population and decrease trust in our political institutions (Sulkin et al 2015).

This is a particular concern for African Americans who, even in the best of times for their racial group, face significant political barriers (Wallace et al. 2017). The lack of a federal legislative response in the face of constant reminders of police violence through videos shot on cell phones and body cameras, attacks on racial history lessons in education, and growing wealth and healthcare disparities among Black and White people have highlighted the pressing need for legislative solutions. The perception that politicians are doing very little as new racial problems appear and old challenges resurface could lead to a sense of powerlessness for African Americans.

We believe that rhetorical representation may have the power to address concerns of unresponsiveness from our elected officials. African Americans have long been cognizant of the obstacles that their group faces in American political institutions (Wallace et al. 2017). They also have a long history of being ignored by both major political parties and even by elected officials who share their race (Gillespie 2010, Frymer 2011, Wallace et al. 2017). To combat these feelings of being overlooked, elected officials can use racial rhetorical representation to demonstrate that they are working on behalf of African Americans, even if the system overall is unresponsive. The presence of a constant ally may serve to keep African Americans engaged in the political process.

The ability of public outreach to build trust and connections with constituents is a valuable byproduct of rhetorical representation. In fact, Dietrich and Hayes (2023) demonstrate that elected officials who speak more about racial issues and tie these issues to prominent civil rights leaders tend to receive higher levels of approval and motivate political participation. The communicative aspect of rhetorical representation makes it easier for individuals to assess how concerned their representative is about their group in ways that other forms of substantive representation generally do not. For example, while a representative's voting record or policy proposals are publicly available, voters are often forced to seek out this information, which can be time-consuming. Additionally, other substantive actions, like coalition building and working with community leaders, are even less publicly visible. Rhetorical representation removes the need for individuals to seek out what their representatives are doing for their group, and instead provides a shortcut through which politicians publicly highlight their priorities and work on behalf of these individuals.

In addition to building connections between representatives and constituents, we contend that racial rhetorical representation also has positive policy implications for underrepresented groups. As African Americans face consistent barriers to normalcy, having political actors use their public platform to frame the debates in a way that highlights the needs of African Americans and keeps pressing racial issues on the agenda increases the likelihood that federal legislation may follow.

Moreover, even if unsuccessful at the federal level, rhetorical representation may set the guidelines for change at the local level. For example, while there was not a successful federal legislative response to protests around George Floyd in the Summer of 2020, many states and cities adopted the policies advocated by members of Congress, including the banning of chokeholds, no-knock warrants, racial sensitivity training for police officers, and changes in police hiring practices.[21] By framing the debate and providing solutions to social problems that African Americans encounter, rhetorical representation can help make tangible changes to a political landscape that appears to be growing increasingly hostile to Black people's political interests.

---

[21] www.axios.com/2020/06/10/police-reform-george-floyd-protest

MEASURING THE CAUSES AND CONSEQUENCES OF RHETORICAL REPRESENTATION THROUGH INTERVIEWS, MACHINE LEARNING OF PRESS RELEASES AND TWEETS, AND SURVEY EXPERIMENTS

Interviews With Communication Directors

Measuring the potential impact of rhetorical representation on policy and symbolic responsiveness requires a wide variety of data sources. First, it is important to learn from the communications directors themselves how they decide to use their public platform to alter the policy debate and/or build connections with constituents. This interview data is instrumental in the development of our theory around the links between identity and rhetorical outreach.

In this spirit, we interviewed 29 communications directors in the 118th Congress (2023–2025). We spoke to communications directors from nine Black Democratic Congresswomen, four Black Democratic Congressmen, seven Latino Democrats, two Latina Democrats, three White Democratic Congressmen, two White Democratic Congresswomen, and two Republican Congressmen. Given that we are interested in the link between descriptive and racially oriented representation, we collected an oversample of communication directors from Black legislators' offices. Our thirteen communication directors in Black representatives' offices represent almost a quarter (22.5%) of all Black representatives' legislative offices. Since communications directors are largely responsible for the messaging coming out of legislative offices, their perspectives shed valuable insight into the decision-making behind legislators' use of proactive or reactive racial rhetorical outreach (See data and methods appendix for more information about our sampling strategies and questions used in the interviews).

Twitter and Press Release Data

Beyond what communications directors tell us, a key source of understanding whether elected officials engage in rhetorical representation and whether they do so proactively or reactively is their actual communication. There are a variety of public mediums through which elected officials can engage in rhetorical representation, including speeches, social media, community meetings, etc. We focus on two forms of communication: press releases and tweets from members of the U.S. House of Representatives. We believe that the combinations of these forms of outreach will best approximate rhetorical representation for several reasons. First, both forms of outreach provide a means through which legislators can reach voters and colleagues (Grimmer 2013). Second, research shows that the media often gets their news stories from the press releases or tweets of political elites (Bennett 1990, Schaffner 2006, Broersma and Graham 2012, Grimmer 2013, Bane 2019). As a result, the messages disseminated by members of Congress are not only available to those who search the member's website or follow them on social media, but also to those who follow political news.

Finally, by using two forms of outreach, which tend to have different targeted audiences, we gain broader insight into how members of Congress communicate. Given that press releases are most effective when picked up by media organizations, members of Congress tend to take a less provocative approach in their outreach. In our interviews with communications directors, many emphasized that press releases were largely aimed at reporters and were reserved for larger pieces of news. When a legislator sponsored a bill, was able to bring something back to their district, or was responding to a major news story, their office tended to issue press releases. By incentivizing cautiousness, elected officials may speak less about particular issues and approach group-based appeals a little differently in their press releases than they would with other forms of communication.

In contrast, the communications directors we spoke to emphasized that those on Twitter tended to be more politically active and partisan. Sometimes what they posted on Twitter would be directed at interest groups and advocacy organizations. Other times, Twitter was used as a way to more quickly get out messages and respond to the day's news cycle. Twitter tends to reward more extreme political outreach and thus incentivizes a different type of political rhetoric (Pew Research). Moreover, Twitter is particularly meaningful to African Americans as a tool to organize and voice their concerns to elected officials (Sharma 2013). Using communication approaches that reward different styles of outreach provides a more comprehensive view of how members of Congress engage in rhetorical representation. It also provides more confidence that our findings would hold across different communication channels and allows us to comparatively explore how racial rhetorical representation may differ on social media and traditional communication approaches.

TABLE 1.1 *Difference in Demographic Partisanship Among Representatives Whose Press Releases We Could Access and Those We Could Not Access in Each Congress. Comparison Data Is Drawn From the Daily KOS Congressional Demographic Profile*

Medium	Congress	Variables	Press Releases Available	Complete Congress	Absolute Difference
Press Release	114	Black	9.82%	10.11%	0.29%
Press Release	114	Female	20%	19.31%	0.59%
Press Release	114	Democrat	44.25%	43.21%	1.04%
Press Release	115	Black	11.61%	10.51%	1.10%
Press Release	115	Female	20%	19.67%	0.17%
Press Release	115	Democrat	46.20%	44.37%	1.83%
Press Release	116	Black	12.76%	11.95%	0.81%
Press Release	116	Female	24%	23.48%	0.16%
Press Release	116	Democrat	53.95%	53.56%	0.39%
Twitter	116	Black	12.13%	11.95%	0.18%
Twitter	116	Female	23.34%	23.48%	0.14%
Twitter	116	Democrat	53.55%	53.56%	0.01%

* Significant at .05 based on Two-Sample T-Test

We draw from two separate data sets to determine levels of Black outreach in Congress. This includes almost the complete universe of press releases for members of the U.S. House of Representatives in the 114th (2015–2017), 115th (2017–2019), and 116th (2019–2021) US Congresses. This data set includes 204,806 individual press releases from 401 members in the 114th Congress, 403 members in the 115th Congress, and 407 members in the 116th Congress. Our dataset represents over 92 percent of the membership in each of the Congresses we examine. The only representatives we were unable to obtain data for were those whose websites did not have an accessible press release section or who retired, and whose websites could not be opened with the internet archive. The representatives from whom we could not get information do not significantly differ from the whole congress in their partisanship, gender, or race (see Table 1.1). Thus, we do not expect that the exclusion of these individuals will systematically bias our results.

Our Twitter data are confined to the 116th Congress (2019–2021). This data set includes 601,303 individual tweets from 411 members of the 116th U.S. House of Representatives. This includes the universe of members of Congress who put out a tweet during our period of interest (January 3, 2019, and January 2, 2021) and/or had an active Twitter account. However, it is possible that deleted tweets were not included in this analysis.[22]

Measuring Racial Outreach

We use press releases and social media posts to determine levels of Black-related rhetorical representation. We consider Black-oriented rhetorical representation to be any discussion of an issue, topic, public figure, event, institution, or organization that is explicitly tied to Black political interests. *Additionally, these discussions must frame Black political interests in a positive or supportive manner.* There is no established measure of Black-oriented outreach, so we create our own codebook for Black political appeals by using a comprehensive review of both our own communication data (i.e., press releases and tweets) and the work of scholars in this area (Metz and Tate 1995, Reeves 1997, Grose 2011, McIlwain and Caliendo 2011, Minta 2011, Gillespie 2010, 2012, Stout 2015, Wamble 2018, Arora 2019, Crowder 2021, Stephens-Dougan 2020, 2021, Dietrich and Hayes 2023).

We supplement this review with an additional audit of Black-centered organizations' websites. This review allowed us to broaden the number of potential topics being covered and ensure that we would not miss key issues. For example, there are several names tied to Black Lives Matter that received low coverage in the media, and several Historically Black Colleges and Universities (HBCUs) that may not be recognizable to the average coder. By including each of the names associated with Black Lives Matter, through a review of the organization's website along with databases tied to political protest like countlove.org and ephrame.com, and each HBCU, we cast a wider net to ensure we are not missing lower-profile cases of Black-related outreach.

Finally, we coded all bill summaries that were issued in the U.S. House of Representatives during our period of interest (2015–2021), which recognized an individual or proposed naming a place after an individual. We then searched Google.com for biographies and photos of each individual named in the summary. While this is an inexact science, we were

---

[22] Unfortunately, we only have Twitter data for a single congress given the time in which we collected this data. However, given that we find relative consistency around racial appeals across congressional sessions with press release data, we have no reason to believe the same pattern would not hold among Twitter users if we obtained the data for the social media site over the complete six-year span.

able to find several individuals who are African American who would not have been included in our initial coding scheme. For example, Kira Johnson was a Black woman who died during childbirth due to prejudiced health care. In recognition of her and all Black mothers who face greater risks during pregnancy, Alma Adams (D-NC) introduced the Kira Johnson Act. While not initially on our coding scheme, the inclusion of this name and people like her increases the probability that a Tweet or press release highlighting this legislation would be appropriately coded as appealing to African Americans.

From our review of research and an exploratory coding analysis of the data that we had available, we created a coding scheme that highlighted fifteen broad themes and provided coders over 500 words and names centered on Black political outreach to reference if they were unsure (see appendix for complete coding scheme). By creating this coding dictionary, we hope to have developed the broadest and most detailed measure of Black political outreach available. We also hope that this comprehensive list of racial outreach can be used as a guide for further research on Black appeals.[23]

We focus on explicit Black outreach because press releases and tweets around these topics demonstrate the most direct and recognizable outreach to African Americans. Moreover, race is a central part of American politics and spillovers into many different domains such as healthcare (Tesler 2016), welfare (Gilens 2001), crime (Mendelberg 2001), and gun control (Filindra and Kaplan 2015). To ensure that the appeals we focus on are made directly to African Americans and are not simply racially tinged, we confine our coding to issues explicitly tied to race. We are not interested in racial outreach, which is meant to harm Black political interests. For example, several posts on Twitter following the murder of George Floyd accused Black Lives Matter of being a violent movement that encouraged rioting. While these forms of outreach make race a salient issue, they do so in a way that harms African Americans. Given that racial rhetorical representation is not simply discussing race but means doing so in a way that advances Black politics, we do not code attacks on African Americans as being forms of rhetorical representation in our analysis.

Given the large number of press releases and tweets, it would be extremely time-consuming and cumbersome to code each one

---

[23] See the appendix of this chapter for these coding themes as well as the dictionary we used for coding.

individually. To circumvent this problem, we use a combination of hand-coding and computer-assisted content coding using RTextTools (Jurka et al. 2012). While much has been written about machine learning content analysis (see Grimmer and Stewart 2013, Barbera et al. 2016), recent research demonstrates that it performs better than dictionary coding approaches and with the proper environment, as well as manual coding (Barbera et al. 2016). Through an iterative process of hand-coding and machine learning, we were able to identify racial outreach with a high degree of intercoder reliability among the hundreds of thousands of press releases and tweets we analyzed. See the data and methods appendix for more details about the process we used to identify and validate our measures of Black-oriented outreach.

SURVEY EXPERIMENTAL DATA

In addition to understanding whether there are differences in rhetorical representation between Black and non-Black elected officials and whether these representatives differ in their use of proactive and reactive forms of rhetorical representation, we are also interested in the electorate's response to this form of racialized outreach. This is vital to understanding the efficacy of proactive and reactive rhetorical representation in building connections with constituents. To better understand whether rhetorical representation matters to the public, we use an experiment conducted via Prolific[24] on a sample of 600 Black and 600 White respondents. In these experiments, we present fictional press releases from a hypothetical Black and White member of Congress that either discusses a non-liberal racial issue, a low-profile (i.e., proactive) racial issue, or a high-profile (i.e., reactive) racial issue. We use the experiment to examine both quantitative and qualitative reactions to candidates who engage in different forms of representation. This allows us to not only assess whether rhetorical representation from descriptive and non-descriptive representatives matters, but also explore *why* potential voters respond to this form of outreach.

By using multiple data sources, which include information from communications directors, legislators' official communications, and

---

[24] Peer et al. (2021) explored different survey platforms across four measures including attention, comprehension, honesty, and reliability. They found that only Prolific respondents scored high in each one of these measures, indicating that Prolific provides high quality data.

quantitative and qualitative responses from everyday citizens, we provide a holistic understanding of the crafting of rhetorical outreach and why it matters. The triangulation of different data sources and our mixed methods approach allows us to empirically investigate the many different sides of rhetorical representation.

CHAPTER OUTLINE

The book is divided into three main sections with the goal of providing readers with a complete understanding of rhetorical representation by using the case study of Black politics. The logic of the chapters is outlined in Figure 1.1. In Chapters 2 and 3, we explore who provides rhetorical representation and why members of Congress engage in this form of outreach.

In Chapter 2, we discuss the rhetorical strategies of congressional offices based on our interviews with twenty-nine communications directors in the U.S. House of Representatives. Our interviews reveal that legislators frequently rely on proactive rhetorical outreach when speaking out on issues that are central to their identity or brand as a legislator. In these instances, legislators use proactive rhetorical representation to advance policy debates and demonstrate their expertise on these issues to build connections with their constituents.

In this section, we also explore *who* provides Black-oriented racial rhetorical representation. This allows us to explore how a racial identity interacts with other key descriptors like gender, age, district composition,

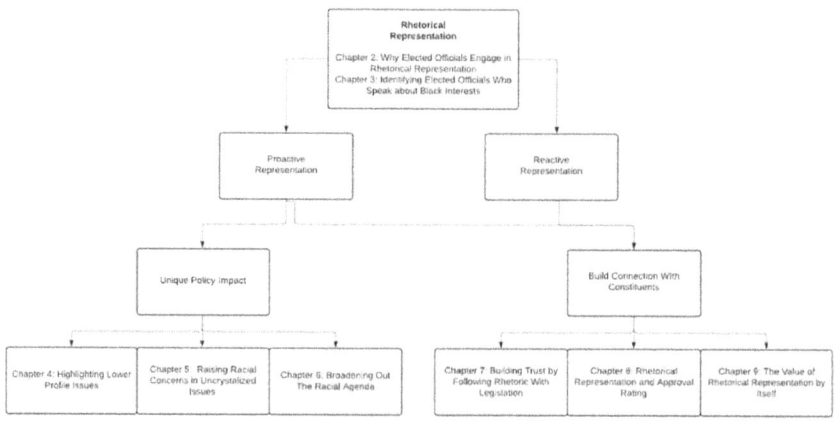

FIGURE 1.1 Outline of the Plan of the Book

and partisanship to shape levels of racial rhetorical outreach. Chapters 2 and 3 provide an overview of the motivations for elected officials to engage in rhetorical representation and provide information on which elected officials use their public platform to advance Black-oriented issues.

In Chapters 4, 5, and 6, we identify the elected officials who are most likely to use their public platform to advance the policy interests of Black people through the use of proactive rhetorical representation. In doing so, we identify three key areas in which speech can alter policy discussions. First, we explore whether Black and non-Black elected officials' rhetorical representation differs in the proportion of high-profile and low-profile outreach. The former represents a reactive form of outreach, while the latter is indicative of proactive racial representation. Using an analysis of over 500 keywords and a case study of the Black Lives Matter movement, we demonstrate that African Americans are the most likely to use their public platform to shed light on lower-profile topics and to keep issues on the agenda when public interest has faded.

The second way in which proactive rhetorical representation improves the legislative landscape for Black people is ensuring that Black political interests are accounted for in emerging policies. To that end, we examine whether Black and non-Black elected officials differ in their discussion of what Mansbridge (1999) describes as uncrystallized issues. Mansbridge (1999) argues that uncrystallized political issues are those that have not been on the political agenda for very long, and political actors have not yet taken public stances. While Mansbridge's (1999) hypothesis was theoretical, in Chapter 5, we empirically demonstrate that Black elected officials are the most likely to speak out on behalf of co-racial individuals around uncrystallized issues using an analysis of racialized press releases and responses to the COVID-19 pandemic.

The final way in which we believe that proactive rhetorical representation may alter the policy landscape is through the discussion of the multiple challenges and opportunities that different groups face in society. We argue that African American legislators' ability to highlight issues of concern to a diverse Black community broadens the recognition of social problems and solutions for this racial group. In doing so, legislators who use proactive rhetorical representation ensure that a broader set of racial interests is in the public domain. In Chapter 6, we use keyword-assisted topic modeling to identify over twenty different topics in both press releases and tweets. We then explore whether Black elected officials differ from others in the number of topics they discuss in their rhetorical outreach. Similar to other areas of proactive rhetorical representation, we find that descriptive representatives speak about a broader set of racial topics than others.

Chapters 7, 8, and 9 explore the symbolic responsiveness aspects of proactive and reactive rhetorical representation. In particular, we explore whether different forms of rhetorical representation can help build trust and approval with constituents. While we think that both forms of rhetorical representation can provide a sense of symbolic responsiveness, it is important to explore whether one is a more effective way to build connections between elected officials and those whom they represent.

The first way that elected officials can use rhetorical representation to build trust is to follow their rhetoric with policy actions. Rhetorical representation can be a powerful tool to inform supporters of the member of Congress' intentions about advancing racial progress in government *if* it is tied to actual behavior. If this is the case, it may be a useful tool to build trust between legislators and constituents. In Chapter 7, we assess whether the use of proactive or reactive rhetorical representation is correlated with a host of legislative activities, including bill sponsorship and co-sponsorship, voting scores, and discussions in committee hearings.

In Chapters 8 and 9, we shift from the trust-building function of public outreach to assess whether proactive and/or reactive rhetorical representation can improve constituents' approval of legislators. In Chapter 8, we use an experiment that presents a large sample of Black and White respondents with a hypothetical press release that discusses a non-racial liberal issue (climate change), a high-profile racial issue (police reform), and a low-profile racial issue (manufacturing employment discrimination). We then ask respondents whether the press release they received improved their perceptions of the elected official and to explain their reasoning.

Chapter 9 explores whether racial rhetorical representation matters in the presence or absence of tangible legislation. To answer this question, we return to our experiment and inform respondents that the topic the elected official spoke about in the press release either became law or failed to become law. After providing information about the fate of legislation, we ask respondents whether this changes their opinion of the elected official's advocacy and why.

In the conclusion, we speak about the growing significance of racial rhetorical representation in demonstrating that elected officials are working on behalf of their constituents in an era of increasing political gridlock. We also connect our findings to the continued importance of Black representation in a period where the salience of race and racial inequality has grown. Not only do we find that Black legislators provide Black people with the most rhetorical representation on race, but we also find that they are more proactive, speaking out on issues that are not widely known and pursuing interests that are not yet part of the national agenda. Black elected officials continue to play a crucial role in advocating for Black interests, and they are necessary for the full and equal representation of Black people.

2

Pushing the Agenda or Reacting to the Moment

Why Communication Directors Engage in Rhetorical Outreach

Members of Congress engage in a large amount of public outreach during any congressional session. On average, members of Congress put out about 100 press releases, 500 Tweets, and 400 Facebook posts in a two-year period (Shoub et al. 2023). These forms of communication play an essential role in U.S. House Representatives' chances for re-election (Grimmer 2013, Hager 2018, Russell 2021). The right message at the right time could catapult the elected official into the national spotlight by increasing their name recognition on a particular issue and improving their legislative opportunities. However, the wrong message could lead to an electoral backlash from the public and provide fodder for ambitious opponents looking to use an elected official's words against them. As a result, rhetorical representation requires a balance between the risks and rewards of any public statement. The uncertainty behind the consequences of rhetorical representation often requires a significant amount of strategizing to determine what elected officials should speak about and when.

This chapter seeks to better understand how legislators make these rhetorical decisions. What leads some legislators to engage in proactive racial rhetorical outreach, while others respond reactively or not at all? Through our interviews with twenty-nine communication directors in the U.S. House of Representatives, we find that a legislator's identity – or brand – plays a central role in these decisions. That is, legislators engage in proactive rhetorical outreach on issues that they see as being a core part of their identity as legislators. For example, a member of Congress who views themselves as an environmentalist should proactively speak out on environmental issues in their public outreach. For the purposes of our study, we argue that Black legislators, whose racial identity is central to how they see themselves as a legislator, should be consistently seeking out opportunities to highlight racial topics and expand the range of Black-centered issues in the public discourse.

In comparison, legislators whose identity is non-racial will often still speak about racial topics in their public statements. However, they tend to do so reactively. Often, these legislators will engage in racial rhetorical outreach in response to an incentive to speak out and will focus on issues that are well-vetted and established. Whether it be in response to a racialized moment which calls for immediate attention, like the passing of Rep. John Lewis or the murder of George Floyd, or perennial topics around discrimination, like voting rights or condemning White supremacy, legislators who engage in reactive rhetorical representation often do so due to public pressures for re-election, career advancement or to remain relevant in the everchanging news cycle. By using a well-vetted script of racial topics and issues that are already in the public eye, elected officials who engage in racial rhetorical representation can still appeal to people of color and advance Black politics using a lower-cost and more narrowly defined form of racial outreach.

In this chapter, we summarize our interviews with communications directors in the U.S. House of Representatives during the 118th Congress. The interviews were semi-structured and took place via phone or on Zoom between February and April 2023 and May and June 2024. We reached out to all communications directors whose legislator identifies as Black and Latino/a.[1] We also reached out to a random sample of communications directors from fifty Democratic and fifty Republican offices. In all, we interviewed communications directors from seven Latino Democrats, two Latina Democrats, four Black Democratic Congressmen, nine Black Democratic Congresswomen, three White Democratic Congressmen, two White Democratic Congresswomen, and two Republican males.[2,3] These legislators cover a wide array of seniority and districts. This is not a representative sample. Nonetheless, the interviews provide important insights into how legislators, particularly racial

---

[1] Legislator identities were determined based upon information provided by the US House of Representatives. https://history.house.gov/Exhibitions-and-Publications/
[2] We hide their racial identity for the sake of confidentiality.
[3] The response rate among communications directors in Black legislators' offices was 22.4%; in Latino/a legislators' offices was 17.3%; non-Black, non-Latino/a Democratic legislators' offices 10%; and Republican legislators' offices 4%.

and ethnic minority legislators, think about and engage in rhetorical outreach.

Through these interviews, we present evidence that legislators think about cultivating an identity or brand based on several factors previously discussed in research around specialization (Asher 1974, Mayhew 1974, Swers 2002, Meinke 2019, Aleman and Micozzi 2023). Namely, members of Congress engage in rhetorical representation on issues tied to their personal identity and experiences, their constituents, and how they are situated in Congress. Once a legislative identity is developed, legislators proactively seek opportunities to speak about that topic as often as possible to both strengthen their brand and to be more effective legislators on that issue.

Conversely, legislators without an identity in a particular area may still respond to key events or topics in this area to appeal to the electorate. However, this responsiveness is often much more limited and cautious. As one communications director for a Black member of Congress said, our "proactive planning goes hand in hand with our overall goals of getting the Congressman's priorities out there. However, Congress is extremely unpredictable, and in addition to proactive planning, we have to do a lot of reactive responding." Overall, the results of our interviews highlight the importance of brand development as a predictor of rhetorical representation and in the distinction between proactive and reactive rhetorical outreach. More particularly, the interviews demonstrate the central role that racial identity and experiences impact how Black legislators engage in racial rhetorical outreach.

LEGISLATIVE IDENTITY AND RHETORICAL REPRESENTATION

Members of the U.S. House of Representatives are but one member in a legislative chamber with 441 members, if you count the non-voting delegates. While the federal legislature is the most high-profile in the United States, it is easy for any single legislator to be overlooked. Members of Congress often work diligently to ensure that they have a specialization or brand in Congress to help them stand out (Asher 1974, Mayhew 1974, Swers 2002, Meinke 2019, Aleman and Micozzi 2023). By developing a brand as an expert in a particular area, elected officials can raise their profiles in their districts, within their political party, and among the national media.

Through our interviews, it became clear that communications directors engage in proactive rhetorical representation in hopes of building and maintaining the brand or reputation of their elected official in this area. Several communications directors highlighted the importance of their legislator's brand in shaping their rhetorical outreach and their personal role in helping maintain that brand. One communications director said that he saw himself as a "brand manager." He said his job was to keep the focus on his legislator's top priorities. In practice, this means he's always thinking about ways to raise his boss' priorities despite the constantly crowded and ever-changing news cycle. Whether that's planning to talk about them at regular intervals regardless of the issue environment or using current events as opportunities to highlight them, communications directors intentionally find ways to speak on their priorities.

But where does this brand come from, and how does the development of this identity differ across members of Congress? In our interviews with communications directors, they echoed much of the research around the development of specializations in Congress. Namely, elected officials' brand development is driven by their own experiences (Burden 2007, Francis and Bramlett 2017), racial/ethnic and gender background (Swers 2002, Hawkesworth 2003, Peay and Leasure 2023), their constituents (Aleman and Micozzi 2023) and the committees that they sit on (Deering and Smith 1997, Hamm et al 2011).

Constituents

One of the most frequently cited factors that shaped the rhetorical strategies of the communications directors in our interviews was the legislator's constituency. Considering that the proximate interest of legislators is reelection (Mayhew 1974), and the important link between branding and homestyles (Fenno 1978), it makes sense that a legislator's constituents play a large role in the development of issue priorities they speak out on. In fact, one communications director said that she doesn't see them "trying to speak to anyone else but their constituents," while another communications director said that about "75 percent" of what they prioritize in their statements is rooted in their constituency. Still another said that their constituents are the first thing he thinks about when deciding what to speak out on.

In our interviews, communications directors talked about the role of their constituency in one of two ways. First, they would talk about their constituency by highlighting how events, circumstances, or conditions within a district led them to develop specific priorities. For instance, one communications director talked about how having a military base in their district has led the legislator to really prioritize military-related issues, as well as advocating for resources for the base itself. Another communications director talked about how a mass shooting in their district led their legislator to prioritize the issue of gun violence. This wasn't an issue that the legislator entered Congress planning to focus on, but having an event like that happen in the legislator's district really impacted the legislator's priorities. Still another talked about how the proximity of their district to the border made the issue of immigration central to their work. This communications director said the issue is "so present" within their district that it's hard not to have that be a focus of their office.

Other communications directors talked about how the relative electoral safety of their district impacted the issues they prioritized. One communications director from a safe district said that because of their electoral safety, they "run communications through a place of authority." This gives them a certain amount of discretion over the issues they prioritize. It allows the legislator to work on issues she personally cares about, which run in harmony with the interests of her constituents. In contrast, a communications director from a swing district talked about how electoral circumstances meant that they were focused on "local, local, local!" Everything this office prioritized centered on the constituency. And yet another communications director said that while they come from a safe district, they're very aware that their biggest vulnerability is from the left. So, anytime there was an opportunity to highlight how an issue that they prioritize speaks to liberal interests, they're going to highlight it.

The second way communications directors frequently talked about their constituency was by highlighting key constituent groups and the role they play in shaping their priorities. Depending upon the district, communications directors emphasized different groups they were trying to reach. One communications director talked about how her legislator was working hard to appeal to different constituent groups in his district, like farmers, veterans, and the middle class. She said he tries to make sure that each of these groups is spoken to throughout the weeks and months. Still another talked about how their legislator was particularly concerned with reaching Latinos, immigrant workers, and senior citizens in their district. This, he said, not only influenced the issues they prioritized but also shaped how they disseminated their message. For instance, their office made sure to reach out to Latino media to reach Latinos and immigrant workers, and cable news to reach senior citizens. While personal backgrounds provide a passion for speaking out about different issues, elected officials are keen to ensure that they reach out to key groups within their constituency.

Personal Background

While much of elected officials' decisions are constrained by their electoral circumstances, previous research demonstrates that an elected official's background before entering Congress is a significant predictor of their actions in government (Francis and Bramlett 2017, Hansen et al. 2019). For example, elected officials who were doctors and/or nurses before they entered Congress are more likely to focus on health care legislation (Christenson 2005). Similarly, individuals who went to a public college are stronger champions for more funding going to public institutions of higher learning (Shorette et al. 2021). We found many elements of this in our own interviews with communication directors and how they crafted their rhetorical outreach strategies. One communications director mentioned that her legislator was a college athlete; therefore, the legislator holds an interest in related issues. Another communications director noted that her legislator came into office with an interest in technology and AI. She continues to hold "a keen interest" in the policy area, so their office regularly speaks out on these issues. Another communications director mentioned his boss' "long standing interest in energy." Any time something pertaining to his legislator's specialized area of energy arises, he makes sure to issue a statement so that he can "remind people that [his] boss is the guy" who knows all about this issue. And lastly, another communications director talked about how his boss' background in education has made her particularly focused on defending academic freedom.

Beyond previous personal experiences, one of the strongest predictors of specialization development in Congress is a legislator's immutable characteristics, like their race/ethnicity or gender. In our interviews, communications directors regularly brought up the racial/ethnic and gender identity of the member of Congress as a key factor in shaping their issue priorities. Many of the communications directors we spoke with indicated that it was their legislators' own experiences within the Black community and with racism and marginalization that shaped their legislators' core priorities. One communications director in a Black Congresswoman's office said, "the congresswoman herself has experienced marginalization," and she wants to use her position to be an "advocate for marginalized communities." Another communications director of a Latino legislator said that "as a child of immigrants," her boss feels a deep connection and understanding with Latino immigrant communities.

Still others highlighted how the social networks of Black legislators provide them a unique perspective on the different issues facing the Black community. For instance, one communications director talked about how a member of Congress identified an issue on Facebook that wasn't gaining any national attention but was being heavily felt within the Black community. Because of the legislator's social network on Facebook, which was largely comprised of co-racial friends and content, this Black legislator identified an uncrystallized issue as important to the Black community. Another communications director of a Black Congresswoman spoke about how her experience at a Historically Black College and University (HBCU) was fundamental in who she is as a legislator. He said that her college experiences exposed her to a "variety of Black folks" with a range of different backgrounds. This, he said, gave her a deeper, more complete understanding of the Black community. He said that "her authenticity was built in the HBCU environment."

Often, identity was mentioned in a way that made it seem like it was serving as a sort of filter through which the office saw everything. One communications director for a Black woman legislator said that "her identity as a Black woman is inherent within most of what she does." The communications director said it shaped the Congresswoman's priorities and how she approached her job. A communications director for another Black Congresswoman said that her identity is very important to the work that she does. She believes she has an "outsized role" to play on gender and racial issues because of her identity. She went on to say that it's important to her to speak out on those subjects and have her perspective heard. Similarly, a communications director from a Latino Democrat's office said that her representative "feels a duty as a progressive Latino" to speak out on issues like immigration, labor rights, and union rights. She said that his "identity shapes his message on multiple levels."

Relatedly, a communications director for a Black Congresswoman mentioned that they've noticed that when racial events occur, people reach out to their office to get her perspective. The communications director recognized this as an important way to build up the legislator's presence and build connections that they can then use to continue to get her perspective out. Another communications director of a Latino legislator from a district with a sizeable Latino population said that because of her legislator's identity as a child of immigrants and a Latino, their office is particularly attuned to the issues impacting these communities. He said that they "feel a moral obligation" to speak out on their needs and interests. Another communications director said that the Congressman brings his own perspective, whether it's his experiences as a Black man, a man of faith, or being from a rural district, and it's important to have his perspective shared on issues. And another said that because of his boss' identity as a minority woman, she understands broader issues and hardships that other marginalized minority communities, co-racial constituents, in her district face, and that they makes a point to speak out on those. These interviews highlight how one's social identity plays a key role in how they see themselves in the legislative sphere and their primary goals as legislators. This deeper-seated interest leads legislators' background to increase their intentionality of engaging in racial outreach.

Committee

A final common theme that communications directors regularly cited was the role that committee assignments played in the setting of their issue priorities. Committee assignments allow legislators to specialize in certain policy areas, making their committee assignment an important component of their legislative identity (Deering and Smith 1997, Hamm et al. 2011). Moreover, because of the role that committees play in the lawmaking process, this is also likely to be where the bulk of their policymaking influence lies. So, when legislators are hammering down their issue priorities and what they want to be known for as a legislator, those covered under their committee's jurisdiction tend to be central.

One communications director said that the Congressman's "committee assignment has dictated his brand to a certain degree." When an issue arises pertaining to the jurisdiction of his committee, particularly that of his subcommittee on which he's a ranking member, "people expect him to speak out as a leader on the issue." Another communications director said that she "use[es] her [the legislator's] position on committees as a way to represent her constituents." The legislator uses her work in committees to demonstrate to constituents what she's doing in D.C. So, she added, "from a communications standpoint, your committee assignment dictates" much of your priorities. Echoing the role of committees in their rhetorical outreach, another communications director from a newly elected Democratic member said that "things really started moving when he got his committee assignments" in terms of the priorities that they are proactively working on.

On the flip side, another communications director highlighted how committee assignments influenced what her boss is able to get done on one of their top issue priorities: housing. She said that because her legislator doesn't sit on a committee with jurisdiction over the issue, they're constrained in what they can accomplish legislatively. While they still speak out on the issue through press releases and social media, the communications director said that they feel somewhat constrained in how they can talk about their efforts on the issue.

WHY COMMUNICATIONS DIRECTORS VALUE PROACTIVE RHETORICAL REPRESENTATION

Once the legislator's issue priorities are set, it becomes the job of the communications director to find ways to regularly raise these issues and highlight the legislator's commitment to them. The activities that legislators take in this area often lead them to engage in proactive rhetorical representation. Because the legislator is deeply immersed in the issue area, they tend to raise low-salient-related topics or previously unrelated topics to the issue area, thereby expanding the scope of the issue. Additionally, legislators engaging in proactive rhetorical representation regularly speak out on this issue area regardless of whether the issue is in the news.

Many communications directors discussed how their office engages in proactive rhetorical representation. One communications director acknowledged that "you can't be out on everything. You need to think about what you want to be known for and make sure you are consistent in prioritizing those issues." As mentioned earlier, elected officials and their staff prioritize certain issues and work hard to speak publicly about these topics repeatedly. One communications director mentioned that the Latina legislator they worked for came into office with core priorities, and these priorities have been the focus of the team's work and communication strategy. Many others mentioned that relatively early on in a session, they highlight three to five issues that their offices prioritize. One referred to these as "pillars" that the entire office revolved around. In this particular case, the "pillars" were so ingrained within the "culture of the office" that the communications director said that staffers almost "reflexively" knew their legislator's position on any emerging issue or current event without speaking to their boss. This allowed them to speak out more quickly and often on this particular topic. Another communications director said that she knows there are "big issues that the congressman cares about and those guide the main [communication's] strategy" of the office. She went on to say that "he's always trying to find ways to highlight those interests." This consistency and intentionality in speaking out about a particular topic is a hallmark of proactive rhetorical representation.

Reiterating the importance of consistency in brand building, another communications director said that she likes to view the issue priorities as "buckets" and every 1–2 weeks, she makes sure to fill the bucket in some way. She said that she has worked really hard to get her legislator to be a leader in three issue areas, and she wants her legislator to remain there. Given that fewer issues arise over time that may fill these "buckets," communications directors must be vigilant in their efforts to identify opportunities to speak in support of their area of specialization. This vigilance often brings to light lesser-known topics and broadens discussions around a particular area.

This same communications director emphasized the importance of maintaining that leadership position on an issue by using rhetorical outreach. As such, she emphasized the importance of regularly highlighting the connection between her legislator and the issue so that when something happens in that issue area, her legislator is thought of as someone who needs to be involved. According to her, "repetition is key" when trying to effectively build a brand. Another communications director from a Black legislator's office drew a connection between her approach to communications and product marketing. She said that research in marketing has shown that it takes "7–10 touchpoints" for a consumer to develop trust and familiarity with a brand. She said that she tries to apply this to her work in communications. She aims to consistently hit on her boss' issue priorities, not deviating too much from the legislator's core brand, so that she develops a reputation among her constituents and others as someone they can trust.

Beyond reminding constituents and key political players that your legislator is devoted to an issue, repetition is also a way to play "lane defense," according to another communications director. This communications director said that by being proactive in speaking out on his top issue priorities, he's trying to ensure that other legislators don't encroach on those issue lanes. By proactively speaking out about a topic consistently, communications directors use proactive rhetorical representation to cement their position as a leader on a topic.

Another communications director talked about how reporters can play an important role in keeping a legislator as a leader on an issue. This communication director discussed the idea of "pushing paper," which is when you steadily give reporters press releases or pieces of information about your legislator working on an issue priority. Another communications director said that she doesn't want to overuse press releases because she's "cognizant of the possibility of callousness to form." But, you want to issue just enough to keep your member of Congress in the back of their mind so that when one of your issue priorities comes up in the news, they'll reach out to you. This then only reinforces the legislator's leadership role on the issue. Again, these actions create a consistency in rhetorical outreach.

Sometimes a legislator prioritizes an issue that they are not well-positioned to advance legislatively, like through bill sponsorship or committee work. Communications directors pointed to the significance of proactive rhetorical representation when they were in the minority or when they faced other constraints in advancing legislation. Given the dim prospects for actually accomplishing anything, legislative offices used rhetorical outreach to remind constituents and others about their activities in a particular area, let concerned individuals know that the legislator had not forgotten about them, and highlight that they would continue to work to advance the goals of specific groups even if such efforts were largely symbolic.

One communications director said that his office knew that there would be no traction on their policy priorities this legislative session because they were in the minority. But this didn't deter them from sponsoring legislation on the issues they care about. Rather, the communications director said that they sponsor "messaging bills." They know these bills are "going nowhere," but they provide the legislator the opportunity to talk about the issues they care about while at the same time showing their constituents that they are still working towards those goals, regardless of the political circumstances.

Other communications directors talked about how they can use different events as ways to highlight their prioritization and work on an issue. For instance, one communications director said that his legislator planned a press conference with a member of Congress from a neighboring district to talk about an issue impacting both of their districts. Rather than just issuing a statement via a press release or Twitter, the communications director said they will use the images and videos from the press conference as part of their outreach on social media. And still another communications director outlined a lengthy communications plan that took roughly eighteen months to implement. In this case, her member of Congress became deeply committed to an issue and wanted to be a leader on it. Because her legislator did not sit on a relevant committee and had little legislative track record on the issue, the communications director built a strategy to have her legislator become a leader in the issue area. This included press releases, holding press conferences, writing op-eds, sponsoring legislation, raising the issue in committee, and finally participating in a high-profile protest on the issue. These examples illustrate the ways that legislators proactively use their public platforms to advance the issues they care most about.

Using Critical Events to Further a Legislator's Brand

The aforementioned forms of outreach are based on the discretion of the elected officials and their staff. However, the communication directors that we spoke to noted that it was not uncommon that their rhetorical strategy would be shaped by factors outside of their control. Legislators are members of parties, committees, and caucuses, all of which have their own priorities and plans for a legislative session. They can place pressure on rank-and-file members to echo a unified message. While at the same time, the ever-changing news cycle continuously reports on the latest natural disaster, political corruption, international war, and global health crisis. This is all to say that, regardless of the extensive planning legislators and their team engage in, they must continually adapt.

It is under these circumstances that legislators try to use the second form of proactive rhetorical outreach: raising new issues or perspectives in response to events or issues that are getting attention. One communications director we interviewed highlighted this nicely when he said that when events out of his control emerge, he tries to view them as "opportunities" to highlight his legislator's issue priorities. Another communications director said that they don't necessarily feel pressure to respond to events; rather, when events emerge, they try to find ways to "tie them back to issues [we] care about."

Overall, there are certain issues that elected officials speak about proactively. Doing so helps them further develop their legislative identity, demonstrate concern for particular groups of voters during periods where legislating is difficult, and help frame issues in a manner that highlights opportunities for the groups that they prioritize. The communication directors spoke about the intentionality and consistency with which they engaged in outreach on issues tied to the "pillars" of their identity. This outreach leads to the characteristics associated with proactive rhetorical representation.

WHY AND HOW MEMBERS OF CONGRESS ENGAGE IN REACTIVE RHETORICAL OUTREACH

It's not always possible, however, to link an issue that emerges directly back to a legislator's core priority. In those cases, legislators and their teams must decide if they need to respond. The legislator may feel pressure to speak out because his or her constituents care about an issue, and if the legislator doesn't engage in outreach, she or he may face electoral consequences. A legislator's office may also engage in reactive rhetorical representation by speaking out about a topic when they want to please party leaders or a particular part of their coalition to advance electorally. Whatever their motivating factor might be, reactive rhetorical outreach occurs when elected officials speak about a topic in a narrower and more established manner.

Most communications directors agreed that they do not need to respond to every new event that emerges. Rather, as one communication director said, they do a "cost benefit analysis" to determine if and how to respond to an event. However, there was some variation between offices around when they felt compelled to respond. On one side of the spectrum was a communications director who made it clear that he didn't want to miss the opportunity to get his legislator's name in a news cycle. As a result, he appeared a bit quicker to issue a statement responding to an emerging issue than some others. On the other end of the spectrum was a communications director who admitted that her approach to communications was "probably more conservative" than most others. She was hesitant to get involved in a news cycle unless it was clear that there was something to be gained or a clear cost for not speaking out.

There were a host of factors that communications directors mentioned that they considered when deciding whether to respond to an event that was outside of an area of specialization. Top among them was when there was a major event happening in their district. For instance, one communications director said that Amazon decided to close a distribution center in their district. There was no question that the legislator needed to issue a statement in response to this. Other events mentioned by communications directors as instances where they felt compelled to respond were mass shootings, police violence, natural disasters, and immigration-related events that occurred in their districts or neighboring districts. Others said that their office almost always responded to tragedies, even if they fell outside of their district. And still another said that any time there is significant legislation that is passed by the House, his office feels compelled to respond. In each of these cases, communications directors speak about reactive rhetorical representation because external forces prompt them to issue a statement.

With a news cycle that's constantly changing, one communications director said that they constantly feel pressure to be the first to speak out on any given event. But, that same director said you don't have to be, "so sometimes you wait." However, others emphasized the importance of holding off on issuing a statement until they saw who else would speak out. One communications director said that he didn't want to be the first person to speak out, but he also didn't want to be the last. When you start seeing lots of legislators speak out, he said he felt more pressure to do so. Another communications director also said that she vigilantly kept track of who was speaking out on an issue. However, for her, it was more important who was speaking out rather than the number of people speaking out. She said once she saw certain legislators and/or advocacy organizations speak out on an issue, then she felt compelled to do so too. The "minimize risk" strategy was most evident among communications directors who did not see a particular issue as being part of their legislators' brand. As a result, they generally refrained from speaking out about the topic unless pushed to do so. The ability to speak out about an issue after the parameters of the event are set makes such outreach less risky. However, such an approach limits the legislator's ability to alter the narrative around the topic because others have proactively set the framing of the issue.

Others highlighted how the desire to minimize opportunities for criticism influenced these decisions. For many, this meant not sticking your neck out and speaking out on something unless it is salient to constituents and/or other key players the legislator values. For instance, a communications director talked about how he felt compelled to lay out "digital datapoints" demonstrating their support for key players. When an event occurred that he knew an important ally, like another legislator or interest group, cared about, he made sure to at least pay lip service to it. Another communications director gave a more concrete example. He said that the National Education Association had been reaching out to member offices asking legislators to oppose Republican sponsored H.R. 5, also known as the "Parents Bill of Rights." The communications director said that his member of Congress agrees with the NEA [National Education Association] around 95 percent of the time, so he's going to issue a post to social media declaring his opposition to the bill and tagging the NEA and other key organizations that would care about it. In many of these cases, the legislators did not have to be creative in their responses or raise novel issues. However, by engaging in reactive rhetorical representation, elected officials were able to demonstrate their attentiveness to key groups.

Other communications directors mentioned the resource costs of drafting a message as a motivation to engage in more reactive forms of rhetorical representation. Both political parties have groups within their leadership that provide messaging support for party members. Other entities, like caucuses or interest groups, also provide these services at times. The Democratic Policy and Communications Committee (DPCC) tries to provide a unified and coordinated party message. It provides key talking points and sample press releases and social media posts that communications directors can customize however much or little they want. Because this can lower the resource costs of drafting statements, one communications director is "60% more likely" to issue a press release or post something to social media if someone gives it to her. Another communications director said that she has found the DPCC to be particularly helpful to newly elected members of Congress who are stretched thin in terms of trying to craft their brand/identity.[4] These prescriptive resources allow elected officials to message toward particular groups. However, the predetermined nature of these resources means that those engaged in this form of outreach are speaking to a much more established and widely discussed set of issues. This is consistent with a reactive rhetorical representation approach.

STAYING SILENT

Of course, beyond rhetorical representation, elected officials often make the decision to make no statement at all. For example, a communications director emphasized that he was really looking to minimize costs. In this vein, the communications director said that he does not hesitate to say "no comment" if it's not something he wants to get involved in. Another

---

[4] In contrast, another CD said that his office rarely uses what the party gives them. His legislator, he said, really prioritizes his individuality. He sees himself as a consensus builder and someone who can work with people on both sides of the aisle, so they really are careful in crafting that image when they speak out. Another said that sometimes their messaging support can be helpful, but they require a lot of customization to make it sound authentically in the voice of their legislator. And still another communications director said that the DPCC does provide good resources, but they're "not always applicable" to a legislator like his who is more moderate and will defy party leaders.

communications director said that he sometimes feels forced to speak out because of the news cycle, but before he does, he always tries to ask himself: "Is our voice really needed here? What do we gain by speaking out?" He then outlined his thought process on an announcement by the Biden administration pertaining to drilling in Alaska. He said, policy-wise, his representative doesn't agree with it. However, no one asked them, it's not one of their main issue priorities, and he doesn't sit on a relevant committee. Moreover, the representatives from Alaska are in support of the policy, and they'd rather not criticize the president, who is of the same party. So, their office did not issue any statement. Another communications director gave a hypothetical example rooted in a real-life situation. He said his boss supports tough-on-crime measures, but every time there is a big drug bust, he's not going to put their office out there and congratulate law enforcement. He's going to wait until all of the facts are in to ensure that, for example, there wasn't some sort of misconduct that occurred during the arrest. He said "why step into something when you don't have to?"

Still another communications director said that sometimes their decision not to speak out on an event stemmed from a lack of resources to do so. One communications director said that, unlike many in her party, her representative, a White male Democrat, did not speak out after the video recording of Tyre Nichols' murder was released. She said his office didn't issue a statement largely because they didn't have the "bandwidth" at that particular moment. She went on to explain that because the incident didn't happen in his district, it didn't directly pertain to one of his issue priorities, and no one asked them to say something; they simply didn't have the resources to respond. Had it happened the next week, then we probably would have issued a statement.

PROACTIVE RACIAL RHETORICAL REPRESENTATION BY BLACK MEMBERS OF CONGRESS

The previous sections have more broadly demonstrated how communications directors approach rhetorical outreach. Upon settling on a legislative identity, communications directors are then tasked with finding ways to proactively speak out on issues pertaining to their legislator's brand. Simultaneously, these communications directors must keep a close eye on the media landscape to see if there are any events or issues that are important for their legislator to speak out on, that don't necessarily speak to their brand, so that they do not miss an important news cycle or suffer electoral consequences. In this sense, the communications director must be prepared to reactively speak out whenever they deem necessary. Though all communications directors engage in proactive and reactive rhetorical outreach, we argue that Black legislators are distinct in their use of proactive racial rhetorical outreach. As a core part of their legislative identity, Black legislators proactively engage in public outreach, which broadens the racial issue agenda by speaking about lower-profile and novel Black-centered topics. This outreach is generally unprompted by public concern, occurring whether or not the public is clamoring for a statement on a particular issue.

Proactive Racial Rhetorical Representation in Practice

Many communications directors in Black legislators' offices talked about how their boss' racial identity led them to identify uncrystallized issues as pertaining to Black interests, even though they are largely not recognized as such. For instance, one communications director talked about how the Black legislator he worked for was scrolling social media when the legislator noticed lots of posts about a health issue, and all of the people in the posts were Black. Recognizing the disproportionate impact this health issue was having on the Black community, this legislator began actively speaking out and working on the issue. Here, the legislator linked Black interests to a low-salient, previously unrelated issue and tried to garner broader attention by proactively speaking on it.

Another communications director talked about how his boss used proactive rhetorical outreach by expanding the narrative around a current event to include the particular impact on the Black community. He said that in response to the baby formula shortage in 2022, his legislator, a Black woman, highlighted the disproportionate impact it was having on Black and Brown children due to lower levels of breastfeeding in these communities. Her position as a Black woman provided her a unique perspective on the issue, and her public statements allowed a previously unrecognized aspect of the shortage to be highlighted.

Other communications directors highlighted the way that their bosses' racial identity shapes how they understand current events, and therefore influences the way they speak out on those events. For instance, when the Boycott, Divestment and Sanctions (BDS) Movement gained attention and a considerable number of members of Congress in both political parties came out to criticize it, one communications director we spoke to said that his boss refused to condemn it. He said that his legislator simply could not condemn boycotts, considering the important role they played in advancing civil rights for Black Americans. When issuing public statements on the matter, this perspective was reflected. Moreover, another communications director said that his boss, a Black legislator, understands that there is a link between the brutality experienced by Palestinians and the brutality experienced by Black people in the US. Therefore, when their office spoke on the issue, this racialized perspective was apparent. This is yet another way that Black legislators engage in proactive racial rhetorical representation.

Others talked about the importance of recognizing the work and accomplishments of the Black community. One communications director of a Black Congressman said that he knows a lot of accomplished people in the Black community, and as such, when they work on something important or achieve something, his legislator wants to recognize that. For instance, in a recent tweet and Facebook post, this legislator congratulated a Black woman who was just named a college president. And another communications director said that it's important for the Black community to "be seen." This communications director said that their office was purposeful in their posts, recognizing the accomplishments of Black Americans. For instance, he said, they paid tribute to Elijah Cummings upon his passing. This was particularly personal to the Congressman because he had worked with him. However, he went on to note other Black people that they recognized during that same congressional session that did not have the national name recognition like Rep. Cummings.

One key figure in the Black community that came up in some of the interviews was Dr. Martin Luther King Jr. One communications director talked about the different ways her office invoked Dr. Martin Luther King Jr. in their outreach compared to the outreach of "some White offices." This communications director said that "she [a Black Congresswoman] understands him very differently" and through her rhetorical outreach she tries to "make the link between what Dr. King really stood for and what the Congresswomen stands for and fights for." Rather than stick to the common and safe tropes that are used to pay homage to MLK, this communications director talked about how she tries to link MLK with a wide array of important issues that disproportionately impact marginalized communities of color. From ensuring people in need get adequate health care and housing, to ensuring a clean environment for inner-city communities, this communications director said, "we're genuinely trying to fight for Dr. King's Dream." This recognition of the Black community demonstrates yet another way that Black legislators expand what's getting discussed in the public sphere.

Why Engage in Proactive Racial Rhetorical Outreach?

When talking with communications directors of Black legislators, they spoke of three primary reasons that they engage in proactive racial rhetorical outreach. First, like every other office we spoke to, they highlighted wanting to demonstrate to their constituents that they are working on their behalf. For some who come from majority–minority districts, where Black Americans alone or in combination with other racial and ethnic groups constitute a majority, they frequently mentioned their effort to demonstrate to these historically marginalized communities what their legislator is doing for them in DC. One communications director from a majority–minority district explained that the vast majority of what he puts out is aimed at showing their constituents "what he's doing for them" in Congress.

However, a growing number of Black legislators are being elected from non-majority–minority districts. Yet, communications directors with legislators from these districts continued to mention speaking to Black Americans as a motivator for their communications. Supporting the concept of surrogate representation, whereby Black representatives seek to represent Black Americans throughout the country (Fenno 2003, Mansbridge 1999), one communications director for a Black legislator whose district has a small minority population, described how his legislator purposefully uses communications to "serve as a surrogate to Black voters" everywhere.

There was, however, some variation in how they talked about it. For instance, one communications director talked about how the district her legislator is from does not have a sizable Black population, but the district is pretty progressive and electorally safe. As a result, she said that her legislator has the freedom to stay true to their priorities and advocate for issues that are important to the Black community. Another communications director from a non-majority–minority district said that his legislator's identity is important in that "it can help folks feel seen or represented," and he speaks out on issues important to the Black community. However, this communications director also characterized the advocacy that the legislator engages in as "broad-based" so that "all boats can be lifted with a rising tide." And still another communications director for a legislator with a seat that is electorally more vulnerable said that her legislator's priorities are clearly shaped by their being "a part of the Black community," but that it's important when advocating for Black interests to make it clear how it helps the broader community.

Second, others echoed the sentiment previously expressed by some communications directors from Latino/a legislators' offices, saying that they feel they have a responsibility to have their perspective heard. One communications director said that his legislator's identity as a Black man is important in part because "it can help folks feel seen or represented." He went on to say that a big part of that is "inserting the Congressman's voice" on important issues of the day. Another communications director for a Black Congressman said that his identity gives him a unique perspective on all kinds of issues, and they feels "an obligation" to get that perspective "out there." Another communications director for a Black Congresswoman held a similar sentiment when she said that their office makes a concerted effort to try to "diversify the media environment." That is, they try to increase the coverage of issues impacting Black and Latino communities, LGBT communities, and women who "aren't always covered by monocultural news." And yet another communications director said that they try to highlight issues that they believe merit national attention, but that are usually ignored because they're centered on minority interests.

Third, some communications directors of Black legislators identified their offices' public communications via press releases and social media as a tactic they use to attain policy change. One communications director of a Black Congresswoman said that "you have to be realistic about American institutions." She operates in an "institution that wasn't built for her." As a result, one of the ways "we push our agenda" is through communications. Even when it's hard, and circumstances are unlikely to produce policy change, "we do whatever we can" to get the issue priority attention and lay the groundwork for future policy action. This, they hope, will help them build traction for policy change. And, in fact, this communications director said that this strategy has worked for them in the past. Their office was able to get one of their issues prioritized in the Build Back Better legislation.

Part of building momentum for policy change, said one communications director, is "bringing people into the coalition" in support of their policy priorities. This communications director viewed communications as a way to expand the existing network of people pushing to advance policy change. In that vein, some communications directors said that when they're issuing communications, they're not just trying to speak to constituents, but also other key "stakeholders," like interest groups, unions, advocacy organizations, party leaders, and "colleagues" at the state and federal level. Sometimes they're speaking out to signal that they are ready and eager to work on an issue with other lawmakers, said one communications director. At other times, their communications are aimed at party leaders and the administration to show them that there is growing momentum on an issue in the hopes that they'll work with them on advancing the issue. Still at other times, communications may be aimed at signaling to activists and other organizations that they have an ally in government. For instance, one communications director said that they're focused on "merging activists with places of power."

SUMMARY

In any congressional session, legislators and their offices must make numerous decisions to ensure that their constituents feel heard and that they position themselves toward the best path for re-election. One decision that legislators and their staff grapple with is how to effectively communicate to the public. Our interviews with communication directors revealed that legislators use rhetorical outreach to bolster their legislative identities and to appeal to important constituencies. In particular, communications directors spoke to the importance of being consistent and intentional in their outreach on issues that were the "pillars" of the legislator's identity. This included outreach, which was not simply responsive to what was in the news each day. Instead, this outreach required the communications director to actively find ways for the legislator to highlight crucial issues and topics tied to their brand. This engagement often led communications directors to speak about more specialized issues around their identity, which helps differentiate them from their colleagues. In doing so, legislators engage in proactive rhetorical outreach and broaden the scope of topics tied to the legislator's identity.

In our interviews, communications directors highlighted three main factors that influenced the development of their legislative identities. Their demographic and professional background, their constituency, and the committees that they served on largely determined the topics they were going to focus on in a particular Congress. Racial/ethnic identity, for a host of reasons, appeared to matter in shaping the communication strategies of the members of Congress. As a result, it would not be surprising to find in later chapters that Black legislators engage in more instances of proactive rhetorical representation based on the role that their racial background plays in shaping their legislative identity.

The communications directors were also candid that they did not have to be out on everything. Outside of one's legislative identity, elected officials were much more likely to engage in a cost–benefit analysis when deciding what to speak about. In general, this form of outreach, while still aimed at addressing concerns of a particular group, tended to be much more cautious with an eye on whether speaking out would cost their legislator votes. When the benefits outweighed the cost, communications directors would speak out. However, these responses tended to be in line with the existing discussions on that particular topic. This narrower form of responsiveness is associated with reactive rhetorical representation. If elected officials saw very few gains for engaging in public outreach, they would withhold from speaking out altogether. The interviews outlined in this chapter have elucidated the strategies that congressional offices use when engaging in rhetorical outreach. In the following chapters, we hope to identify which elected officials engage in racial rhetorical outreach and distinguish which factors are tied to proactive and reactive forms of rhetorical representation.

3

Who Racializes? Exploring the Demographic Factors of Members of Congress Who Provide Racial Rhetorical Representation through an Intersectional Perspective

To say that African Americans have been historically underrepresented in Congress would be an understatement. It was not until 1928 that Oscar DePriest became the first African American to be elected to the U.S. House of Representatives in the twentieth century. As the lone Black member in Congress, DePriest felt intense pressure to represent Black interests nationally (Teague 2024). In his tenure in Congress, DePriest advocated for national anti-lynching legislation, introduced a bill that would provide pensions to ex-slaves, and used his public platform to defend the Scottsboro boys who had been wrongly accused of raping two White women (Teague 2024).

Like DePriest, most African American representatives in this period had the dual responsibility of speaking out for their local constituents and advocating for Black people nationally. Louis Stokes, a founding member of the Congressional Black Caucus, stated, "The thrust of our elections was that many [B]lack people around America who had formerly been unrepresented, now felt that the nine Black members of the House owed them the obligation of also affording them representation in the House. In addition to representing our individual districts, we had to assume the onerous burden of acting as congressman-at-large for unrepresented people around America."[1] The small number of African Americans in Congress for much of the twentieth century created an "all hands-on deck" situation, were each Black member carried the additional responsibility of being the representative for Black people nationally.

---

[1] https://cbc.house.gov/history/#:~:text=%E2%80%9CIn%20addition%20to%20representing%20our,1971%20by%2013%20founding%20members.

Black representation in Congress has grown significantly since this period. In the forty years between 1982 and 2022, the number of Black members in Congress tripled. African Americans now represent the same percentage of Congressional representatives as they do in the national population. This increase in the number of elected officials of color brings with it significant diversity within each racial/ethnic group. For most of the twentieth century, the only Black members of Congress were men. Shirley Chisholm became the first and only Black woman to serve in Congress in 1969. Forty years later, in 1999, there were twelve Black women in Congress. In 2022, the number doubled to twenty-five. In the 118th Congress, there are Black members from every generation, from the Silent Generation (1928–1945) to Generation Z (1997–2012), and Black congresspeople represent a greater variety of districts than ever before and identify with both major political parties.

While DePriest and others served in a period where their small numbers necessitated racial rhetorical outreach, in the current period, African American elected officials may have more leeway to specialize in non-racial issues and remain silent on Black-oriented topics. This deracialized approach among Black leaders is becoming more common in the current political context (McIlwain and Caliendo 2011, Gillespie 2012). In fact, several studies in political science have found that due to the moderation that comes with political incorporation and electoral constraints tied to racialized language, Black elected officials no longer uniformly speak out in support of Black political interests (Gillion 2016, Price 2016, Haines et al. 2019, but see Dietrich and Hayes 2023).

In this chapter, we seek to establish whether a link between descriptive and rhetorical representation exists in a period where African Americans have made significant numerical gains in Congress. Moreover, we analyze whether the dramatic changes to the diversity of Black congressional membership lead some African American elected officials to provide greater levels of rhetorical representation than others. In particular, we assess whether the intersection of race with gender, age, partisanship, and the racial composition of the representative's district can help us identify which Black elected officials are the most likely to engage in racial rhetorical representation. This intersectional approach helps us better understand where the link between descriptive and rhetorical representation is strong or weak.

African Americans are not the only racial/ethnic minority group to experience sharp increases in representation. In the past 20 years, the number of Latino/a and Asian American members of Congress has grown by about 250 percent. Like African Americans, this increase in membership among Latinos/as and Asian Americans brings with it diversity in terms of gender, age, and partisanship, among other factors. While others have explored disparities in representation among Black and White members, this chapter moves beyond the Black–White binary and explores whether there are differences in rhetorical representation among non-Black elected officials of color (i.e., Latino/a and Asian American elected officials). By taking a more holistic view of who engages in Black rhetorical representation, we provide crucial insight into identifying how elected officials' identities, backgrounds, and electoral pressures shape their willingness to be strong proponents of African American political interests in government. In doing so, we provide a snapshot of who is engaging in Black-related rhetorical representation.

AFRICAN AMERICANS AND BLACK RHETORICAL REPRESENTATION

A long line of literature finds that descriptive representation is a significant predictor of substantive representation (Canon 1999, Barreto 2007, Tate 2003, Minta 2011, Grose 2011, Schwindt-Bayer and Mishler 2005). Namely, elected officials who share the identity of those they represent are much more likely to take proactive steps in government to advance their group's interests (Canon 1999, Tate 2003, Barreto 2007, Grose 2011, Minta 2011). There are numerous reasons for the link between descriptive and substantive representation. The first is largely centered around the shared experiences between individuals of the same identity. These experiences provide important insight into problems sometimes unnoticed by others (Mansbridge 1999, Dovi 2002, Fenno 2003). Well-meaning White elected officials who want to address racial inequality are sometimes not aware of the subtle and not-so-subtle ways in which symbols and policies may disempower people of color. In contrast, descriptive representatives' identities make them better able to identify issues that could affect their racial group and work to counteract them when possible.

These experiences also make elected officials feel more passionate about addressing problems facing their group. By rectifying racial inequalities, descriptive representatives not only improve the lives of those who share their identity but also improve their own opportunities. Despite their high-profile positions, African American elected officials are not immune to the same problems that rank-and-file members of their community face (Dawson 1995). For example, numerous studies have shown that law enforcement systematically treats African Americans differently from White people (Weitzer and Tuch 2002, Peffley and Hurwitz 2007, Legewie 2016). These inequities have led to high-profile cases of African American legislators being subjected to police harassment. Former Black congresswoman Cynthia McKinney was stopped by Capitol police officers after they failed to recognize that she was a member of the U.S. House of Representatives (Allen et al. 2008). Black U.S. Senator Tim Scott described being stopped numerous times by law enforcement when he was a member of the South Carolina state legislature for frivolous reasons.[2] Given these experiences, it is not surprising that Black elected officials are often the most vocal in advocating for racial justice around policing (Dancey and Masand 2019, Stout et al. 2017). While these examples are centered on law enforcement, there are a myriad of other experiences that provide descriptive representatives with insights into problems faced by their community and inspire the passion to address them.

Even when descriptive representatives do not share the same experiences as those who share their identity, these elected officials are often sympathetic to the plight of co-racial individuals. This is in part driven by people's greater concern for in-group members. Social psychologists demonstrate that as individuals develop salient identities, they become more sympathetic to those who share their background (Tajfel and Turner 1982, Maeda and Hashimoto 2020). This often manifests in greater outreach and support for co-identifiers. This in-group preference is particularly strong around race and for racial groups who have experienced significant discrimination, like African Americans (Tate 1994, Dawson 1994).

Given African Americans' long socio-historical legacy of discrimination, they have developed a strong group identity (Tate 1994, Dawson 1994). This identification leads African Americans to view their own opportunities as tied to their racial group and is powerful in shaping their political behavior. Elected officials are no different, as this sense of a common fate has been documented to lead African American members of Congress to go the extra mile to eradicate barriers faced by their racial group (Minta 2011). Broockman (2013) shows that African American elected officials demonstrate an intrinsic motivation to assist those who

---

[2] https://www.npr.org/2016/07/14/485995136/watch-black-gop-senator-says-hes-been-stopped-7-times-by-police-in-a-year

share their race. This manifests itself in African American elected officials doing work that is often unrecognized and does little to improve their chances of being re-elected (Grose 2011, Minta 2011, Broockman 2013). Based on this previous research, we strongly expect that Black elected officials will provide the strongest levels of rhetorical representation to co-racial individuals.

LATINO/A AND ASIAN AMERICAN MEMBERS OF CONGRESS AND BLACK RHETORICAL REPRESENTATION

While there is good reason to suspect that Black elected officials will be more likely to engage in Black-oriented rhetorical representation, less research has explored whether a broader coalition of elected officials of color speaks out for all underrepresented groups. On the one hand, there is literature that argues that people of color's position in American society will lead to more competition rather than cooperation (Kauffman 2003, Wilkinson 2014, 2015). This is particularly true in conditions of political and economic scarcity (Kauffman 2003). For example, when African Americans, Asian Americans, or Latinos/as compete over elected positions or employment, rivalries develop, which lead to fewer cases of cooperation (Meier et al. 2004, McClain et al 2006). Given the limited number of seats held in majority–minority districts and increased competition within urban areas among people of color, Asian American and Latino/a elected officials may be less amenable to speaking out for Black political interests.

Asian Americans and Latinos/as may also work to differentiate themselves from African Americans to assimilate into the American political mainstream (Perez et al. 2023). Instead of forming coalitions with others from underrepresented groups, some elected officials of color may view the best path to advance their group's interests is to tie themselves with the dominant group in government (i.e., White people). To curry favor with White elected officials, non-Black elected officials of color may emulate their largely deracialized approach. Even more, they may work to actively keep Black politics at arm's length to demonstrate their independence from African Americans. This may manifest itself in lower levels of Black-related rhetorical outreach among Asian American and Latino/a elected officials.

On the other hand, there is reason to believe that people of color's shared status as minority groups in the United States and their common interests in combating racial inequality may lead to cooperation among these groups (see Hero and Preuhs 2013, Tyson 2016). This, in turn, may lead Asian American and Latino/a elected officials to be more willing to speak out for Black political interests than their White counterparts. A 2021 Pew poll asked individuals whether "there is a lot/some/only a little/no [of] discrimination against each group in society."[3] Responses revealed that at least some discrimination was perceived by 95 percent of Black respondents, 83 percent of Latinos/as regarding co-ethnic individuals, and 87 percent of Asian Americans concerning their own group. In contrast, only 48 percent of White people said that their racial group faced some or a lot of discrimination. While they may not confront the same forms of discrimination, their shared experiences may lead non-Black elected officials of color to be more sympathetic to the plight of African Americans. This may increase their motivation to speak out in support of this group.

Moreover, because of overlapping racial biases, when elected officials condemn discrimination or highlight policies that address systematic racism for their group, there is likely a spillover effect for all people of color. For example, Meier et al. (2004) show that while Black and Brown people often are in conflict when competing for limited positions on school boards, they cooperatively address racial inequalities when they share the same spaces on these boards. By addressing racial inequities in learning for students of color, they advance opportunities for both in-group and out-group members. Within Congress, Tyson (2016) shows that linked political fate brings together legislators of color to advocate for equality and social justice. Similarly, Hero and Preuhs (2013) showed that Latino/a-focused organizations, like the National Hispanic Leadership Agenda, and Black-focused organizations, like the NAACP, often select the same pieces of legislation when assigning congressional scores, demonstrating overlapping interests between these two groups. When speaking in support of policies that limit police violence against people of color or recognizing individuals who fought for Civil Rights, non-Black elected officials of color may be simultaneously providing rhetorical representation for their in-group and for African Americans.

Additionally, given common circumstances around racial/ethnic discrimination, people of color may believe that coalitions among members of underrepresented groups may improve their chances of furthering their

---

[3] www.pewresearch.org/fact-tank/2021/03/18/majorities-of-americans-see-at-least-some-discrimination-against-black-hispanic-and-asian-people-in-the-u-s/

agenda. While Whites will make up a plurality of the electorate for the foreseeable future, people of color will make up the majority of the nation by 2045.[4] If united, people of color may be able to enhance their representation in government. Elected officials of color, as a result, may work to cultivate connections across racial groups, and one tool for doing so is through discussing issues and topics of importance to African Americans.

HOW INTERSECTING IDENTITIES MODERATE THE RELATIONSHIPS BETWEEN RACE AND RHETORICAL REPRESENTATION

While we anticipate that there will be large differences in racial rhetorical representation between racial groups, we also believe that it is important to explore within-group variation. Rather than treat all racial/ethnic group members as a monolith, we suspect that there will be some identities that intersect with race that amplify a representative's levels of racial rhetorical representation. In this section, we focus on four main cleavages: gender, age, party, and the racial makeup of the representative's district.

Race, Gender, and Rhetorical Representation

There is a significant amount of work that demonstrates that race and gender intersect to influence political behavior (Reingold 1992, Bratton and Haynie 1999, Bratton et al. 2006, Brown and Gershon 2016, 2017). Much of this work is rooted in intersectionality theory (Crenshaw 1989), which purports that overlapping social categories and identities inform the politics of Black women. While race is a dominant social cleavage (Mansbridge and Tate 1992, Robnett and Tate 2023), Black women often experience the world differently than their co-racial male counterparts (Crenshaw 1989, Simien 2005, Alexander Floyd 2012). For example, Black women earn a lower wage than both Black males and White women, while also being more likely to be the head of household,[5] are more likely to report not being taken seriously by medical professionals,[6] and are more likely to be sexually assaulted.[7] Black women political elites

---

[4] www.brookings.edu/articles/the-us-will-become-minority-white-in-2045-census-projects/
[5] www.pewresearch.org/social-trends/2023/03/01/the-enduring-grip-of-the-gender-pay-gap/
[6] www.pewresearch.org/science/2022/04/07/black-americans-views-about-health-disparities-experiences-with-health-care/
[7] www.apa.org/topics/sexual-assault-harassment/black-women-sexual-violence/

are also more likely to be marginalized in social movements and receive less electoral support in comparison to groups with other intersecting identities (Robnett 2000, Philpott and Walton 2007).

The double bind that women of color face with regard to racial and gender discrimination often leads to a stronger sense of racial and gender group consciousness (Gay and Tate 1998). Simien (2005), for example, demonstrates that Black women's strong group consciousness often makes them more aware of the plight of marginalized groups and more likely to take political action to address inequality. Brown (2014) finds that this relationship also holds among Black women's political elites. In interviews, Brown (2014) demonstrates that Black women legislators prioritize a broader set of Black priorities than elected officials with other intersectional identities. Brown attributes this activism to Black women legislators' greater awareness of how race, gender, and the intersection of the two identities influence opportunities for marginalized groups.

Along the same lines, Ford Dowe (2023) shows that Black women political elites continue to advocate for Black political interests regardless of their circumstances. While previous research demonstrates that Black elected officials focus less on race as they move up the political ladder (see Price 2016, Tate 2020), Ford Dowe (2023) finds that political advancement does not curtail racial outreach among Black women. Instead, she argues that continued racial advocacy is driven by Black women's community-based approach to legislating. In essence, Black women's political ambition is largely shaped by their interest in addressing concerns in their community. This desire does not abate even as they serve in office for a long period. Given this research, we hypothesize that Black women will provide co-racial individuals with stronger levels of rhetorical representation than Black men.

While we expect that Black women should be the strongest advocates for Black political interests, we also anticipate that White, Latina, and Asian American women will be more likely to speak out about racial issues in comparison to the men who share their racial/ethnic identity. Previous research demonstrates that there is a significant gender gap in American politics, where women are generally more liberal than their male counterparts (Barnes and Cassese 2017, Condon and Wichowsky 2017). This ideological divide is present in Congress as well (Thomsen 2020). Given that most issues addressing race are tied to liberal politics, one way this gap may manifest itself is through more Black-oriented outreach.

Beyond the ideological divide, it is likely that the marginalized status of women makes them more sympathetic to African Americans. While White women's racial asymmetry in positions of power limits the amount of discrimination they face, their gender increases barriers to normalcy (Bejarano et al. 2021). Moreover, Latina and Asian American women often face similar double binds as Black women. These experiences with discrimination may increase the recognition of systematic biases in our political system. This recognition may also lead to increased activism to combat discrimination in all forms (Gurin 1985). The greater awareness of systemic inequalities among women may lead female elected officials to be the most outspoken for underrepresented groups, including African Americans.

Race and Age

Beyond gender, research shows that the generation a person was born into plays a key role in shaping one's politics (Jennings 1984). Recent research also demonstrates that this matters for elected officials as well (Gillespie 2010, Tate 2020). While we anticipate that generation will shape levels of racial rhetorical outreach, we anticipate that it will matter differently for Black and White elected officials. Older African American elected officials should be the strongest proponents of Black political interests through their outreach. Gillespie (2010) argued that because younger African Americans generally did not experience the same levels of overt racism and were removed from the Civil Rights movement, they are more likely to engage in a deracialized approach to public service. Moreover, the fact that younger African Americans were socialized in a period where Black and White political leaders highlighted the need for a color-blind society may lead them to be more hesitant to speak about racial issues publicly (Smith 1996).

Additionally, younger African Americans have witnessed co-racial politicians reach the upper echelons of politics by moderating their stances around racial topics. This may lead younger African Americans who hope to advance politically to remain silent on racial issues compared to their older counterparts. Along these lines, Tate (2010, 2014) finds that as younger African Americans move into the mainstream of the Democratic Party, they soften their focus on race to assimilate. We anticipate this same logic should apply to Asian American and Latino/a elected officials as well. Overall, we suspect that younger elected officials of color should be the least likely to provide racial rhetorical representation.

In contrast, younger White people in the population tend to display a greater recognition of racial discrimination as a systematic problem than their older co-racial counterparts (Engelhardt 2021). Younger White people also tend to be more ideologically and racially liberal (Hagerman

2020). These factors should lead younger White members of Congress to think more about race as part of their outreach strategy. In contrast, given that many older White people were socialized in a period where overt racism was more common, more may hold more negative attitudes toward people of color (Nteta and Greenlee 2013, DeSante and Watts Smith 2020). Moreover, many older White politicians held political office in a period of a less diverse America, where outreach to African Americans was likely not a necessary component of a successful political coalition. These differences in racial attitudes and experiences with a different set of electoral conditions may lead older White elected officials to refrain from speaking out in support of Black people.

Race and Partisanship

While it may seem self-evident, it is important to explore the magnitude of the differences in racial rhetorical representation based on race and partisanship. We suspect that Democrats within each racial group should be more likely to speak about racial issues than Republicans. This may be tied to the fact that Democratic members of Congress tend to be more ideologically liberal on racial issues (Minta 2020, Dietrich and Hayes 2023). As a result, many of the issues that they advocate for are going to include some appeals to Black people.

Strategically, it also makes sense for Democratic members of Congress to speak about racial issues to appeal to their political base. It is no secret in American politics that African Americans are strong supporters of the Democratic Party (Grossman and Hopkins 2016, White and Laird 2020). Given their centrality in the Democratic coalition and growing pressure among even White Democrats to address racial inequality (Grossman and Hopkins 2016, Stout 2020), Democrats should have more of an incentive to provide racial rhetorical representation.

Republicans, in contrast, should be less likely to engage in racial outreach. This is driven by their own ideological preferences for more racially conservative policies and or/ a color-blind approach to governing (Tesler 2016). Their lack of interest in discussing racial issues may also come from their political base, which is increasingly displaying higher levels of antagonism to racial policies (Tesler 2016, Valentino et al. 2018). While Democrats would be incentivized to provide racial rhetorical representation, Republicans might face a backlash from their base for this same behavior. Fewer Republicans should speak about progressive racial issues as a result.

Racial District Composition and Representation

While identity matters in shaping the decisions of elected officials, re-election is the dominant motivation of almost all members of Congress (Mayhew 1974). As a result, we suspect that the constraints and opportunities tied to the demographic characteristics of each district should play a large role in determining representatives' levels of racial rhetorical representation. A significant amount of research demonstrates that elected officials consider the demographic makeup of their district when deciding what topics to focus on (Canon 1999). As expected, the larger a particular group is in the district, the more elected officials will weigh their concerns (Canon 1999). Given this, we anticipate that members in districts with a larger percentage of the Black population should be more likely to speak about their issues when given the opportunity. Such outreach would be necessary to attract Black support when they are a key constituency.

While we anticipate that the size of the Black population should be a strong predictor of racial outreach for all elected officials, we anticipate that this variable will be a particularly strong predictor for non-Black elected officials. Black elected officials, regardless of their rhetoric, are perceived as being stronger champions for Black people (Williams 1990, Harris 2012, Stout 2018). As a result, they receive some benefit of the doubt even if they remain silent on racial topics. Moreover, as was discussed previously, Black elected officials tend to be more intrinsically motivated to speak about racial topics regardless of electoral incentives (Minta 2011, Broockman 2013, see also Chapter 2 of this book). The combination of factors should make the size of the Black population in Black elected officials' districts less consequential in their decisions to engage in racial rhetorical representation.

In contrast, the size of the Black population in non-Black representative districts should play more heavily in their calculus to engage in racial rhetorical representation. When there are few African Americans in the district, many non-Black elected officials may prefer to be silent on racial issues. However, as the size of the Black population grows, non-Black elected officials may feel more pressure to speak up to attract this group of voters. Moreover, unlike Black elected officials, non-Black members of Congress are not assumed to be empathetic to the Black population (Garcia and Stout 2022). As a result, non-Black representatives must engage in more racial rhetorical representation to appear as caring to African Americans (Garcia and Stout 2022).

DATA

To analyze who provides Black-related rhetorical representation, we turn to our content-coded press release data from the 114th, 115th, and 116th Congresses and Twitter data from the 116th Congress. In this analysis, we calculate the average number of press releases or Tweets that members of Congress put out that included a Black-related appeal in each Congressional session. For example, in the 116th Congress, we took the sum of press releases or tweets that each U.S. House Representative put out which contained Black-related outreach (coded dichotomously as one if such outreach is present and zero if it is not) and divided that by the total number of press releases or tweets the member of Congress put out between January 3, 2019 and January 2, 2021 (or the period of the 116th Congress).

We repeated this process for the 114th and 115th Congress for press releases. Over this time span, we collected press release data for 1,213 observations for 572 unique members of Congress. This includes 58 Black members of Congress, 50 Latino/a members of Congress, 452 White members of Congress, and 18 Asian American members of Congress. We are also able to collect Twitter data for 410 U.S. House Representatives, including 48 Black Representatives, 36 Latino/a Representatives, and 13 Asian American/Pacific Islander Representatives. For Twitter, we only analyze the 116th Congress.[8]

We used Daily Kos' Demographic Guides to the 114th, 115th, and 116th Congress to identify demographic information such as the age, race, gender, and partisanship of the elected official, and validated these measures with each member of Congress' biography where available. We also used data from the American Community Survey to find the estimated percent of African Americans in each congressional district for each congressional session.

RACE, ETHNICITY, AND RHETORICAL REPRESENTATION: GROUP-BASED SUMMARY STATISTICS

To determine whether there are racial differences in levels of Black-related rhetorical representation, Figure 3.1 presents the average levels of racial

---

[8] Mixed race members were coded as being part of both racial groups. For example, Bobby Scott (VA-3) who is African American and South Asian is coded as being both Black and Asian American.

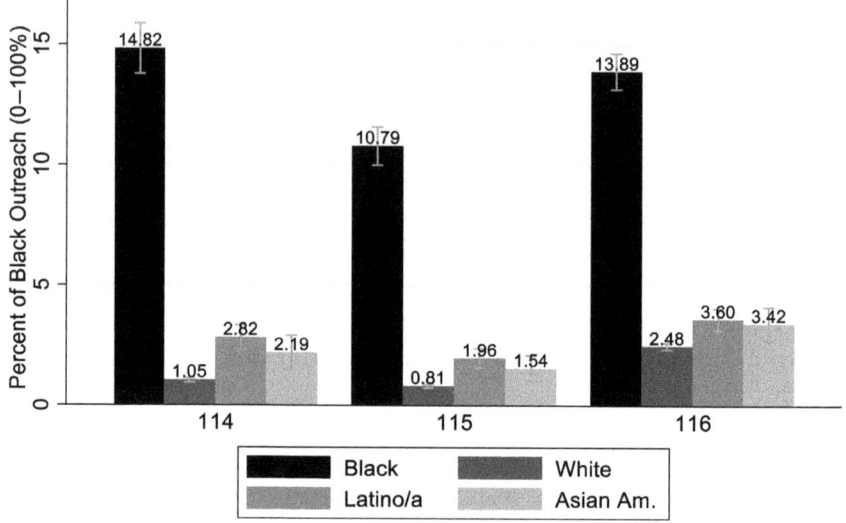

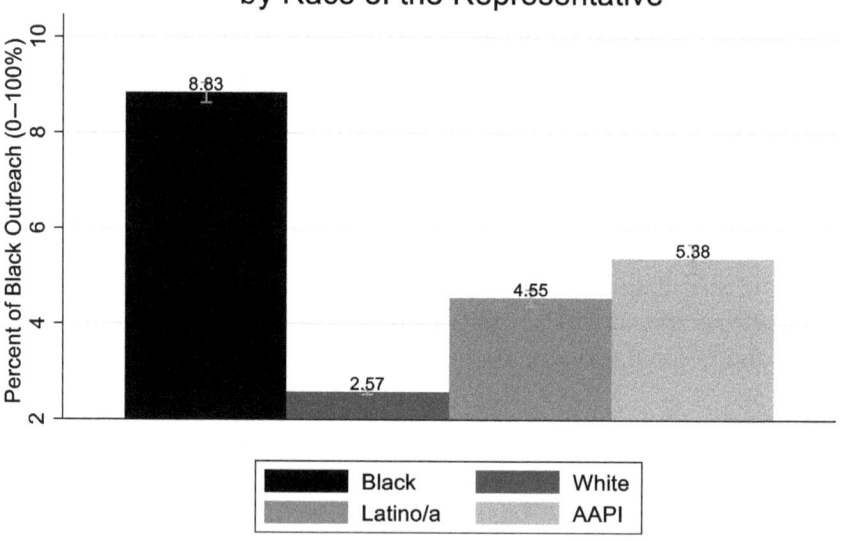

FIGURE 3.1 Average Levels of Racial Rhetorical Representation in Press Releases (2015–2021) and Tweets (2019–2021) Across Racial/Ethnic Groups and Congressional Session
Notes: These scores are calculated by dividing the number of press releases or tweets that contain Black-related outreach for each U.S. House Representative by the total number of press releases or tweets the member of Congress issued during each congressional session. T-tests are used for comparison.

outreach by the race/ethnicity of the member of Congress.[9] Figure 3.1 is disaggregated into A: Press Releases and B: Twitter. Press release averages are disaggregated for each Congressional session between the 114th and the 116th Congress. The bars in each figure display the average racial representation score along with 95 percent confidence intervals.[10]

As anticipated, Black members of Congress are by far the most likely to engage in co-racial rhetorical representation. In fact, on average, Black elected officials issued about 6.25 percent more Black-oriented tweets in the 116th Congress than White elected officials. This gap widens outside of Twitter. The gap between Black and White elected officials in their issuing of Black-oriented press releases is 13.77% in the 114th Congress, 9.98% in the 115th Congress, and 11.41% in the 116th Congress. Black elected officials across both mediums were also statistically significantly more likely to speak about Black-related issues than were Latino/a elected officials and Asian American elected officials. Albeit the gap between Black elected officials and other elected officials of color is much smaller on Twitter (about 3 to 4 percent) and in press releases (about 12 percent in the 114th Congress, 9 percent in the 115th Congress, and about 10 percent in the 116th Congress) than the same disparity between Black and White members of Congress.

Comparing just the 116th Congress, it appears that the disparity in racial rhetorical representation among Black elected officials and others is greater in press releases than it is on Twitter. This is because Black elected officials post a higher percentage of Black-oriented press releases than tweets, and non-Black elected officials speak about race more on Twitter than they do in press releases. Differences in audiences between the two platforms may explain this result. Nonetheless, it is important to note that while qualitatively similar, there are magnitude differences in racial disparities in rhetorical representation depending on the platform for outreach being analyzed.

---

[9] There are too few Native American members of Congress to draw meaningful inferences about this group.

[10] While we display descriptive statistics here, in the appendix, we show we arrive at the same substantive findings for Blacks in comparison to other groups in both Twitter and in Press Releases if we controlled for key factors like party and percent of the Black population in the district. Latino/a elected officials also put out more Black-related press releases in comparison to White elected officials when controlling for other factors. This relationship was absent in our Twitter data. Asian American and White elected officials do not differ in their racial outreach on either platform when controlling for these different factors.

Latino/a and Asian American elected officials are significantly more likely to engage in Black-oriented outreach than their White counterparts. On average, across each congressional session, Latino/a and Asian American elected officials put out about 1 percent more Black-related press releases than White members of Congress. This gap widens a little bit when examining Twitter. Black and Asian American elected officials issue over 2 percent more tweets discussing racial issues than White U.S. House Representatives. Given the overlapping concerns between these groups, this finding demonstrates that increasing diversity in Congress can benefit African Americans.

Within Racial Groups

While it is important to consider differences across racial groups, it is also essential to understand whether there is a key difference in demographic factors within each racial group. Table 3.1 presents the average percentage of Black-oriented appeals issued in press releases and tweets for Black, White, Latino/a, and Asian American members of Congress. These percentages were calculated by dividing the total number of press releases or tweets that contain a racial appeal by the total number of press releases or tweets the member issued over our period of interest (114th, 115th, 116th Congress for press releases and 116th Congress for tweets). Empty spaces indicate that there were not enough participants of that racial group in that category.

While the largest differences in racial rhetorical representation are between racial groups, there are important internal differences in Black-oriented outreach within these groups. Female Black and White elected officials are significantly more likely to engage in Black-oriented rhetorical representation than their co-racial male counterparts. This difference is greatest among Black women, who are more than 5 percent more likely to speak about Black issues in press releases and over 2 percent more likely to speak about race in their tweets than Black men. In contrast, Latino and Asian American men are slightly more likely to engage in Black-related appeals than their female counterparts. These differences, while small in magnitude (less than 2 percent in all cases), are statistically significant. This reinforces previous research, which demonstrates that Black women are the strongest proponents of Black political interests. As Simien (2005), Gay and Tate (1998), Brown (2014), Wright-Austin (2023), and Ford Dowe (2023) show, Black women's unique position in society plays a key role in their passion for advancing the interests of underrepresented groups.

TABLE 3.1 *Percent of Racial Outreach in Press Releases (2015–2021) and Tweets (2019–2021) for Black, White, Latino, and Asian American Members of Congress*

	Press Release				Twitter			
	Black	White	Latino/a	Asian Am	Black	White	Latino/a	Asian Am
All	12.48%	1.45%	2.86%	2.50%	8.76%	2.51%	4.59%	5.11%
Gender								
Female	15.48%	2.12%	2.32%	2.38%	9.88%	3.65%	4.86%	6.20%
Male	10.36%	1.26%	3.04%	2.60%	7.55%	2.16%	4.46%	4.43%
Generation								
Silent Generation	15.47%	2.22%	7.62%	2.02%	7.65%	3.60%	4.01%	.
Baby Boomers	13.02%	1.43%	2.49%	4.14%	9.82%	2.58%	5.76%	7.64%
Gen X/Millennial	8.84%	1.24%	2.46%	1.89%	7.21%	2.23%	4.17%	4.64%
Party								
Democrat	12.86%	2.37%	3.42%	2.50%	8.81%	3.71%	5.03%	5.11%
Republican	1.13%	0.60%	0.28%	.	3.67%	1.08%	0.69%	.
District Black Composition								
Percent Black <5%	2.41%	0.98%	2.23%	2.01%	2.63%	2.25%	3.69%	6.30%
Percent Black >5% & <30%	12.97%	1.57%	2.61%	2.52%	9.12%	2.65%	5.10%	3.92%
Percent Black >30%	13.87%	4.22%	11.17%	6.67%	9.54%	3.84%	4.40%	.

Source: Data compiled by authors. "."=Indicates Not Enough Data to Make Statistical Inferences. T-tests and Chi-Square tests used for Comparison.

As has been found in other studies (Gillespie 2010, Tate 2014), older African American elected officials are the most likely to speak out in support of Black political interests, and the youngest Black elected officials tend to be the least likely to engage in this form of outreach. In press releases, Black elected officials who are from the silent generation are almost twice as likely to provide Black rhetorical representation as those from Generation X or Millennials. This divide persists even on Twitter, which tends to be a platform dominated by younger people (Pew Research 2021).

We find a similar relationship for elected officials of other races/ethnicities. For Latino/as, those from the silent generation are similarly more vocal in support of the political interests of African Americans. For White and Asian American elected officials, this gap in Black-oriented representation is minimal among the generations. Still, it is older White and Asian American elected officials who speak out most on racial issues. There are several possibilities for this unexpected result, particularly with White elected officials. First, older White elected officials may worry most about being perceived as racially insensitive, given stereotypes that it is older people who harbor the most racially biased attitudes.[11] To combat this perception, they may speak about race more often. Second, unlike generation X and millennials who were socialized in a period focused on "colorblindness," older White politicians, and in particular, older White Democratic politicians, may be more aware about the role of racism in limiting Black people's opportunities given their lived experience with the Civil Rights Movement of the 1950's and 1960's. This may lead them to want to speak out in support of African Americans more often.

For every racial/ethnic group and for each public medium, Democrats are statistically significantly more likely to speak about Black political interests than Republicans of the same race. The largest difference again is among African American elected officials. Black Democrats are about 11.5 percent more likely to put out a Black-related press release than are Black Republicans. Similarly, Black Democrats issue 5 percent more race-based tweets than co-racial Republicans. It should also be noted that while Black Democratic elected officials are the most likely to speak about race, White, Latino/a, and Asian American Democrats provide stronger rhetorical representation than Black Republicans. However, Black Republicans are much more likely to provide Black rhetorical representation than Republicans of other races/ethnicities.

---

[11] www.pbs.org/newshour/nation/americas-racism-problem-far-complicated-think

Beyond individual-level characteristics, the districts that elected officials represent play a large role in shaping their levels of Black rhetorical representation. As expected, Black, White, Latino/a, and Asian American elected officials from districts with a larger percentage of Black constituents are more likely to speak about racial issues in both their press releases and on Twitter. However, this effect appears to be largest for non-Black elected officials. Blacks who represent districts that are between 5 percent and 30 percent African American have similar racial rhetorical representation scores on both Twitter and in press releases as Black elected officials whose districts are 30 percent or more African American. In contrast, non-Black elected officials who represent districts that are 30 percent or more African American engage in over twice as much rhetorical representation in press releases compared to co-racial/ethnic individuals who represent districts in which African Americans make up between 5 and 30 percent of the district. This result suggests that African Americans are more intrinsically motivated to provide co-racial individuals rhetorical representation than their non-Black counterparts.

SUMMARY

In this chapter, we explored *who* provides racial rhetorical representation with a focus on differences between and within racial/ethnic groups. Our findings echo a robust literature that demonstrates that descriptive representatives – those who share the race of their constituents – are the most likely to take actions to advance the goals of their group (Canon 1999, Tate 2003, Barreto 2007, Grose 2011, Minta 2011). Our analyses demonstrate that Black elected officials are by far the most likely group to speak out in support of Black political interests. In fact, all other variables, including the partisanship of the elected official and the racial composition of the district, while significant, pale in comparison to the magnitude of the effect of descriptive representation on Black-related outreach. Even Black Republicans consistently provide Black citizens better rhetorical representation than White, Latino/a, or Asian American Republicans.

While to a much lesser degree than Black politicians, we also find that Latino/a and Asian American elected officials are more likely than White elected officials to speak out in support of African Americans. This is significant given that Latino/as are the second largest racial/ethnic group in the United States and have more than doubled the size of their U.S. House delegation over the past 20 years. Asian American elected officials are also a rapidly growing group in the United States and among the ranks of politicians across the country.[12] The concurrent growth of Black, Latino/a, and Asian American elected officials in Congress increases the levels of rhetorical representation that African Americans should expect to receive.

While White women provide substantially less racial representation compared to Black women, we find that White women are significantly more likely to engage in racial rhetorical outreach than White males. The growth in the representation of women, while still far below their proportion in the population, provides another opportunity for African Americans to gain in their levels of rhetorical representation in Congress.

In addition to these broader differences, our analysis also helps us identify which characteristics increase White, Black, and Latino/a elected officials' likelihood of providing racial rhetorical representation. For African Americans, the largest discrepancies occurred with gender, age, and partisanship. Older, female, Democratic Black members of Congress were more likely to provide rhetorical representation than their younger, male, and Republican counterparts. This work is in line with existing research, which shows that not all Black politicians represent Black political interests equally. This is true with regard to rhetorical representation as well.

The percent of Black constituents in a congressional district is a consistent and powerful predictor of an elected official's likelihood of speaking out in support of African Americans. The effect is particularly pronounced for the percent of Black people in each district for non-Black elected officials. White, Latino/a, and Asian American elected officials appear to be especially motivated by the size of the Black population in their district in deciding their levels of Black-related racial outreach. This finding speaks to the importance of the redistricting process and racial gerrymandering. Blacks who are relegated to districts without a large percentage of co-racial individuals are not only less likely to be descriptively represented, but they are also less likely to have representatives who speak out in support of their interests. As a result, creating districts with fewer African Americans decreases the likelihood that Black people are adequately represented.

Finally, this study provides an important comparison across medium of communication. This is the first study that we are aware of that

---

[12] https://www.nbcnews.com/news/asian-america/california-asian-americans-find-growing-political-power-n866611

explores the racial content of the discussions across forms of communication. We largely find consistency in this area. The same elected officials who provide rhetorical representation on Twitter are also issuing press releases around the same topic. While the degree to which they speak about Black-related issues differs across platforms, the comparisons across racial/ethnic groups and even within racial/ethnic groups provide generally consistent differences in rhetorical representation. This indicates that researchers should have confidence that the platform they select to analyze racial speech will provide consistent results to other mediums of public outreach.

While this chapter provides details on *who* provides racial rhetorical representation, the question remains whether Black and non-Black elected officials engage in public racial outreach *differently*. In the next chapters, we will examine whether Black elected officials are more likely to provide proactive racial representation at a greater rate than others through exploring differences among high- and low-profile racial appeals, uncrystallized racial outreach, and the variety of Black-oriented outreach.

4

The Highs and the Lows

Predicting Racial Rhetorical Representation around High- and Low-Profile Racial Events

On June 19, 2015, America celebrated the 150th anniversary of Juneteenth. While slavery had officially ended when President Abraham Lincoln issued the Emancipation Proclamation on January 1, 1863, the practice of slavery would not be over until the Confederacy surrendered. The Union army would make great strides over the next few years, but it would not be until June 19, 1865, when the last slaves would be free. On this date, Union troops reached Texas and freed more than a quarter of a million slaves. The National Museum of African American History and Culture dubbed this day, known as Juneteenth, as "America's Second Independence Day."[1]

Juneteenth was hardly a widely celebrated or even a recognizable event when the country celebrated the sesquicentennial of this unofficial holiday. In fact, only ten members of the U.S. House of Representatives put out a press release commemorating this important moment. One of those ten was Texas U.S. House Representative Sheila Jackson Lee. In her press release, she spoke about the importance of Juneteenth as a national symbol to motivate action for social justice and as a way to recognize African Americans' contributions to American democracy.

Juneteenth reminds us of the power we have to meet the challenges that communities of color and so many others continue to face in the pursuit of justice and equality. As we celebrate the jubilee, let us resolve to end the indignity and violence of bigotry, discrimination, and hatred in all its forms.

---

[1] https://nmaahc.si.edu/explore/stories/historical-legacy-juneteenth

June 19, 2015, would not be the first or last time that Representative Sheila Jackson Lee would speak about Juneteenth in a press release. She would do so again in 2016, when only she and six of her colleagues would issue press releases commemorating the holiday. She would also do so again in 2021, when Juneteenth became a national holiday. Only this time, as public attention focused on this celebration, she would be one of at least seventy U.S. House members to issue a press release about Juneteenth.

Elected officials who engage in proactive rhetorical representation do not wait for critical moments to use their public platform to speak about their issue priorities. Instead, they speak about issues and topics that are rarely in the public eye to advance the aims of their group by highlighting topics of interest. Speaking about lower-profile topics, like Juneteenth, can serve to educate the public about important moments or individuals in Black History, which tend to receive little attention. Discussion of lower-profile topics can also cover policies and issues that draw a lot of attention at a particular moment and then fade from public discourse.

Elected officials who engage in proactive rhetorical representation can have a meaningful, substantive impact by speaking about topics that are not well-known or trendy. For example, having members of Congress like Sheila Jackson Lee, Gwen Moore, Barbara Lee, and Steve Cohen be consistent in their discussions about Juneteenth raised awareness about this historical date. In doing so, they educated the population about the event and inspired activists and their colleagues to advocate for a formal recognition of Juneteenth. This outreach was instrumental in laying the groundwork for Congress to pass the Juneteenth National Independence Day Act in 2021.

In this chapter, we explore which elected officials are the most likely to engage in proactive rhetorical representation by speaking about lower-profile racial issues. We argue that much of the racial outreach that non-Black elected officials engage in will be discussions of higher-profile topics that are well-known by the public and thus reactive. In contrast, Black elected officials will speak to a greater diversity of topics, including those that are low salience. By raising awareness about lower-profile issues, descriptive representatives' use of proactive rhetorical representation may lay the groundwork for official actions to be taken by the government.

To test differences in the discussion of high-profile and low-profile racial issues, we return to our examination of racialized press releases from the 114th through the 116th Congresses and tweets from the 116th Congress. Using this data, we create a list of topics that are high-profile over this period using a dictionary of over 500 racial terms and an analysis of Google search trends over our period of interest. We define high-profile issues as those that are highly searched by the public on Google. These terms include names and topics that would be well-known to the public as forms of racial outreach, like voting rights, Martin Luther King Jr., white supremacy, and removing the Confederate Flag. Lower-profile issues include the discussion of lesser-known racial justice activists, legislation, and topics. We find that Black elected officials are more likely to make statements about a combination of high-profile and low-profile racial topics than are non-Black elected officials in both their press releases and tweets. In contrast, we find that non-Black elected officials gravitate more to higher-profile topics.

We further test this hypothesis by exploring whether the salience of a topic matters in the volume of outreach tied to that topic among Black elected officials and non-Black elected officials. By exploring dynamic interest in topics tied to Black Lives Matter through Google searches, we show that non-Black members of Congress almost exclusively speak out about Black Lives Matter topics when the issue is publicly salient. In contrast, Black elected officials speak about the issue even when it is not in the public eye (i.e., has a lower profile). The results of this chapter demonstrate that descriptive representatives are more likely to be proactive in their racial outreach by ensuring that racial issues that get less attention are in the public discussion and keeping higher-profile topics on the agenda even when they are less salient.

SPEAKING BROADLY TO SPECIFIC GROUPS OF VOTERS

Elected officials engage in group-based appeals in large part to increase their chances of re-election (Hersh and Schaffner 2013, Holman et al 2015, Burge et al. 2020). As congressional staff have become more professionalized and as new technologies have provided politicians with both the information and the means to reach out to specific populations, politicians have engaged in microtargeting (Endres and Kelly 2018, Nteta and Rice 2021). Microtargeting refers to the idea that elected officials will put out specific messages to different electorates in hopes of demonstrating their support for that group. By ensuring that the politician has spoken to a large enough collection of unique groups, elected officials hope to put together strong electoral coalitions. Democratic elected officials, at points during a congressional session, will likely make specific group appeals to people of color, women, members of the

LGBTQIA+ community, and labor unions. Republican elected officials will engage in some form of outreach to groups like Evangelicals, gun owners, and business owners. Such outreach makes voters in these groups feel appreciated by the elected official and has the potential to increase support for them (Hasell and Monson 2014, Barreto and Collingwood 2015, Bonilla 2022).

While appealing to subgroups of the population is important for the politician to succeed, *how* they appeal to these groups is also likely important. Some research suggests that while politicians focus on specific groups, they often do so in broader, less specialized terms (Barbu 2014). For example, when targeting liberal female voters through abortion-based appeals, elected officials would likely talk broadly about women's overall right to choose. They may be less likely to focus on more specialized topics like access to Mifepristone (the abortion pill). Similarly, when conservatives appeal to gun owners, they may speak more broadly about the Second Amendment and less about opposition to more specialized legislation like red flag laws.

These broader appeals to specific groups are advantageous for several reasons. First, appeals that are more recognizable make it easier for the voter to understand that the candidate is speaking to their group. As a result, higher-profile targeted appeals are much more likely to be received as such and not be overlooked because of a lack of knowledge about the topic (Carmines and Stimson 1980, Cobb and Kuklinski 1997, Johnston and Wronski 2015). Second, more salient topics are often well-vetted because they have been in the public discourse for a longer period (Carmines and Stimson 1980). This makes it so that elected officials already know generally how the targeted group will react to such appeals. Third, and related to the second advantage, elected officials better know whether well-vetted and high-profile issues are almost universally supported by the targeted group (Dawson 2001). For example, targeting Black voters through condemning racial hate crimes is likely more universally appealing to this racial group than is support for policies tied to reparations, which are more rarely discussed and have the potential to be more divisive among African Americans. Given these advantages, it is likely that elected officials whose primary goals are to be re-elected through attracting the attention of a specific group of voters will focus on high-profile and easily recognizable forms of outreach.

In addition to issuing statements as a form of group-based appeals, one of the reasons elected officials may speak out about a particular topic is to gain notoriety (Krutz 2005, Grimmer 2013). There are periods of time when elected officials discuss race to gain press coverage because the population is thinking about the topic at that moment. For example, many elected officials discuss what they are doing to commemorate holidays that celebrate prominent African Americans, such as Martin Luther King Jr. Day or Black History Month. These moments provide an opportunity for elected officials to make appeals to African American voters and others who are also thinking about this topic on that day. It also offers elected officials an opportunity to get their name in the press. As local media outlets often cover Martin Luther King Jr. Day and Black History Month, they may look to what local elected officials are doing to celebrate. The congruence between press releases on these topics and media attention may provide an opportunity for an elected official to get notoriety and make group-targeted appeals.

Beyond moments of celebration, moments of tragedy also require elected officials to take a position to ward off criticism of inattentiveness or insensitivity (Milita et al. 2014). However, pressure to take a stand only occurs when the public and the media are paying close attention to a particular incident. In these moments, like the murder of George Floyd or the shooting of Black parishioners in the Emanuel AME church in South Carolina, voters will expect that their elected officials take a public stand. Silence on such high-profile events raises questions about whether the elected official is paying attention or, even worse, does not want to condemn such events. While there has been growing acceptance of racially insensitive rhetoric in recent years (Valentino et al. 2018), hate crimes and violent attacks based on race continue to be disliked by the general population. Thus, during salient, tragic racial events, elected officials who remain silent on the topic run a greater risk of electoral punishment than if they condemn such actions. In contrast, moments or topics that are not in the public discourse do not provide the same incentive to speak out. The result should be more silence on these topics for elected officials who are centrally concerned with limiting discussions of race as a means to advance electorally (Milita et al. 2014).

SO WHY SPEAK ABOUT LOW-PROFILE RACIAL TOPICS?

Given the numerous electoral advantages of high-profile racial appeals, why would legislators engage in outreach to specific groups by focusing on less salient topics? For example, why would a person tout legislation naming a post office after a lesser-known Civil Rights Activist like Clara Luper, who would not be readily known to the public, instead of legislation commemorating the 50th anniversary of the 1965 Voting Rights Act, whose implications for racial equality are better known?

As discussed in our interviews with congressional communications directors, elected officials work hard to carve out an area of specialization (Esterling 2007, Adler and Wilkerson 2013). This perceived expertise provides more opportunities for elected officials to position themselves as leader on a topic by engaging in proactive rhetorical representation. This leadership can then be used to gain notoriety through newspaper coverage or in internal party discussions about who should speak/lead on legislation tied to group-specific issues. One way that elected officials may demonstrate their expertise and passion for a particular topic is by differentiating themselves from others by focusing on lower-profile issues.

To better illustrate this point, we will use police violence against people of color as an example. When elected officials spoke about this issue in 2020, most press releases and tweets centered on George Floyd, Ahmaud Arbery, and Breonna Taylor. Mentioning these individuals signals that the elected official cares about this topic. However, because mentions of these individuals are so widespread among members of Congress, signaling support for these individuals is unlikely to lead an elected official to stand out. However, an elected official who mentions these names, as well as lower-profile cases tied to police brutality (which happened in the same period), such as Andre Hill, Casey Goodson Jr., and David McAtee, may demonstrate a deeper commitment to this issue. These discussions would make them unique in their breadth of discussions about police brutality. Mentioning a greater variety of individuals who were murdered by vigilantes and law enforcement may signal a specialization in the topic. As a result, elected officials who want to develop a perceived expertise around the issue of police violence will proactively speak about overlooked incidents around this topic rather than react to what is salient in the public. In doing so, they will speak to both higher-profile and lower-profile instances of police brutality.

While focusing on lower-profile topics may make it less likely that an elected official gains national media coverage in most periods, such outreach may get them more coverage in specialized and local media sources. The national media is unlikely to consistently focus on cases of racial inequality, given that the public generally has a limited appetite for this topic (McAdam 2017). As a result, press releases and tweets about lower-profile racial issues are often going to be overlooked by large media outlets. However, Black-focused newspapers are consistent champions of Black political interests regardless of the national saliency of the topic

(Walton 1985, Jennings 2000). These outlets are often more likely to cover lower-profile racial topics, which larger media outlets tend to ignore (Mastin et al. 2005, Dolan et al. 2009). When elected officials speak about a lower-profile racial topic, they may gain interest from Black-centered newspapers. In doing so, they not only are better able to define a topic they care about to an attentive audience, but they also increase their name recognition in this key constituency. In fact, in our interviews with communications directors, several mentioned that an important part of their job was building connections with a variety of media outlets and knowing when and where to pitch different stories. Among communications directors for Black lawmakers, without prompting, many said that they prioritize sending stories they know will resonate with the Black community to Black newspapers.

Additionally, elected officials who are genuinely concerned about an issue and want the public to be more informed about it may feel freer to engage in public outreach around lower-profile topics. This may lead elected officials to speak more about things that are not yet in the public discourse in hopes that they raise interest in the topic. Moreover, it allows them to recognize individuals whom they believe are worthy of recognition, even if they are not well-known. While higher-profile outreach is important to signal interest and empathy for a targeted group, lower-profile outreach may better help people hone in on the issues the elected officials are most passionate about.

In addition to building a specialization around a particular topic, elected officials who are associated with an issue generally want to advance policy on it (Alder and Wilkinson 2013, Volden et al. 2018). An important tool that elected officials have to advance their legislative priorities is keeping a particular issue salient to the public. There are often short policy windows around particular events in which the public is putting pressure on elected officials to address a social problem through legislation (Crawford 2021). By focusing on examples of a problem even when the topic is not salient to the public, elected officials may be better able to keep a topic in the public's eye. This may improve the likelihood that an individual is able to pass legislation.

Moreover, by regularly raising an issue in press releases and tweets, legislators are able to position themselves as someone who should be included in policy discussions on that issue. For instance, one communications director said that part of the reason he repeatedly issues communications on the same topic, even when little public attention is being given to it, is to position their legislator as a leader on that issue.

He said that he's trying to show other lawmakers and the administration that his legislator is ready to work on issue-related policy. When the issue garners public attention or other lawmakers are ready to work on the issue, he wants to make sure that his legislator is thought of and included in the policymaking process.

Returning to our police brutality example, the public may be most focused on Black Lives Matter-related issues around the murders of George Floyd, Breanna Taylor, and Ahmaud Arbery, but the fervor for legislation may wane as the public focuses on a different issue. To keep the issue salient, resourceful elected officials may point out continued incidents of police brutality even if the public or the media is no longer paying attention, and these incidents get less coverage. This serves to both try to regain momentum for an issue which has gone past its policy window and to build up examples of the social problem. This strategy requires more commitment and dedication to the problem and has the potential to improve the chances of success in the long term.

WHO SHOULD SPEAK OUT ABOUT LOWER-PROFILE ISSUES?

Based on our review, it is likely that lower-profile issues will be discussed much less often than higher-profile issues. This disparity in the types of topics being discussed may be tied to the identity of the elected official. We anticipate that elected officials who are less deeply committed to a particular topic will put out a higher proportion of high-profile topics in their racial outreach. High-profile outreach likely represents either a less nuanced form of outreach or is more likely to be reactive. In contrast, we anticipate that elected officials who are more deeply committed to an issue will be the most likely to talk about the issue using a combination of higher- and lower-profile outreach. The former signals to the electorate that they, too, care about the issues that are given the most coverage. The latter indicates a proactive commitment to the group by keeping a particular topic in the public discussion, informing individuals about group-centered issues which are often overlooked, and/or moving legislation around a particular topic.

Based on this, we anticipate that Black elected officials will be more likely to use a combination of high- and low-profile racial outreach than non-Black elected officials, who will mostly engage in racial outreach using high-profile racial appeals. African Americans' high level of concern for those who share their race will make it so that they should feel the most passionate about addressing issues tied to racial equality (Tate 2004,

Minta 2011, Stout et al. 2021). This fervor to improve the lives of rank-and-file African Americans will likely keep them engaged in racial outreach regardless of the salience of the racial topic. As a result, they will be more likely to engage in proactive actions, including searching out and amplifying the voices of African Americans who are overlooked by the population (Williams 2000). This may manifest in a greater proportion of lower-profile racial outreach.

Additionally, African American elected officials likely have more knowledge about the different ways in which co-racial individuals face discrimination and may be more interested in lower-profile African American public figures (Mansbridge 1999). Indeed, Black people tend to be the most likely to seek out topics around African American history and African American studies (Marable 2000). When lower-profile events occur or there is an opportunity to recognize individuals who have worked toward racial justice, African American elected officials may be the least likely to want to see these moments pass without recognition. This may lead them to be more likely to engage in lower-profile racial outreach at a greater rate than non-Black elected officials.

Additionally, Black elected officials may work to specialize and develop a perceived expertise in issues around racial identity. Previous research shows that elected officials work to cultivate a specialization that is informed by their own personal experiences (Burden 2007). As African American elected officials experience what it means to be Black in the United States, many may work to demonstrate their expertise by showcasing their knowledge around more specialized topics tied to Black political interests. In doing so, the elected official could amplify the messages they care most about when the media and voters, who already have a pre-inclination to look to descriptive representatives during periods of racial crises (Arora et al. 2025), seek out information from these elected officials.

TESTING THE DIFFERENCE OF HIGH- AND LOW-PROFILE RACIAL OUTREACH

To better understand whether Black and non-Black elected officials differ in the ways in which they engage in racial outreach, we began by using a systematic analysis to identify high-profile racial topics. To accomplish this goal, we used a dictionary of racialized terms.[2] This list included over 500 topics identified through a review of racialized press releases, tweets,

---

[2] See introduction for more information about the creation of this list.

congressional legislation, and outside sources (see the appendix of the introduction for a full list of terms). To determine the salience of each topic, we searched each term from our dictionary on Google Trends over our period of interest (January 3, 2015–January 2, 2021) and limited the queries to only include searches conducted in the United States. Google Trends examines the relative number of searches on Google over a period of time from the public, indicating the level of interest each topic has. In fact, several research projects use Google Trends as a measure of the salience of a topic and/or advocate its usage as a way to approximate public interest (Mellon 2013, 2014, Lee et al. 2016, Chykina and Crabtree 2018)[3]

We argue that topics that get searched for most often are those that attract the interest of the population.[4] We used Martin Luther King Jr. as a baseline score given his prominence in discussions around race. Any topic that received a Google Trends score of 8 or greater out of 100 (in comparison to Martin Luther King Jr.) at any point during our period of interest was labeled as being high-profile. This accounts for about 10 percent of all the words in our dictionary. While there are numerous cutoff points that could be used here, we selected eight because it gave us the closest round number cutoff point to get to the 90th percentile of attention scores. Moreover, dropping the Google trend score cutoff to 7 or 6 or expanding the number to 9, 10, and 11 provided the same substantive results. While there is no pre-established rule on what would be considered high profile, we believe that the consistency of our results across cut points provides confidence in the replicability of our findings. The list of high-profile terms is in Table 4.1.[5]

---

[3] To further validate our measure of salience, we explored the number of times the keywords presented in Table 4.1 appeared in a New York Times (NYT) article over our period of interest. We also explored how often a random sample of 56 words from our dictionary which are not featured in Table 4.1 appeared in an NYT article. While we focus on google searches, other studied have used NYT articles as a measure of salience (Epstein and Segal 2000, Kiousis 2004). On average, the words on our high-profile list appeared in 1,049 articles over our period of interest. The median number of articles our high-profile keywords appeared in was 362. In contrast, keywords in our non-high-profile random sample appeared in 98 articles with a median score of 21.5. Fifty-five of the fifty-six words appeared in more NYT articles than the median of the low-profile topic (12.5).
[4] We focus on the nation overall rather than subsamples of the population, because we are interested in the national salience of the topic, rather than the salience among a particular part of the population.
[5] To ensure that these names/topics were included we used variations where necessary. For example, on Twitter George Floyd was often written as GeorgeFloyd to save space. We combined each name and used some alternative searches to ensure we had the correct information.

TABLE 4.1 *List of High-Profile Topics*

Martin Luther King Jr	Chuck Berry	Jim Crow
Black Lives Matter	Elijah Cummings	Lynching
Muhammad Ali	Rayshard Brooks	Voting Rights
Kobe Bryant	Dylann Roof	Stephon Clark
George Floyd	Elijah McClain	Nia Wilson
Aretha Franklin	Selma	Jackie Robinson
Juneteenth	Chadwick Boseman	Fourteenth Amendment
Jacob Blake	NAACP	Voter ID
John Lewis	March On Washington	White Supremacy
Confederate Flag	Toni Morrison	Tulsa Massacre
Greensboro Sit-In	Gwen Ifill	Kamala Harris
Freddie Gray	Black History Month	Charlottesville
Ahmaud Arbery	13th Amendment	Slavery
Colin Kaepernick	Police Brutality	BB King
Ferguson	Malcolm X	Walter Scott
Harriet Tubman	Rosa Parks	Dick Gregory
Sandra Bland	Marvin Gaye	Breonna Taylor
Shelby County	Philando Castile	Emanuel AME Alton Sterling	Civil Rights

We then searched a subsample of press releases and tweets that included racial outreach for any mentions of terms from our high-profile dictionary. This included 5,439 press releases, which represent 2.65% of all press releases in our dataset, and 21,894 tweets, which represent 3.6% of all tweets issued by U.S. House Representatives over our period of interest. Racialized press releases and tweets that included at least one of the terms listed in Table 1 were categorized as high-profile racial outreach and given a score of 1. All those that did not have these terms were coded as being lower-profile racial outreach and given a score of zero. Given that we focus only on press releases and tweets that contain positive forms of racial outreach in our analysis, we can rule out the possibility that elected officials are using these terms in a negative manner.

Following this coding procedure, we created our dependent variable, which is the proportion of high-profile racial appeals among all racial appeals issued in press releases or tweets in each congressional session. Our measure only includes representatives who put out a racial appeal in each Congress. Those who never put out a racial appeal in a congressional session would not be included in this model. Thus, we are exploring *when* elected officials engage in racial outreach, and how much of these appeals are high-profile forms of rhetorical representation. We are interested in whether Black elected officials are the least likely to focus only on high-profile forms of racial outreach. As a result, we disaggregate our models by the race/ethnicity of the elected official.

RACIAL DIFFERENCES IN HIGH- AND LOW-PROFILE RACIAL OUTREACH

Figure 4.1 presents the percent of racial appeals that are high-profile among all racial appeals for Black, White, Latino/a, and Asian American elected officials.[6] We further disaggregate White Members of Congress by their partisanship. As a result, Figure 4.1 shows, among all racial appeals made by members of Congress of a certain race/ethnicity and party, what percentage included one of the terms mentioned in our high-profile dictionary. Thus, we are exploring the proportion of racial appeals that are high- and low-profile and not the absolute number of these forms of racial outreach. In addition to being disaggregated by race, Figure 4.1 is also divided by the platform of delivery (i.e., press releases and Twitter) and includes 95 percent confidence intervals.

The results in Figure 4.1 provide support for our expectations that the race of the elected official influences the ratio of high-to-low profile racial outreach. The vast majority of Black-centered press releases contain at least one of the terms in our high-profile dictionary. High-profile outreach was common and included press releases which discussed the Voting Rights Act, like Jan Schakowsky's (D-IL) 2018 press release entitled "Schakowsky Statement on the Anniversary of the Voting Rights Act" or Bradley Byrne's (R-AL) 2020 tweet "John Lewis, a son of Alabama, became the conscience of America. He was a good friend who never failed to inspire, and I miss him already" which recognized John Lewis after his death. The topics that captured the attention of the nation made up a majority of Black-oriented outreach among members of Congress.

With that said, there are significant differences based on the race/ethnicity and party of the elected official. African Americans, on average, tend to make lower-profile racial appeals relative to higher-profile racial appeals than most of the other racial/ethnic groups. On average, 58% of

---

[6] For the sake of simplicity, here we present the averages without any controls. In the appendix of this chapter, we demonstrate the same substantive results for both press releases and Twitter when controlling for the partisanship of the elected official, the gender of the elected official, the partisanship of the district, the percent of Black people in the congressional district and the congressional session (w/ press release data).

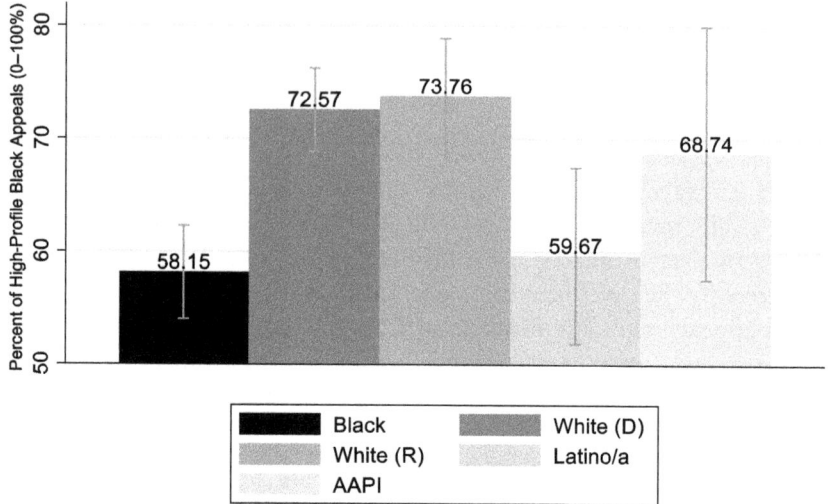

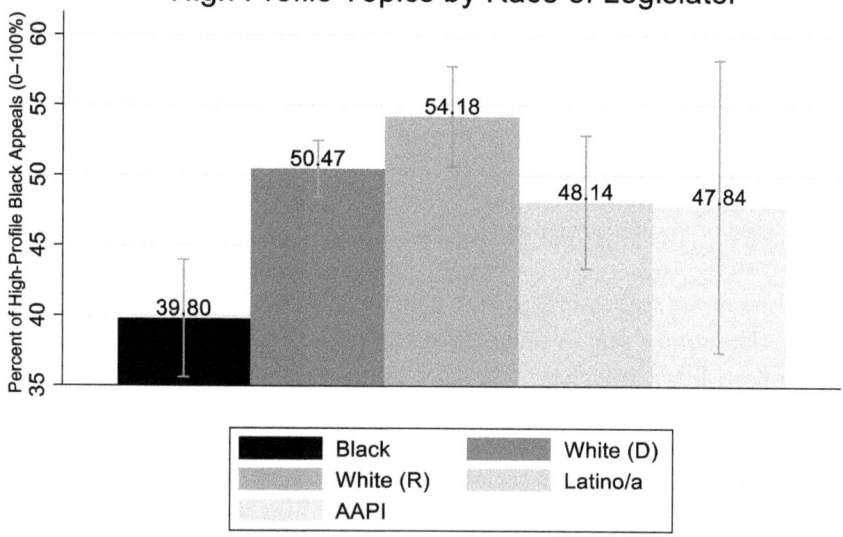

FIGURE 4.1 Percent of High-Profile Racial Appeals among Only Racial Appeals for Elected Officials of Different Racial/Ethnic Groups in Press Releases and Twitter W/ 95% Confidence Intervals
T-tests are used for comparison.

race-related press releases put out by Black elected officials include at least one high-profile racial term. This is a 15% lower ratio of high-to-low profile racial outreach than for White Democratic elected officials (73%), a 16% lower ratio than White Republican elected officials (74%), and an 11% lower ratio than Asian American/Pacific Islander members of Congress (69%). Each of these differences in comparison to Black elected officials is statistically significant. Latino/a elected officials only have about a 2 percent greater proportion of high-to-low profile racial outreach in comparison to Black elected officials. This difference is not statistically significant. This finding suggests that Latino/a politicians, like African American politicians, engage in a wider variety of racial outreach in comparison to White members of Congress in their press releases.

While there are large differences across groups, a review of what members discuss when speaking about lower-profile topics does not reveal systematic differences. What largely makes them lower-profile is the fact that they are generally one-off press releases like the ones in which Maxine Waters (D-CA), Barbara Lee (D-CA), and Robin Kelly (D-CA) recognized the passing of former member of Congress Ron Dellums. Or when Mo Brooks (R-AL) called for a federal building to be named after Mary W. Jackson, the first Black woman NASA engineer. Others dealt with lower-profile pieces of legislation, like when several members, including Ro Khanna (D-CA), James Clyburn (D-SC), and Yvette Clarke (D-NY), advocated for the passage of the Legal Assistance to Prevent Evictions Act of 2020, which they noted would protect "Low-income women, especially racial minorities, [who] are at particularly high risk of eviction."[7]

Unlike press releases, where a larger percentage of outreach is centered on high-profile racial topics, the ratio of high- and low-profile racial outreach is much less pronounced on Twitter. This may be driven by the fact that Twitter makes a direct connection to its audience and does not need the approval of traditional media outlets to amplify its voice the same way as press releases. As a result, congressional communication teams do not have to worry that lower-profile outreach will not reach their intended audiences on Twitter.

While racial appeals on Twitter are less likely to contain a higher-profile racial term, we arrive at similar conclusions in our comparisons across racial groups. Namely, African Americans have a lower proportion

---

[7] https://khanna.house.gov/media/press-releases/release-rep-khanna-majority-whip-clyburn-sen-bennet-reps-price-and-clarke

of high-to low-profile racial appeals than other groups. Unlike for press releases, this difference is statistically significantly lower for Black elected officials compared to each of the comparison groups. Less than half (40%) of African American elected officials' Black-related tweets contain discussions of a high-profile issue. This 40% proportion of high-to low-profile racial outreach for Black elected officials is 10% less than that of White Democratic elected officials (50%), 14% less than that of White Republican elected officials (54%), and 8% less than that off Latino/a and Asian American elected officials (48%).

While we focus on the ratio of low- to high-profile racial outreach only among press releases and tweets that contain a racial appeal, it is important to note that we arrive at similar conclusions if the denominator changed from only racial outreach to all press releases/tweets. African Americans, on average, speak more about both higher- and lower-profile racial topics than all other groups in both press releases and on Twitter. Moreover, the largest relative differences between Black and non-Black elected officials are between lower-profile forms of racial outreach on both platforms.[8]

EXAMINING RACIAL RHETORICAL REPRESENTATION DURING LOW- AND HIGH-PROFILE MOMENTS OF POLICE BRUTALITY

Police reform is one of the most commonly appearing racial topics in the period that we examine. The time frame that we analyze comes just months after the murder of Michael Brown in Ferguson, Missouri put Black Lives Matter on the map in August of 2014 (Freelon et al. 2016) and continued to the summer of 2020 in which the murder of George

---

[8] Five percent of all press releases for Black elected officials are low-profile racial appeals (i.e., racial appeals which do not contain a term from our dictionary). In comparison, .4 percent of all press releases for non-Black elected officials are low-profile racial appeals. 7.4 percent of all press releases for Black elected officials are high profile racial appeals compared to 1.1 percent of all press releases containing these same topics for non-Black elected officials. Thus, Black members of Congress engage in low-profile rhetorical representation 12.5 times more than non-Black politicians and engage in high-profile racial rhetorical representation 6.7 times more often than the same group in press releases. We find a similar pattern in discussions of low- and high-profile racial outreach on Twitter. 5.2% of all tweets from Black elected officials contained a lower-profile racial appeal compared to 1.3% of the same type of tweets for non-Black elected officials. In comparison, 3.4% of all tweets from Black members of Congress contained a high-profile form of racial outreach compared to 1.2% of the same type of tweets for non-Black elected officials. Again, the ratio of Black-to-non-Black racial appeals is greater for lower-profile racial rhetorical representation (4) than high-profile forms of racial outreach (2.83).

Floyd led to an explosion of interest on the topic (Reny and Newman 2021). While topics around Black Lives Matter are considered high-profile as measured by our criteria discussed above, the salience of Black Lives Matter increases and wanes over time depending on media coverage around the murder/harassment/injury of African Americans, generally at the hands of law enforcement or vigilantes. Given its prominence during our period of study and the fact that public interest in the topic ebbs and flows over time, we can examine whether outreach tied to Black Lives Matter changes based on the salience of the topic in the public and whether this differs based on the race/ethnicity of the elected official. This allows another avenue to explore whether public salience drives racial rhetorical representation equally for Black and non-Black elected officials.

To examine the impact of the salience of police reform on discussions of the topic in press releases and tweets, we searched for 141 terms and names that are tied to Black Lives Matter. These terms were collected from a review of Blacklivesmatter.com and from protest data around racial justice from countlove.org and ephrame.com. The terms in our dictionary, include mentions of the movement (i.e., Black Lives Matter, #Blacklivesmatter), legislation tied to the movement, such as the JUSTICE Act and the Justice in Policing Act, police reform terms like body cameras, racial profiling, excessive use of force, popular names tied to Black Lives Matter such as Trayvon Martin, Breonna Taylor, and George Floyd, and lesser-known names like Dion Johnson, Edson Thevenin, and Jameek Lowery. A full list of our Black Lives Matter dictionary can be found in the Appendix. We gave a score of 1 to any press release or tweet that contained a Black Lives Matter term from our dictionary. For each individual legislator, we then divided the number of Black Lives Matter terms mentioned in each month by the number of press releases the legislator put out in each month or the number of tweets they put out in each month. For example, in June of 2019, if a legislator put out one of ten press releases that mentioned a word from our Black Lives Matter dictionary, they would be given a score of 10%. We would repeat this process for Tweets for the same legislator in the same month. This percent of mentions of Black Lives Matter topics in press releases and tweets serves as our dependent variable.

Our independent variable measures the salience of the topic in the public through searches for Black Lives Matter on Google Trends. We use Google Trends to look up the relative volume of searches for "Black Lives Matter" monthly between January 2015 and January

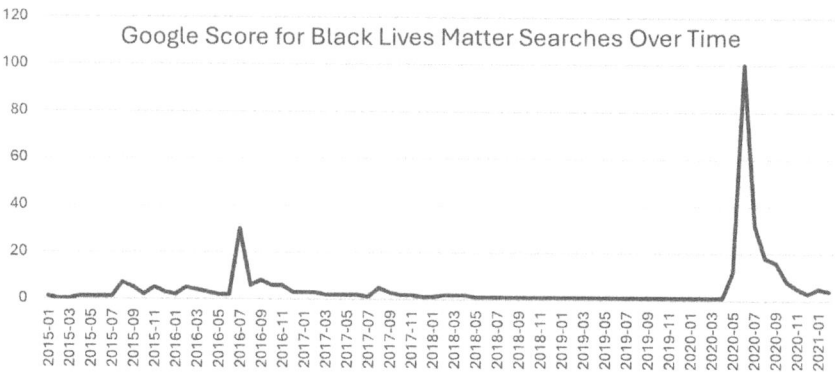

FIGURE 4.2 Google Trends Search Scores for Black Lives Matter From 2015–2021

2021 in the United States. Figure 4.2 presents the average Google Trend score over our period of interest, which ranges from 0, indicating relatively few searches around Black Lives Matter, to 100 in June of 2020, indicating the highest levels of searches for this term. Using the press release/Twitter data and this Google Trends data, we estimate the average levels of Black Lives Matter press releases/tweets at each level of Google Trends scores for Black and non-Black elected officials.

SALIENCE AND BLM DISCUSSIONS IN PRESS RELEASES AND TWEETS

Figure 4.3 presents the average percent of mentions of Black Lives Matter topics in A: Press Releases and B: Tweets by Google Trends scores for Black and non-Black members of Congress. Our period of interest is between January 2015 and January 2021 for press releases and January 2019 through January 2021 for tweets. The graphs also include 95 percent confidence intervals. The data provides more evidence that the salience of a topic (i.e., whether it is high profile or not) matters more for non-Black elected officials than for Black elected officials. Following the murder of George Floyd, mentions of Black Lives Matter topics were significantly higher for non-Black elected officials than they were in other months for these legislators. In fact, 15.5% of all press releases and 7.7% of all tweets put out by non-Black elected officials in the month of June 2020 mentioned a Black Lives Matter topic.

Almost all of these were tied to the murder of George Floyd, Breonna Taylor, or Ahmaud Arbery, or support for the George Floyd Justice in

Salience and BLM Discussions in Press Releases and Tweets 87

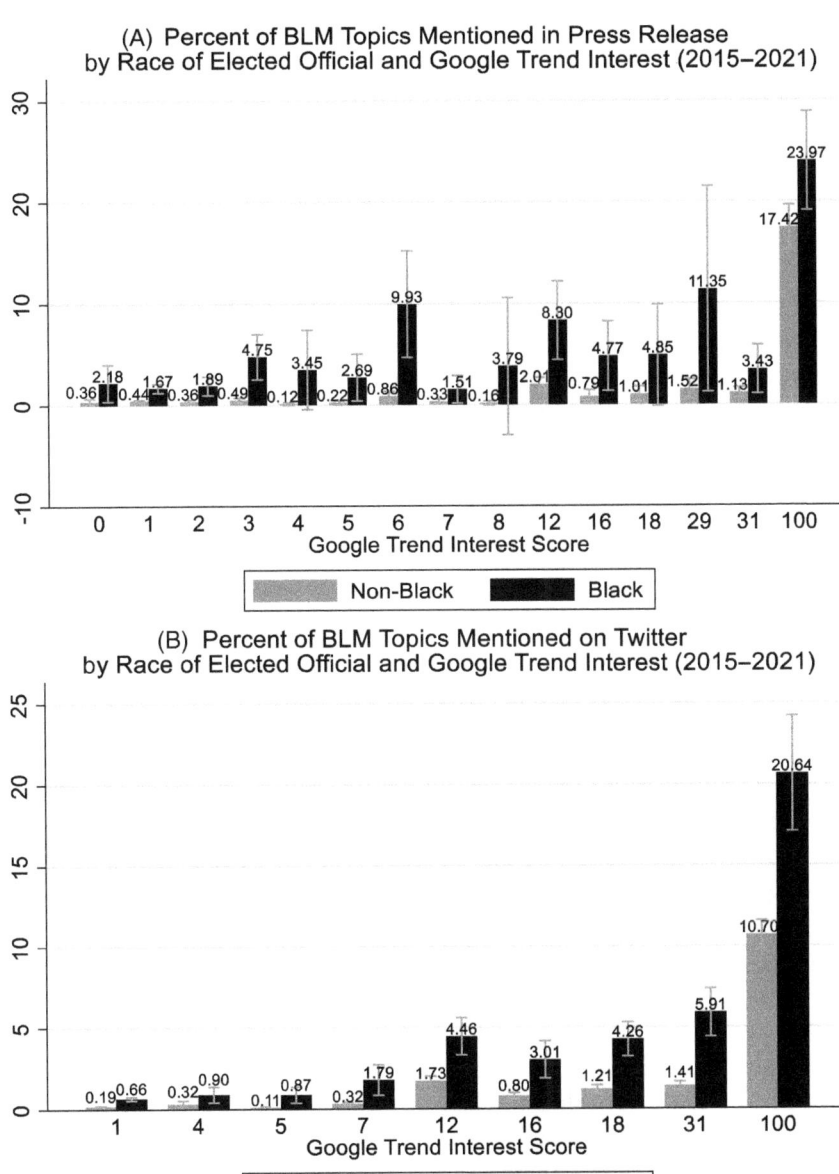

FIGURE 4.3 Percent of BLM Topics Mentions in Press Releases Monthly by Race of the Elected Officials and Google Trend Search Scores (2015–2021) W/ 95% Confidence Intervals

Policing Act or the JUSTICE Act. For example, Representative Ted Lieu (D-CA) put out a press release a few days after Floyd's murder stating, "Watching Minneapolis police officers murder George Floyd shook me to my core. All the officers involved must be prosecuted to the fullest extent of the law. I share the pain and frustration that Americans feel in this moment. Black Lives Matter." Even Republicans like Tom Cole (R-OK) echoed this sentiment, saying, "The events of the last few days have been distressing to every American. The reprehensible treatment of George Floyd that resulted in his death is unacceptable. There should be and will be a full local, state, and federal investigation of the event." Others used press releases during this moment to talk about their support or role in legislation to curb police violence. For example, Representative Jason Crow (D-CO) used a press release to signal his support for police reform to his constituents. "Jason Crow today voted to pass the Justice in Policing Act, the first-ever bold, comprehensive approach to hold police accountable, change the culture of law enforcement, and build trust between law enforcement and our communities." Unsurprisingly, a few topics this month encapsulated the vast majority of outreach.

However, outside of June 2020, when interest in Black Lives Matter was low, non-Black elected officials were much more likely to remain silent on this issue. Non-Black Elected officials put out 2 percent or fewer press releases and 1 percent or fewer tweets including at least one Black Lives Matter term in every month outside of June 2020. These were mostly centered on lower-profile figures tied to Black Lives Matter. For example, in December 2015, a month with a BLM interest score of 2, Steve Cohen (D-TN) discussed the shooting of Laquan McDonald in Chicago to further police reform legislation. "[Rep. Cohen] cited the shooting of Laquan McDonald by Chicago police on the House floor while renewing his call for a federal law to encourage states to use independent prosecutors in cases involving police use of deadly force: the Police Training and Independent Review Act (H.R. 2302)."

Others, like Mark Pocan (D-WI), spoke about Black Lives Matter-related deaths in their state or district. He said, "The loss of this young life is a tragedy, and my deepest sympathy goes out to the family of Tony Robinson at this very difficult time. My hope is that out of this tragedy comes an opportunity for our community to grow stronger together. People of color across the country and right here in our community are arrested at disproportionately high rates." On average, non-Black elected officials mentioned a Black Lives Matter term in less than half of a percent of all press releases or tweets when fewer people were paying attention to the topic (i.e., outside of June 2020).

Like non-Black elected officials, Black Members of Congress were much more likely to speak about Black Lives Matter in June 2020 than they were in other months. On average, 23.97% of Black legislators' press releases and 20.64% of their tweets contained at least a single Black Lives Matter topic in June of 2020. Both differences were statistically significantly greater than the percent of Black Lives Matter topics put out by non-Black elected officials in the same month.

Black elected officials were also statistically significantly more likely to speak about Black Lives Matter in almost every month than non-Black elected officials. Thus, regardless of the salience of the event, Black elected officials continued to speak about Black Lives Matter topics. Even when the Google Trends score was zero, indicating little to no interest from the public, 2.18% of press releases put out by Black elected officials mentioned Black Lives Matter topics. Similarly, when the Google Trends scores for Black Lives Matter searches were below average between 2015 and 2021, Black elected officials issued six times as many press releases mentioning Black Lives Matter terms as White elected officials and 8.5 times as many press releases mentioning these topics as Latino/a elected officials. Similarly, Black elected officials tweeted about Black Lives Matter issues about 7.5 times more often than White and Latino/a elected officials when the Google Trend score for Black Lives Matter for the 2019–2021 congressional session was below average.

Black elected officials used their public platform to highlight the murders of lesser-known figures tied to Black Lives Matter during low salience months. In November 2015, a month with a BLM attention score of 5, Gwen Moore (D-WI) put out a press release calling for an investigation into the shooting of a Black man named Dontre Hamilton, which occurred 18 months earlier. "I am especially saddened by the Department of Justice's decision not to bring criminal civil rights charges against Officer Christopher Manney. More than eighteen months have passed since Officer Manney fatally shot Dontre Hamilton, an unarmed Black man struggling with mental illness, and many unanswered questions still remain." This was a common theme among Black elected officials to not only highlight lower-profile figures tied to Black Lives Matter, but to do so when interest around these individuals had faded.

Another example of this is when Frederica Wilson tweeted that she continued to highlight the fact that the Miami police department had shot seven Black men in seven months, eight years earlier. "It's too soon to declare mission accomplished. Back in 2011, I fought for a DOJ investigation after seven black men in Miami were shot and killed in 7 months and still believe we have work to do to make our community safer for all." She used her public platform to argue that more oversight is necessary in a month when few were discussing the topic (April 2019). In another month where BLM was less salient, September 2016, Barbara Lee issued a press release putting pressure on Congress to take action tied to police reform. In doing so, she highlighted the murder of Michael Brown, which happened over a year earlier. "Since Michael Brown was shot in Ferguson two years ago, 2,195 people have been killed by police in our nation. As a mother of two black men and the grandmother of five black grandchildren, I worry that someone I love could become number 2,196."

While both Black and non-Black elected officials respond to the salience of an event when deciding to speak about Black Lives Matter issues, Black elected officials speak out about this topic even during periods when the population is not as interested. They also appear to work to keep an issue on the agenda even when public interest fades. This provides additional evidence that the high-profile nature of a topic is a stronger driver of support for racial rhetorical representation for non-Black elected officials than it is for Black elected officials.

SUMMARY

In this chapter, we find strong evidence that Black and non-Black elected officials differ in how they engage in racial outreach. While Black members of Congress speak about a combination of higher- and lower-profile racial topics, non-Black elected officials tend to gravitate toward racial issues that have more notoriety. This follows our expectations that when non-Black elected officials engage in racial outreach, they do so in a way that is reactive to public expectations. Such outreach ensures that the targeted group recognizes the overtures that the elected official is making to connect with this group. It also signals that non-Black elected officials focus more on a racially expected script rather than speak about topics/issues the public is not paying close attention to when they engage in rhetorical representation. In this way, non-Black elected officials are more likely to engage in reactive rhetorical representation than Black elected officials.

In contrast, Black elected officials use a greater combination of low- and high-profile racial outreach in their press releases and tweets. As a result, Black elected officials tend to be more likely to speak about racial issues that fly under the radar. Black elected officials likely do not want policies that address race or lower-profile Black public figures to be overlooked, even when the public is not paying attention to these topics. African American elected officials also appear to want to build a specialization in caring about racial issues. As a result, they tend to engage more in proactive rhetorical representation. Rather than waiting for pressure from their constituents to speak out about racial issues, Black elected officials are proactive in searching for opportunities to highlight racial inequality.

We find more evidence that Black elected officials engage in proactive rhetorical representation in our examination of Black Lives Matter discussions over time. Proactive rhetorical representation is more likely to occur when elected officials speak out about a topic, even when the public is not interested in that issue. We show that non-Black elected officials are more reactive to speaking out about police reform, mostly when Black Lives Matter-type issues become more salient. While still responsive, Black elected officials speak about this topic even when there is little interest from the public.

The results of both sets of analyses suggest that Black elected officials are more likely to engage in proactive rhetorical representation where they bring attention to topics that are not in the public eye and work to keep already well-known issues on the agenda when the public is not paying attention. In doing so, descriptive representatives raise awareness about important issues and lay the groundwork for future action. Also, speaking about issues whose time on the public agenda has passed elongates the policy window and places pressure on fellow policymakers to accomplish something around the topic. The use of proactive racial rhetorical representation in this way has tangible benefits to make the government more responsive to communities of color.

5

Crystal Clear

Rhetorical Representation and Defining Novel Racial Issues

On March 11, 2020, the World Health Organization declared that the COVID-19 outbreak was officially a global pandemic. Two days later, former President Donald Trump declared COVID-19 a national emergency, investing fifty billion dollars to combat the spread of this new virus. Congress spent much of 2020 introducing legislation to provide healthcare workers the tools they needed to treat patients with the disease, fund grants for scientists who were working to find effective treatments, and provide resources to businesses and communities ravaged by the virus.

While COVID-19 did not discriminate, the systematic inequalities built into the health care and economic systems in the United States meant that African Americans were more severely affected by the outbreak than others. In the first month following the emergency declaration, Black Americans were about four times more likely to die of COVID-19 than their White counterparts.[1] Black people were also consistently more likely to contract the virus, given that they disproportionately live in cities and work in jobs that were not able to go remote. Black Americans were also more likely to need hospitalization than White Americans.[2] Outside of the health effects of COVID-19, African Americans faced a greater financial strain because of the pandemic. A report by the Rand Corporation, entitled "Laid Off More, Hired Less: Black Workers in the COVID-19 recession," showed that the unemployment disparity between Black and White workers doubled in the first few months of the recession. Overall,

---

[1] www.washingtonpost.com/health/2022/10/19/covid-deaths-us-race/
[2] www.mayoclinic.org/diseases-conditions/coronavirus/expert-answers/coronavirus-infection-by-race/faq-20488802

the COVID-19 pandemic created a set of unique challenges for people of color.

As Congress was addressing the pandemic, Black elected officials were vocal about the need to pay attention to how COVID-19 was exacerbating racial inequality. In the first few months of the pandemic, a group of Black and Brown legislators led by Danny Davis (IL-7), Barbara Lee (CA-13) and Terri Sewell (AL-7) wrote a letter to the then Speaker of the House Nancy Pelosi and Minority Leader Kevin McCarthy asking for more resources and attention to be paid to the particularly harmful effects of COVID-19 on people of color. The letter raises awareness that COVID-19 has a differential effect on Blacks and Latino/as and asks for resources aimed at helping people with sickle cell disease.

> The undersigned Members of Congress are gravely concerned about the impact COVID-19 is having on African Americans and Latinos in the US and particularly, on individuals living with sickle cell disease (SCD), who often live with long term heart and lung problems (multiple severe co-morbidities) and are at higher risk of life-threatening complications if infected... We are suggesting authorization language for $30 million that is modeled on a demonstration program included in the recently passed legislation...

Outside of health effects, Black U.S. House Representative Joyce Beatty (OH-3) introduced a bill to "Ban the Box" on Paycheck Protection Program (PPP) loans. By forcing business owners to report even minor legal infractions in PPP applications, the program would be less likely to invest in minority-owned businesses. Given inequities in our justice system, Beatty points out that asking about minor legal offenses disproportionately hurts Black businesses.[3]

> As Congress debates a cash infusion into the Paycheck Protection Program (PPP), U.S. Congresswoman Joyce Beatty (OH-03) and U.S. Congressman Joe Kennedy III (MA-04) today called on Congressional leadership to fix a glaring flaw in the program that disqualifies small business owners with even minor offenses from critical relief. As it becomes increasingly clear that the COVID-19 pandemic has disproportionately impacted communities of color, these exemptions will only penalize the same communities that have been most prejudiced by a broken criminal justice system.

These press releases represent the significance of Black elected officials' ability to recognize problems that would affect those who share their race in new legislation and introduce solutions.

---

[3] https://beatty.house.gov/media-center/press-releases/reps-beatty-and-kennedy-ban-the-box-for-coronavirus-small-business-loans

Identifying racial disparities that have been largely undiscussed demonstrates a proactive approach to rhetorical representation, which has important policy implications. The aforementioned press releases represent the importance of descriptive representation in advancing Black interests in an area which Mansbridge (1999) describes as uncrystallized policy issues. Mansbridge (1999) argues that uncrystallized political issues are those that have not been on the political agenda for very long, and candidates have not yet taken public stances. As a result, those engaged in proactive racial rhetorical representation use their public platform to frame the terms of the debate in ways that recognize their groups' interests, thereby expanding the racial issue agenda. COVID-19 represents such an issue, and the examples above conform to Mansbridge's (1999) expectation that descriptive representatives will fight for their groups' policy preferences.

Discussions of uncrystallized issues also represents a key component of proactive rhetorical representation. By being vocal about the racial consequences of undeveloped policy solutions, proactive elected officials can ensure that their fellow legislators are aware of how their decisions may impact underserved communities. Descriptive representatives who speak about race on uncrystallized topics further ensure that the interests of those who share their identity are accounted for in any policy solution.

While Mansbridge's (1999) hypothesis was theoretical, in this chapter, we set out to empirically assess whether Black elected officials speak out on behalf of co-racial individuals around uncrystallized issues more than non-Black elected officials. To accomplish this goal, we review Mansbridge's (1999) seminal research and explain the significance of descriptive representatives in the policy process. We then discuss why Black representatives should play an important role in identifying and shaping the terms of debate around uncrystallized issues using proactive racial rhetorical representation. We assess whether Black elected officials discuss Black-centered uncrystallized issues more than others by using the hand coding of press releases, which included a race-based appeal in the 114th through 116th Congresses. We find that Black elected officials are much more likely to highlight the significance of race in their discussions of uncrystallized issues than other members of Congress. In doing so, we provide empirical evidence in support of Mansbridge's (1999) hypothesis around descriptive representation and uncrystallized issues.

We follow this analysis up with a case study of discussions about racial issues in press releases and tweets that mentioned the pandemic in the first six months of the outbreak in the United States. We argue that the pandemic provides a strong case study as an uncrystallized issue because it was an unexpected and extremely salient new social issue that attracted a lot of attention from elected officials. However, in spite of its salience, the novelty of the pandemic meant that there were no established positions around the racial implications of COVID-19 in the early parts of the outbreak. Similar to our previous analysis, we find that Black elected officials were the most vocal about the impact of the COVID-19 pandemic on racial inequality. We conclude the chapter by demonstrating that through racial rhetorical representation of uncrystallized issues, Black elected officials ensure that co-racial individuals are not ignored in the framing of debates around new political issues.

THE SIGNIFICANCE OF DESCRIPTIVE REPRESENTATION IN UNCRYSTALLIZED ISSUES

In 1999, Jane Mansbridge published the article "Should Blacks Represent Blacks and Women Represent Women? A Contingent 'Yes.'" In the article, Mansbridge (1999) explores the circumstances in the legislative process in which descriptive representation matters most. She argues that the legislative process has multiple components. Two important portions of this process are the deliberative stage and the aggregative stage. The deliberative stage occurs when legislators are at the beginning of a policy proposal. During this stage, elected officials discuss and debate the terms of a specific problem. Ideally, in this stage, elected officials are able to arrive at a legislative solution. It is important in this stage of the legislative process to have more voices in the room to maximize the equality of the legislative outcome. Without the availability of people from different backgrounds, it becomes likely that any resulting legislation may intentionally or unintentionally be biased toward those who were present during the discussion.

For example, if the debates are only occurring among the financially well-off, then it is likely that the resulting legislation will be biased against those in the working class. This bias occurs because poorer representatives' absence from the process means their unique perspectives are not accounted for in the discussion. In contrast, those who are wealthier and more involved in the process will be better able to articulate their group's interest. Moreover, even those who want to create more equitable legislation are unaware, due to a lack of experience, of how the decisions they make may inadvertently affect poorer individuals. The lack of information from a variety of voices increases the likelihood that legislation is written more narrowly around the present groups' interests. This is why President John Adams once argued that Congress "should be a portrait, in miniature, of the people at large. As it should think, feel, reason and act like them."[4] By having more voices in the room, legislators at the deliberation stage can be better assured that they are representing the interests of the people at large and incorporating a wide variety of perspectives.

The next stage of the legislative process, according to Mansbridge (1999), is the aggregative phase. During this stage of the process, the different stakeholders have outlined their goals to best represent their groups' policy preferences. From here, there needs to be compromises to adjudicate between a list of competing demands. As a result, representatives must not only outline their group's interest, but they must follow that up with actions that ensure that their group's demands are accounted for in the legislative process.

The actions of legislators in these two phases are the most consequential for uncrystallized issues. As mentioned earlier, uncrystallized issues are those in which there are few pre-established positions or solutions. These issues arise during new crises or when previously overlooked topics become salient. The latter often occurs when new groups become politically incorporated and are able to raise novel legislative concerns. Given their lack of representation in government, minority and women's political interests were generally not well defined in the marketplace of political ideas. In fact, for most of American history, the political goals of marginalized groups only existed on the fringes of political discourse (Tate 2010). Hence, they were uncrystallized.

While crystallized topics have a track record that legislators can refer to so that they may better understand the implications of their decisions, uncrystallized issues provide no such guide. Descriptive representatives, Mansbridge (1999) contends, have the best understanding of how uncrystallized policies may affect their racial group and, if vocal about their concerns, are invaluable in creating a more equitable policy process. Mansbridge (1999) argues that descriptive representatives play a key role in shaping uncrystallized issues at key junctures of the policy process. First, descriptive representatives play an important role in framing the debate around uncrystallized issues. This is driven by the fact that descriptive representatives' personal histories naturally generate perspectives and interests in line with the marginalized group (Fenno 2003, Tate 2003).

---

[4] www.senate.gov/artandhistory/history/common/generic/exerpt-thoughts-on-government-adams-1776.htm

It also makes descriptive representatives vital in identifying potential blind spots in legislation that elected officials of a different identity may miss.

A pertinent example of descriptive representatives addressing blind spots in legislation can be found in discussions of the aforementioned PPP. The PPP was a new program instituted as part of the government's response to the COVID-19 pandemic. The novelty of the program meant that parties likely had not staked out a position on this legislation. Moreover, there were likely blind spots in the legislation that, if not identified, would have led to a disproportionate number of people of color being left out of the program. The evolving debate around the nature of the program provided descriptive representatives opportunities to identify areas where people of color were being excluded or disadvantaged. In the early debates, several Black elected officials spoke out in protection of their racial group's interests. For example, as discussed in the introduction, Joyce Beatty (OH-3) argued that asking PPP applicants if they had ever had felony charges in the application would make it harder for African Americans, who face biases in the criminal justice system, to obtain a loan. Small infractions around marijuana use, for example, would make it so that Black business owners would not be able to participate in the program. Given that such infractions were disproportionately more likely to reach the level of a felonious charge for Black people, it would mean that previous inequalities in the justice system would exacerbate racial disparities in the PPP.

Along the same lines, Black U.S. House Representative Steven Horsford (NV-4) spoke to the small business sub-committee in Congress to argue that stipulations in the PPP, which excluded small gaming operators, would mean that fewer minority-owned businesses would be able to obtain Small Business Administration loans. In his testimony, Representative Horsford argued, "minority, women and veteran-owned businesses have not gotten an equal share of the funding either. So, while I am voting for this bill today, I call on this committee to join with me and the members of our delegation to fix this issue that prohibits gaming businesses from getting their share of the money..." In both instances, Black members of Congress were able to both highlight blind spots around a new issue and advocate for legislation to change to reflect the issues that affect their communities.

What makes African American elected officials better able to identify blind spots? As mentioned in Chapter 4, their own experiences with discrimination and their connections with others who have faced these obstacles make them more aware of how vague policy could lead to greater problems for those who share their race. In arguing for more protection for Black Maternal Care, Barbara Lee (D-CA) speaks of her own mother's experience and those with whom she has personal connections as a motivating factor to create legislation to combat disparities in racial maternal morbidity.

> My mother, Mildred Parish Massey, fought for me from the day I was born. She needed a cesarean section to deliver me, but the hospital refused to admit her because she was black. When – after a long ordeal – she was finally admitted, it was too late for a C-section. My mother became unconscious and nearly died as a result… I know personally the tragedy of infant and maternal mortality rates that women of color disproportionately suffer… In honor of my beloved mother, last week I announced my support for the Mothers and Offspring Maternal & Morbidity Awareness (MOMMA) Act.[5]

Barbara Lee's mother's experience with poor maternal care due to racism likely made her aware of the role that race can play in access to quality health care. These traumas tied to race would also make her more vigilant of how policies can disproportionally affect one's group. This likely increases Black elected officials' likelihood of speaking about race in areas that are uncrystallized.

In addition to framing the debate, Mansbridge (1999) notes that elected officials who hope to achieve the integration of their group's interest into uncrystallized legislation must advocate strongly for their position. Mansbridge (1999) writes that women and minorities need descriptive representation to get their "uncrystallized substantive interests" represented with sufficient vigor (1999: 648). She adds, "[p]articularly on issues that are uncrystallized or that many legislators have not thought through, the personal quality of being oneself a member of the affected group gives the legislator a certain moral force in making an argument or asking for a favorable vote on an issue important to the group" (1999: 648).

It is here too that descriptive representatives' personal histories with discrimination toward their group may make them stronger advocates for their group's positions (Fenno 2003, Tate 2003). Black members of Congress not only raise the terms of debate, but they are also active in advancing policies aimed at improving opportunities for their group. For example, it is not uncommon in press releases around COVID-19 for Black members of Congress to use words like "urgent," "crucial," and

---

[5] https://lee.house.gov/news/press-releases/congresswoman-lee-marks-mothers-day

"vital" to describe policies that address racial disparities in response to the pandemic. For example, U.S. House Representative Anthony Brown (MD-4) pressed Maryland's governor to provide resources to communities of color during the pandemic.

> Congressman Anthony G. Brown (MD-04) and Majority Leader Steny Hoyer (MD-05) wrote a letter to Maryland Governor Larry Hogan laying out **urgent** priorities to address racial disparities exacerbated by the novel coronavirus pandemic. The lawmakers highlight the need for additional resources for testing, hospital surge capacity, public health education, and data collection in Prince George's County. They also urge Governor Hogan to develop plans to address long-standing health care disparities in communities of color.[6]

This example demonstrates that not only do Black elected officials shape the terms of the debate, but they often are the strongest advocates to make sure that these new reforms are implemented. Based on this review, we strongly expect that Black elected officials will be the most likely to raise racial concerns in uncrystallized issues.

DATA

To examine the link between the race of the representative and their likelihood of raising racialized concerns with uncrystallized issues, we use two different strategies. First, we completed hand-coding of all press releases that were identified as being tied to Black political interests using the data set described in the introduction. This step required the hand-coding of 5,439 Black-centered press releases from our universe of 204,910 press releases put out by U.S. House Representatives in the 114th, 115th, and 116th Congresses to identify uncrystallized racial outreach. Given that we are interested in racialized uncrystallized outreach, we only code press releases that were identified in our original analysis as being Black-centered. While Mansbridge (1999) gives a broad framework for uncrystallized issues, the application of this description toward individual-level outreach is original.

We coded uncrystallized racial press releases as those which deal with a novel and unestablished racial issue and as being a position not staked out by either political party. For example, given the long-standing discussions and settled positions around voting rights, police reform, or affirmative action, these issues were not coded as uncrystallized. Instead, press

---

[6] https://hoyer.house.gov/content/hoyer-brown-write-letter-governor-hogan-laying-out-urgent-priorities-address-alarming-racial

releases were coded as uncrystallized when they raised issues that addressed a new and rarely discussed racial topic. This often happened when legislators highlighted inequality in novel ways. For example, Bobby Rush (D-IL) wrote a press release asking the U.S. health commissioner to get more people of color included in clinical trials. While legislators often speak about health-related issues, Rush's focus on increasing the representation of people of color in these trials is rarely discussed by elected officials. As a result, we coded it as an uncrystallized racial appeal. Similarly, several legislators were coded as making uncrystallized racial appeals when their press releases denounced the Internal Revenue Service (IRS) for what they viewed as discriminatory audits of African Americans. Again, legislators engage in discussions of uncrystallized issues when they raise the often-overlooked issue of racial discrimination in IRS audits in their press releases. By raising new racial issues in a generally deracialized space (tax audits), these elected officials were engaging in uncrystallized racial outreach. Press releases that were uncrystallized were substantive rather than symbolic. While Mansbridge (1999) considered some symbolic acts to be uncrystallized as well, we used a narrow definition to simplify the coding process.

We coded discussions of uncrystallized racial topics in press releases as one. We labeled press releases that did not feature an uncrystallized topic as being zero. Following this process, we took the average number of press releases that mentioned an uncrystallized racial topic and divided that by the total number of press releases the member of Congress put out in each congressional session. This serves as our main dependent variable.

To complement this hand-coded analysis, we also take a case study approach. As discussed throughout this chapter, COVID-19 represents a novel social and medical problem that legislators rushed to react to. It is the prototypical uncrystallized issue because the exogenous shock of COVID-19 meant that 1: it was a new social issue which had not been on the political agenda, and 2: parties and policymakers would not have time to stake out a position on this issue. This is particularly true in the early part of the pandemic.

To examine whether Black elected officials took the lead in identifying racial disparities tied to this uncrystallized issue, we look at the percent of race-based appeals which included the words "COVID-19," "Coronavirus," or "pandemic" among all mentions of any these same words in the first six months of the pandemic (3/1/2020–9/30/2020). We use a six-month cutoff because it allows enough time for elected officials to raise new concerns and navigate the twists and turns of a developing pandemic. The time frame is also not too long, in that we see repeated discussions around the same topic.[7] We perform this analysis for both press releases and for tweets put out for members of the 116th U.S. House of Representatives. Our dependent variable for this analysis is the percent of COVID-19 discussions that raise Black issues through press releases and tweets. Our independent variable of interest is the race/ethnicity of the elected official.

RESULTS

Press Releases from the 114–116th Congress

Figure 5.1 presents the percent of uncrystallized racial issues discussed in press releases by Black and non-Black U.S. House Representatives in the 114th, 115th, and 116th Congresses. The figure also includes labels for the average percent of press releases across racial groups and Congressional sessions with 95 percent confidence intervals. Unsurprisingly, discussions of uncrystallized issues in press releases make up a minority of all outreach in each Congress. This is in large part because members of Congress generally speak to issues that are established. In the 114th Congress, .14 percent of all press releases, or less than 1 percent, addressed race in uncrystallized issues. In the 115th Congress, a scant .20 percent of all press releases addressed these topics, and in the 116th Congress, .7 percent of all press releases discussed Black interests in uncrystallized issues.

While small in numbers, discussions around uncrystallized issues grew over the course of our data set. The large growth in discussions of uncrystallized issues in the 116th Congress, which represents about a 500 percent growth in these discussions compared to the 114th Congress, are likely tied to the key events which occurred in 2020. First, as mentioned throughout this chapter, the COVID-19 pandemic raised significant opportunities for elected officials to address race in this uncrystallized topic. Second, the racial awakening that occurred as a result of the murder of George Floyd likely led more members of Congress to be aware of the different ways that new policies could exacerbate racial inequality.

---

[7] However, it is fair to note that this time frame could be elongated or shortened. To ensure that our results are not driven by our choice of six months, we replicated the results using a 3-month and 9-month cutoff. Our results are consistent to these bandwidths.

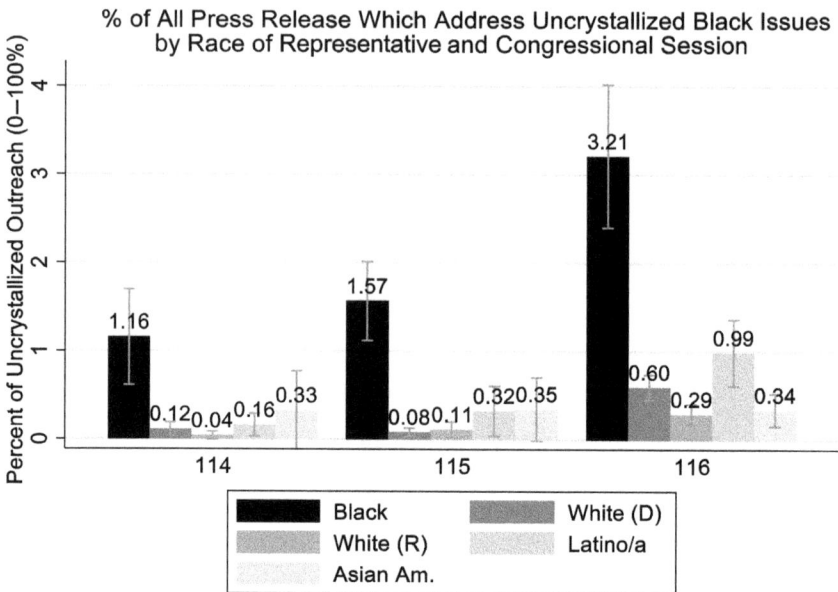

FIGURE 5.1 The Percent of All Press Releases Issued in the 114th, 115th, and 116th Congresses Which Include Mentions of Uncrystallized Black Issues by the Race of the Representative W/ 95% Confidence Intervals[8]
T-tests are used for comparison.

In addition to the growing number of public statements around uncrystallized racial issues, the gap between non-Black and Black elected officials' mentions of these topics also increased over this period. This was particularly true for differences between Black and non-Black Democrats. In the 114th Congress, the gap between Black and non-Black Democratic elected officials in their discussions of uncrystallized racial issues was about 1 percent and was statistically significant based on a two-sample t-test. By the 115th Congress, this disparity grew to 1.5 percent and was also statistically significant based on a two-sample t-test. By the 116th Congress, Black elected officials put out about 2.6 percent more press releases which mention uncrystallized issues than non-Black elected officials. This gap was also statistically significant based on a two-sample t-test. It should be noted that we find similar patterns in racial disparities

---

[8] Total Black Uncrystallized Press Releases by Group: Black=398, White Democrat=207, White Republican=48, Latino=70, Asian Am=19

when we examine the percent of crystallized issues among only racial appeals. Given the dearth of Black Republicans, it is difficult to know if Black GOP members of the House discuss racialized differences more than their non-Black co-partisans. Across, all three congresses we examine the average Black member of Congress (2%) puts out 1.8 percent more press releases which mention uncrystallized issues than non-Black elected officials (.20%).

We also find that overall, non-Black Democrats discuss uncrystallized racial issues in about .35 percent of all press release which is statistically significantly greater than the same discussions from non-Black Republicans (.17%). However, these differences across party are much smaller than the differences by race.[9] Overall, this analysis demonstrates empirically that Black descriptive representatives are the strongest proponents of advancing racial interests around uncrystallized issues.

It is also important to note that discussions of uncrystallized issues covered important topics. For example, several members of Congress raised the disproportionate impact that government shutdowns would have on people of color. Judy Chu (D-CA), for example, issued the following statement in opposition the 2018 U.S. Government Shutdown. "This pattern of lurching from crisis to crisis while ignoring the requirements of real, long-term budgeting must end. Such reckless governing negatively impacts the most vulnerable in our society, including communities of color." Others like Maxine Waters (D-CA) and Keith Ellison (D-MN) issued statements to the government agencies to warn them about the implications of new regulation changes on people of color.

Today, Congresswoman Maxine Waters (D-CA), Ranking Member of House Financial Services Committee, and Congressman Keith Ellison (D-MN) led a cohort of Congressional Democrats in a letter to Federal Communications Commission (FCC) Chairman Tom Wheeler, urging the reclassification of mobile broadband as a common carrier. This move would protect communities of color who disproportionately rely on mobile devices for internet access.

While most of our coded cases discuss uncrystallized issues around government actions, some used their public platforms to speak to private industry. Bobby Rush (D-IL), for example, joined the Hispanic conference

---

[9] The substantive differences hold when we estimate a regression analysis and control for several factors including the demographic and political factors of the elected officials and the districts they represent. See appendix for these models.

to ask the cable company comcast to work with the channel STARZ to ensure that more diverse voices were represented in television.

Today, U.S. Representatives Bobby L. Rush (D-Ill.) and Tony Cárdenas (D-Calif.), joined by members of the Congressional Hispanic Caucus, sent a letter to Comcast Corporation, calling on the company to negotiate in good faith with regards to its dealings with STARZ and to ensure diverse perspectives and programs.

These examples show that members of Congress remain vigilant and speak about issues that are generally not on people's radar to highlight the impact of decisions for members of underrepresented groups.

Uncrystallized Issue Case Study: COVID-19

As mentioned earlier, the COVID-19 pandemic provides an ideal case study to examine the discussion of race around an uncrystallized topic. COVID-19 represents an exogenous shock to the social system which created a new and highly salient social problem. While parties quickly drew lines in the sand around this issue, in the first few months of the pandemic, both parties worked to find policy solutions for this crisis. One way that legislators can influence the policy process is by raising concerns about the issue for their specific group in their public communication. This allows them to raise concerns about the disproportionate impact of the pandemic and any resulting legislation for their racial group.

To examine discussions around race and COVID-19, we examine all press releases and tweets put out in the first six months of the pandemic (3/1/2020–9/30/2020) and explore the percent of COVID related press releases which included Black outreach. Black outreach is measured by our hand-coded/computer assisted analysis described in the introduction. A score of "1" indicates Black outreach and a score of "0" indicates otherwise. Our dependent variable is simply the percent of all press releases/tweets which are coded as Black outreach and include a pandemic related word ("COVID," "Coronavirus," or "pandemic") divided by the total number of press releases/tweets which include at least one of the pandemic related words.

Before we discuss the general differences between the groups, it is important to assess how elected officials spoke about COVID-19 in the first few months of the pandemic. A cursory review of our data set of press releases and tweets shows that the vast majority of COVID-19 Black-oriented outreach was centered around support for specific bills or calls to the president, federal agencies, and/or state or local governments to address the pandemic's disproportionate impact on communities of color.

For policy, many of these focused on supporting policies like the HEROES Act or more specific bills like the Equitable Data Collection and Disclosure on COVID-19 Act. Some of these highlighted changes that individual members made to larger bills. For example, Marc Veasey (D-TX) highlighted an amendment to the HEROES Act that he added to improve internet access for people of color in a press release. "Congressman Marc Veasey (TX-33) announced he will introduce legislation that will bolster access to broadband for low-income and minority individuals who are facing unprecedented challenges during the spread of the Coronavirus pandemic."

Others used their public platform to ask federal agencies or other administrators to take action to address racial/ethnic inequalities that were exacerbated due to the pandemic. For example, Elaine Luria (D-VA) highlighted actions she and her colleagues took, urging the FDA to collect more data on vaccine trials for people of color in the early months of the pandemic.

> In an effort to ensure inclusivity in COVID-19 vaccine development, Congresswoman Elaine Luria joined a letter urging the Food and Drug Administration (FDA) and the Department of Health and Human Services (HHS) to collect and report the aggregate sex and race data of all participants in COVID-19 vaccine trials. This data collection will be imperative to ensuring that a vaccine will have demonstratable efficacy and safety for communities of color, which are disproportionately affected by COVID-19.

Similarly, Barbara Lee (D-CA) chastised her Republican colleagues in the Senate for blocking legislation that would require the Food and Drug Administration (FDA) to collect data on how the pandemic was affecting racial groups differently.

> Every day, we are seeing more evidence that communities of color are more affected by COVID-19. In Chicago, African Americans make up 70% of those who have died from COVID-19 despite only making up 30% of the city's population. This is unconscionable. If we are to ensure everyone's safety and security, we need the facts on who is being affected.

While calls to action or highlighting the pandemic's disproportionate impact on people of color was the modal form of outreach on Twitter and in press releases, a few highlighted how the pandemic's impact on Black people may have worsened the anguish they felt following the murders of George Floyd, Ahmaud Arbery, and Breonna Taylor. In a discussion with community leaders, Frank Pallone (D-NJ) highlighted his plan to address the multitude of challenges that Black people faced in the Summer of 2020. "Pallone outlined legislation in Congress that would help stop the disproportionate use of force, reform the criminal justice system, and end racial disparities in the response to the coronavirus pandemic." While some of the tweets and press releases connected COVID-19 to the murder of Floyd, even these press releases often spoke about substantive actions to address these inequalities. In addition to speaking about police reform, in the same press release mentioned above, Pallone (D-NJ) also spoke about pushing the Trump administration to close gaps in health care. "As Chairman of the Energy and Commerce Committee, I've called on the Trump Administration to work with Congress so we can close the gaps in our health care system." As a result, the vast majority of Black-oriented outreach which also addressed the pandemic took substantive actions which are in line with Mansbridge's (1999) definition of uncrystallized outreach.

Moving to a more quantitative analysis of racial outreach around the COVID-19 pandemic, Figures 5.2 and 5.3 present the average number of press releases (Figure 5.2) and tweets (Figure 5.3) which mentioned racial topics among all pandemic related press releases or tweets for members of the U.S. House of Representatives. The models are disaggregated by the race/ethnicity and party of the elected official. The graphs also include 95% confidence intervals. Among all discussions of the COVID-19 pandemic, 1.8 percent of press releases and 2.1 percent of tweets were coded as being tied to Black political interests.

The results in both Figures provide more evidence that descriptive representatives are the most likely to bring up group centered issues among a critical uncrystallized topics in their public outreach. This again, was particularly true for Black elected officials. On average, Black elected officials raised concerns tied to race in about 6 percent of press releases and tweets mentioning the pandemic. This represents 4.4 percentage points more COVID-19 related press releases and 3.6 percentage point more COVID-19 related tweets mentioning racial issues than non-Black elected officials. In both forms of outreach, the differences between Black and non-Black members of Congress are statistically significant. The results provide more evidence that Black elected officials raise concerns about race in uncrystallized issues at a greater rate than their non-Black counterparts.[10]

---

[10] We arrive at the same results when we control for potential confounders such as the racial and partisan composition of the district and the age and gender of the member of Congress. This analysis can be found in the appendix.

Summary

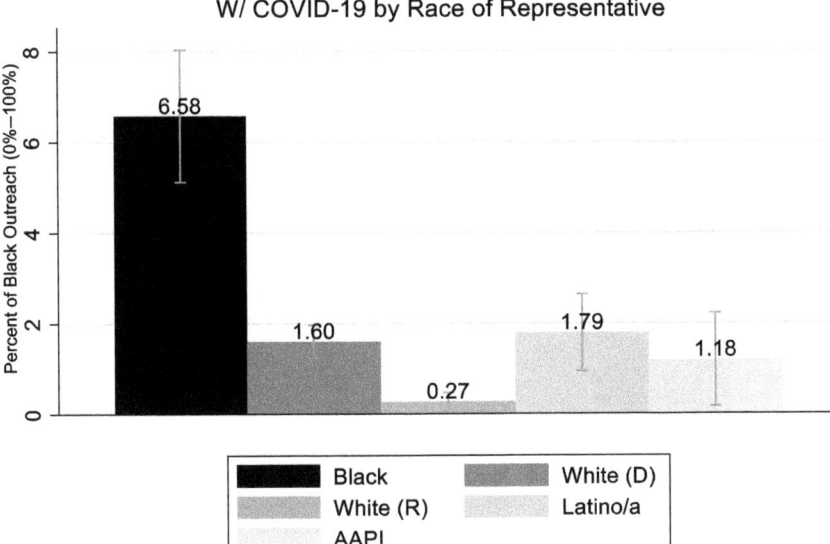

FIGURE 5.2 The Percent of COVID-Related Press Releases in the First Six Months of the Pandemic Which Include Racialized Outreach With 95% Confidence Intervals
Note: The total number of COVID-related Black press releases by racial/ethnic Group: Black$_N$=74, White (D)$_N$=75, White (R)$_N$=7, Latino/a$_N$=17, Asian$_N$=5

SUMMARY

As new issues arise in political debates, it is crucial that a diverse group of legislators proactively voice their concerns about how policies may benefit or harm their group. In her seminal research on descriptive representation, Mansbridge (1999) notes that it is in this deliberative phase of the policy process where descriptive representation can matter most. By helping to frame the debate around uncrystallized issues in a way which accounts for Black political interests, descriptive representatives expand the scope of racial policy interests and ensure that their group is represented in any policy solution.

While Mansbridge's (1999) argument was largely theoretical, this chapter explored whether descriptive representatives follow through in race-based discussions around uncrystallized issues in practice. Public outreach is a powerful way to gauge whether elected officials are framing the debate in a way which benefits their group. Moreover, the shaping of

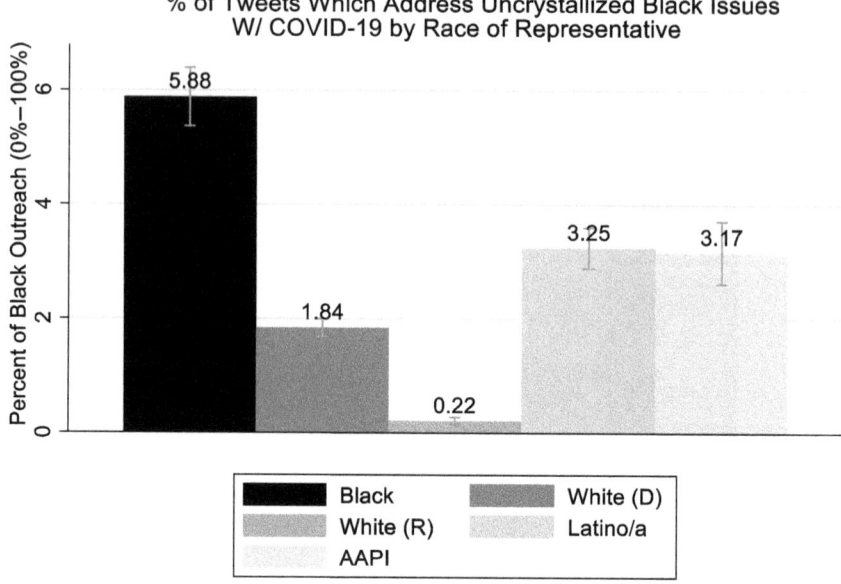

FIGURE 5.3 The Percent of COVID-Related Tweets in the First Six Months of the Pandemic Which Include Racialized Outreach With 95% Confidence Intervals
Note: The total number of COVID-related tweets by racial/ethnic Group: Black$_N$=452, White (D)$_N$=495, White (R)$_N$=37, Latino/a$_N$=276, Asian Am$_N$=122. T-tests are used for comparison.

solutions around uncrystallized issues is a potentially important benefit of racial rhetorical representation.

Our results provide more evidence that descriptive representatives provide stronger levels of proactive racial rhetorical representation than others. This holds for a key component of rhetorical representation, the discussion of uncrystallized issues. During key debates around new social problems, like COVID-19, the presence of Black elected officials to articulate the unique challenges these new issues pose to co-racial individuals ensures that their voice is heard during the policy process. This raises awareness of racial inequalities in areas which are often perceived as being non-racial. Through the unblinding of the racial implication of new issues, proactive rhetorical representation around uncrystallized issues puts pressure on elected officials to craft policies which will not ignore people of color.

6

Depth and Breadth

Exploring the Breadth of Racial Topics Members of Congress Speak About When They Engage in Racial Rhetorical Representation

While African Americans come from a wide variety of social classes, reside in different types of neighborhoods, and vary in numerous phenotypical characteristics such as skin tone, most will experience some form of racial discrimination. A Kaiser Family Foundation Poll taken in 2020 found that nearly three-quarters of African Americans say they have been mistreated because of their race during their lifetime.[1] In spite of experiencing the world in different social contexts, so many African Americans report facing racial discrimination because racial inequality is endemic in American society and permeates almost every facet of American life. African Americans face numerous racial hurdles in their day-to-day lives from the undervaluing of one's home based on race (Howell and Korver Glenn 2018, Kamin 2020), to doctors providing worse care to Black people based on assumptions about race (Assari et al. 2017), to Black children facing more severe punishments for similar behaviors as White children (Gregory et al. 2011). The fact that racism is so prevalent means that it does not matter the path that Black people in the United States take, they will likely face some hostility based on their skin color.

The multifaceted nature of racism in the United States means that a singular focus on addressing racial inequality is likely insufficient. Focusing on one area of racial discrimination may miss the way in which some Black people face discrimination. For example, a singular focus on

---

[1] www.kff.org/racial-equity-and-health-policy/press-release/poll-7-in-10-black-americans-say-they-have-experienced-incidents-of-discrimination-or-police-mistreatment-in-lifetime-including-nearly-half-who-felt-lives-were-in-danger/

voting rights is likely to be more meaningful to Black people in Republican-led states, which have made political participation more difficult in recent years (Grumbach 2022). However, this same outreach may be less personally meaningful to Black people in states like Oregon, California, and Washington, which have expanded access to the ballot box (Grumbach 2022).[2] Similarly, discussions about racial inequality in learning outcomes are likely to be more personally meaningful to African American adults with children than they might be for African Americans with few personal ties to the education system.

Given the multiple ways in which African Americans experience discrimination, the strongest levels of rhetorical representation will not only be deep in terms of the number of statements tied to race, but they should also be broad in terms of the number of racial topics discussed by the elected official. By highlighting achievements of African Americans, calling out racial inequality in various arenas, and/or furthering discussions around the multiple ways that race manifests itself in society, elected officials who engage in proactive racial rhetorical representation will work to reach a wider swath of Black people.

This proactive approach, which uses a broader racial rhetorical strategy, will likely make more African Americans feel that they have an ally in government and a voice in the political process. This broader discussion may better highlight the contributions of Black people to American life and make people more aware that racial disparities are not tied to a single area but are a systemic issue. In doing so, highlighting the many ways that Black people face discrimination increases the likelihood that the government will not take a one-size-fits-all approach to addressing racial inequality.

In this chapter, we explore whether Black and non-Black elected officials differ in the breadth of discussion around racial issues. In previous chapters, we demonstrated that Black elected officials spoke about race differently than non-Black elected officials in that they focused more on racial issues, which flew under the radar (i.e., lower profile forms of racial outreach) and spoke about uncrystallized racial issues. Another unique way that African American elected officials engage in proactive racial rhetorical representation is that they speak about race in more categories than non-Black elected officials. This broader outreach may be driven by Black elected officials' greater ability to identify racial concerns in

---

[2] This is not to say that voting rights would not be meaningful to all Black people given that their fates are often tied together (Tate 1994, Dawson 1994).

multiple areas, their social networks informing them about a wide variety of issues of importance to African Americans, and their own personal experiences with race in the United States.

To assess whether Black and non-Black elected officials differ in the breadth of their racial outreach, we examine press releases and tweets that include Black-centered appeals from almost the complete universe of U.S. House members. Using this data, we estimate categories of race-based appeals using keyword-assisted topic modeling (Eshima et al. 2024). This form of semi-supervised computer-assisted content coding identifies themes in the ways that members of Congress appeal to the Black community. In our analysis, we identify twenty-three unique themes of race-based appeals over our period of interest in press releases and twenty-four unique themes on Twitter in the 116th Congress. We use this information to explore the number of categories in which the elected official issued at least a single press release or tweet. We then take the sum of the different categories that the elected official spoke about at least once to measure the breadth of racial rhetorical outreach.

We find that Black elected officials speak about race more broadly than their non-Black counterparts in press releases and more so than White and Latino/a elected officials on Twitter. By demonstrating that Black elected officials tap into more topics when engaging in racial rhetorical representation, we show that Black elected officials provide a more proactive form of racial outreach than non-Black elected officials. By speaking out about a broader set of topics, elected officials are alerted to the many ways that race influences opportunities and challenges for people of color. This awareness can matter in pushing legislators to take a broader approach to reach the diverse Black community.

WHO SPEAKS OUT BROADLY?

A large body of research demonstrates that one's experiences play a significant role in how they legislate (Mansbridge 1999, Burden 2007, Ditmar et al. 2017, Sobolewska et al. 2018). As mentioned in the introduction, a vast majority of African Americans will face discrimination during their lifetime. These personal experiences with discrimination are particularly potent in making one aware of this problem and increasing vigilance of prejudicial behavior (Purdie-Vaugns and Eibach 2008). For example, experiences of being passed up for a promotion in one industry based on one's race may make the victim more aware of racial discrimination in other facets of hiring and promotion. It may also make them more aware of discrimination in other areas, such as with school admissions or judicial proceedings. This greater awareness of racial discrimination may lead an individual to be more alert to the possibility of discrimination in understanding seemingly non-racial events and issues.

Mansbridge (1999), for example, describes a routine vote in the U.S. Senate which, in part, allowed the Daughters of the Confederacy to continue to use the Confederate flag in their design. While this seemed innocuous to some, given its prevalence at the time, Carol Moseley Braun, the first Black female U.S. Senator in American history, and the only Black member of the Senate at the time, called out the design for its racial insensitivity. Mansbridge (1999: 647) notes, "The most important reason for [Moseley Braun's] action seems to have been the particular sensibility, created by experience, that led her to notice the Confederate flag and be offended by it." In this example, Mansbridge (1999) describes Moseley Braun's experience as a Black woman as making her keenly aware of racist imagery that others have overlooked.

This example illustrates the importance of descriptive representation. Co-racial elected officials' greater abilities to identify the potential harms or benefits of legislation to Black people that others may miss provide a unique and necessary lens to maximize representation in government (Mansbridge 1999). While non-Black elected officials may be more alert to think about racism in high-profile topics, like voting rights or police reform, their lower levels of vigilance may lead them to miss the racial implications of other types of legislation, like promotion in the military or education funding. African Americans' experiences may make them better able to see the racial opportunities and pitfalls in more areas. This attentiveness may increase the number of topics that Black elected officials use to speak about race.

Experiences with discrimination also lead people to be more passionate about combating prejudice (Wallace 2014, Childs 2002). While discrimination can have negative effects with regard to one's emotional state, some research suggests that those who face discrimination become more active in preventing racial biases in the future. For example, Hope et al. (2022) found that young Black people who experienced racism were the most likely to engage in race-based activism. Minta (2011) argued that experience with discrimination and levels of linked fate also shape how Black legislators work to advance Black political interests in Congress. Minta (2011) notes that these experiences make Black elected officials more active in speaking out for Black people in oversight hearings.

Highlighting racial inequality and calling out racism play a significant role in addressing the problem (Devine et al. 1991, Monteith 1993). When people are made aware of racial discrimination, they become more likely to alter their behavior in this area. This is particularly true for issues/decisions which are expected to be non-racial. For example, Pope et al. (2018) found that a National Basketball Association report highlighting racial bias in foul-calling altered the behavior of referees. By making an implicit action explicit, referees were more likely to check themselves on foul calling against Black players, and this reduced racial disparities. Given that African American elected officials work hard to root out racial discrimination, many may be more likely to call out racism where they see it, even if the topic is largely non-racial. In doing so, Black elected officials may speak about race in a wider variety of areas.

Beyond personal experiences with discrimination, social networks play a significant role in making people aware of social biases (Paluck 2011, Stout and Baker 2018). A common way in which people learn about discrimination is through personal narratives, which can be effective in highlighting a social problem and encouraging action (Broockman and Kalla 2016). African Americans are often better connected with individuals who share their race (Ajrouch et al. 2001, McKenzie 2004). These stronger social connections may make them more aware of the different ways in which discrimination is affecting a broader group of African Americans. For example, while Black cisgender males will not give birth, their greater proximity to Black women may make them more aware of Black women's greater risk in childbirth and their generally worse maternal medical care. This information may make them better able to recognize the specific form of discrimination that Black women face in childbirth and increase their likelihood of speaking out about this problem compared to their non-Black counterparts. Multiplying this example by numerous intersectional identities provides Black elected officials greater knowledge about different forms of discrimination and increases the likelihood that they make Black-focused appeals in multiple areas.

Of course, discrimination is not the only area in which African Americans appeal to individuals who share their race. Another way in which Black elected officials may advance co-racial political interests is by highlighting the achievements of their racial group and by recognizing Black political figures. The same factors that would make Black elected officials more likely to call out discrimination in several areas will also make them more likely to speak about a broader array of African Americans than non-Black elected officials. This recognition of African

Americans outside of traditional racial areas, like Civil Rights, may lead to greater diversity in racial outreach.

Black elected officials' higher levels of group identity will make them more cognizant of the successes of those who share their race (Tate 1994, Minta 2011). This greater awareness and interest in improving perceptions of their group should lead Black legislators to be more likely to highlight Black advancement in several areas. For example, Representative Robin Kelly (D-IL) put out a press release congratulating Roz Brewer for being named as part of Amazon's board of directors. "Robin Kelly... released this statement applauding the appointment of Rosalind 'Roz' Brewer - the first African American, person of color and African American woman - to Amazon's Board of Directors."[3] The personal experiences of Representative Kelly as a Black woman may make her more interested in highlighting the successes of those who share her intersectional identity. Representative Kelly ends this press release by noting, "It is my hope that this barrier-breaking appointment serves as an example to other industry leaders regarding the positive economic, business, innovation and inclusion benefits offered by increasing board diversity." In recognizing the achievement of Black businesswomen, Kelly also pushed for the inclusion of diverse voices in boardrooms. This recognition of African American achievement in a traditionally non-racial area (business) broadens the ways in which race is discussed.

Black elected officials' greater connection to co-racial individuals should also lead them to recognize lower-profile public figures in the Black community. For example, Alma Adams (D-NC) wrote about the passing of one of her previous mentor, Black business advocate Andrea Harris. "I am heartbroken by the loss of my dear friend Andrea Harris... but most of all, I'll remember her as a faithful friend and mentor."[4] Adams' personal connection to Andrea Harris likely motivated her to speak out about her friend's death. Given that Harris is not a household name, it is likely that non-Black elected officials would not issue a press release about her or what she meant to the Black business community in North Carolina.

Along the same lines, in one of our interviews, a communication director mentioned a press release congratulating a Black woman on becoming a college president. When asked why, the CD said that her

---

[3] https://robinkelly.house.gov/media-center/press-releases/congresswoman-robin-kelly-applauds-roz-brewers-barrier-breaking

[4] https://adams.house.gov/media-center/press-releases/adams-statement-passing-andrea-harris

representative "had a personal connection to her." The greater number of personal connections to African Americans should allow Black elected officials the opportunity to issue more statements recognizing co-racial individuals in a broader set of areas outside of civil rights and politics.

In contrast to Black elected officials, non-Black elected officials may make more traditional forms of outreach to African Americans. As was demonstrated in Chapter 4, non-Black elected officials tend to focus on higher-profile racial issues, such as voting rights and Black Lives Matter. Non-Black elected officials generally focus on these issues when discussing race because they are better known to the public. As was highlighted in the example of Daughters of the Confederacy, there are many issues that even well-meaning non-Black elected officials may miss around racial discrimination because they are unaware of the racial connection or consequences.

This is likely exacerbated by the fact that non-Black legislators, like African Americans, are more likely to connect with individuals who share their race/ethnicity (Ajrouch et al. 2001). These social networks may make White elected officials even less aware of the different ways that racial discrimination occurs. Given that non-Black elected officials do not have the same experiences with discrimination and have more limited networks, which can make them aware of the many ways in which structural racism limits opportunities of African Americans, non-Black elected officials may concentrate their racial outreach in fewer areas that are more well-known. The overall result should be that Black members of Congress speak about race in a broader set of areas than non-Black elected officials.

MEASURING BREADTH IN RACIAL OUTREACH

To identify the different ways that members of Congress engage in rhetorical representation, we begin by sub-setting all press releases and tweets that were coded as making Black-centered outreach. In doing this, we identified 5,439 Black-centered press releases put out in the 114th, 115th, and 116th U.S. House of Representatives. We also identified 21,894 tweets that included instances of racial rhetorical representation in the 116th Congress. To identify the different ways in which members of Congress engage in Black-centered rhetorical representation, we use a keyword-assisted topic modeling approach (Eshima et al. 2021).

Based on our review of the corpus of press releases and tweets, we identified twenty-three distinct but commonly occurring categories in our press releases and twenty-four commonly occurring categories among our Twitter data. We provided keywords that we found to be frequently occurring and generally distinct in each topic. While we identified numerous common themes, we could not be sure that our topics covered every frequently occurring form of outreach. As a result, we allowed the keyword-assisted topic modeling to find up to five additional categories in both the press releases and the tweets, which were not defined by us. While these mostly included random language indicating that they were not coherent topics, a few new categories appeared in press releases (discussion of the Charleston AME Church shooting) and tweets (discussions of facial recognition software and announcements about meeting with constituents).

Following this process, we placed each document into a single category based on its highest probability topic.[5] Table 6.1 presents the keywords we used to identify each topic, along with the five most commonly occurring words in each topic. In the appendix, we show intercoder reliability to ensure that the algorithm properly coded the press releases and tweets into the correct categories. While we find substantial overlap between the computer and hand coder, the intercoder reliability scores (Cohen's Kappa$_{\text{press releases}}$=.79, Cohen's Kappa$_{\text{Twitter}}$=.73) are within the substantial rather than strong agreement category. As a result, our analysis should be interpreted with some caution. Also, not every press release or tweet fits into a topic, but a vast majority (>95% of racialized press releases and racialized tweets) were placed in one of the topics listed in Table 6.1.

In total, we identified twenty-three topics in our press releases and twenty-four topics for our Twitter data. The topics presented in Table 6.1 address many of the most pressing issues regarding race in the United States between 2015 and 2020. These topics include issues such as policing, COVID-19, voting rights, and discussions about President Trump. They also include the recognition of Black leaders from the past, such as discussions about Martin Luther King Jr., and the mourning of prominent Black legislators who passed away during our period of interest, like Elijah Cummings, John Conyers Jr., and John Lewis. The list also includes Black-centered topics that intersect with non-racial areas. For example, a sizeable number of Black-focused press releases and tweets centered on race and education, race and the economy, and race and gender.

---

[5] We arrive at the same results if we use different cutoff probabilities from the keyword assisted topic modeling. See the appendix.

TABLE 6.1 *Common Topics in Press Releases and Tweets, Author Selected Keywords, and Highest Probability Words in Each Category*

Variable	Keywords
Black Celebrations	history, month, juneteenth, **blackhistorymonth**,
Black Organizations	caucus, cbc, naacp, tri-caucus
BLM/George Floyd	floyd, arbery, police, breonna, policing, protests, **blacklivesmatter, blm, georgefloyd, breonnataylor, ahmaudarbery**
Business	business, employment, bank, financial, jobs, wage, salary
Census	**census, undercount, 2020census, counted**
Charleston	-
Civil Rights Movement	selma, movement, civil, marches, **freedomriders**
Confederacy	slavery, confederate, statue, confederacy
Courts	court, decision, judge, supreme
Democratic Pres.	obama, kamala
Education	college, university, hbcu, stem, school, student, education
Environment	environment, climate, population, sustainable, **environmentaljustice**
Facial Recognition	-
Gender	women, girls, brother, sister, mother, mom
Health	covid, health, aids, diabetes, coronavirus, sickle, aca, obamacare, cdc, medicare, Medicaid
Honorees	medal, honor, award, tribute
Immigration	**immigrant, immigration, refugee, africa, border**
John Lewis	lewis, icon
Legislation	act, legislation, bill
LGBTQIA+	**lgbt, pridemonth, trans, lgbtq, lgbtqia+, pride, lesbian, gay**
Martin Luther King Jr.	martin, luther, king, mlkday
Military	army, navy, military, war, veteran
Nomination	nominee, nomination, appointment
Passing	passing, death, widow, **rip**
Town Hall	-
Trump	trump, Bannon
Voting Rights	voting, shelby, suppression, voter, purging, **vra**
White Supremacy	supremacy, racism, bigotry, violence, hatred, kkk, nazi, charlottesville

Text in bold indicates that the topic and keywords are Twitter-specific. Charleston is the only category that is press release-specific.

WHAT ARE THE MOST COMMON FORMS OF RACIAL RHETORICAL REPRESENTATION IN THE 114TH, 115TH, AND 116TH CONGRESSES?

Before we examine differences across legislators, we begin by exploring the most common topics that members of Congress discuss when they engage in racial rhetorical representation during our period of interest. Table 6.2 provides the percent of times each topic is discussed among all members of the 114th, 115th, and 116th U.S. Congresses by the four largest racial/ethnic groups in the United States. In this case, we only include press releases in which elected officials engage in racial rhetorical outreach. As a result, this table provides information to the question: which topics do elected officials speak about *when* they engage in rhetorical representation? As a result, the denominator is not of all press releases the member put out during our period of interest, but instead only includes those that already discuss what we deemed as a Black-centered appeal. If we simply look at the percent of times racial rhetorical representation occurs in all press releases and tweets issued over our period of interest, African Americans put out a higher percentage of communications around each topic than all other racial groups by a large margin.[6]

In addition to engaging in racial outreach at different rates, members of Congress from different racial groups also vary in the number of topics they discuss when engaging in Black-centered rhetorical representation. We begin by focusing on our press release data. Fifteen percent of White Democrats' and 12.5 percent of White Republicans' racial rhetorical outreach occurred around police reform or Black Lives Matter, tied to the murder of George Floyd. Moreover, a vast majority (over 90%) of this outreach came in response to the murder of George Floyd in the Summer of 2020. This is not terribly surprising given the significant increase in interest in this topic in the public during the summer of 2020, the large-scale protests nationally (Pressman et al. 2022), and the overwhelming support for Black Lives Matter and police reform during this period (Reny and Newman 2021). For White Democrats, this was the

---

[6] For example, the greatest disparity between Black and White legislators in their press releases is with regards to race and education. Blacks put out about 11.7 times more press releases discussing this topic than Democratic elected officials and 12.28 more race and education press releases than White Republicans. The smallest disparity is around police reform which were overwhelmingly press releases tied to the George Floyd Justice Act and the JUSTICE Act. In this case, Black elected officials put out over twice as many press releases tied to this topic than White Democrats and White Republicans.

TABLE 6.2 *Proportion of Black-Centered Press Releases in Each Topic for White, Black, Latino/a, and AAPI Members of Congress*

Topic	Black Mean	White Democrat Mean	White Republican Mean	Latino/a Mean	Asian American Mean
Black Celebrations	**8.46%**	6.66%	4.04%	**14.32%**	5.62%
Black Organizations	6.12%	1.47%	1.62%	5.16%	**9.55%**
BLM/George Floyd	7.06%	**15.01%**	**12.53%**	**17.37%**	**14.61%**
Business	5.10%	1.86%	1.62%	3.52%	1.12%
Charleston	1.59%	1.30%	2.83%	0.94%	1.69%
Civil Rights Movement	1.77%	6.04%	3.03%	1.17%	2.81%
Confederacy	0.49%	0.79%	0.20%	0.47%	0.56%
Courts	2.57%	1.64%	0.00%	2.35%	3.37%
Democratic Pres.	1.81%	0.85%	0.00%	0.70%	0.56%
Education	**8.49%**	3.95%	**14.14%**	5.16%	4.49%
Environment	0.68%	0.40%	0.20%	1.17%	0.00%
Gender	1.17%	1.47%	0.00%	1.17%	0.00%
Health	**8.34%**	4.80%	2.42%	**6.34%**	1.69%
Honorees	4.34%	2.77%	5.25%	2.11%	4.49%
John Lewis	1.51%	2.93%	4.24%	1.17%	1.12%
Legislation	**12.00%**	**10.27%**	**17.17%**	**12.21%**	**16.85%**
Martin Luther King Jr.	2.42%	4.51%	6.26%	3.99%	3.93%
Military	1.51%	1.13%	0.61%	1.41%	0.56%
Nomination	3.62%	3.33%	0.61%	2.82%	2.81%
Passing	**8.15%**	6.38%	6.67%	2.82%	**7.30%**
Trump	2.60%	4.06%	0.61%	3.29%	0.56%
Voting Rights	4.79%	6.38%	2.02%	4.93%	5.62%
White Supremacy	3.40%	6.94%	**12.53%**	5.40%	**8.99%**

Bold indicates the topic is in the Top 5 for the Racial/Ethnic Group. Black N=2,649, White Democrat N=1,772, White Republican N=495, Latino/a N=426, Asian American N=178 most common racial press release that they issued during our period of interest.

White Democrats and White Republicans also discussed race and legislation as a key part of their legislative outreach. White Republicans' highest levels of racial outreach in press releases were tied to legislation. Almost 1 in 5 (17.2%) racialized press releases from Republicans came from discussions of legislation. This comes as a surprise, given that Republicans introduce far fewer Black-oriented pieces of legislation in comparison to their Democratic counterparts. However, the vast majority of discussions around race and legislation were centered on a single piece of legislation, the JUSTICE Act, which was introduced as a Republican's response to the George Floyd murder. In fact, 40 percent of legislation based on racialized press releases introduced by White Republicans was tied to Black Lives Matter and policing.

Several other press releases issued by White Republicans in the race and legislation category explained their opposition to Black-oriented legislation while at least insinuating that they would support unnamed alternatives. For example, in explaining her "No" vote for the Strength in Diversity Act of 2020, Representative Cathy McMorris Rodgers wrote, *"racial isolation or concentration of poverty is something we must address.* However, instead of finding a bipartisan solution, Democrats pursued a top-down, big-government approach that prioritizes teacher's unions over families."[7] Several other White Republican members of Congress wrote about Black-oriented bills they had introduced, including Rep. French Hill speaking about introducing a bill tied to expanding funding for HBCUs[8] and Rep. Jim Sensenbrenner advocating for a renewal of the Voting Rights Act.[9]

White Republicans (12%) and White Democrats (7%) also issued a sizeable portion of their press releases around White supremacy. For both groups, a sizable percentage of these discussions condemning White supremacy were tied to the Unite the Right rally in Charlottesville, VA, in 2017. For Democrats, several press releases related to White Supremacy called out Trump for his infamous "both sides" comments. Republicans largely confined these press releases to be focused on

---

[7] https://mcmorris.house.gov/posts/my-votes-week-of-september-14th
[8] https://hill.house.gov/news/documentsingle.aspx?DocumentID=1205
[9] www.wispolitics.com/2019/u-s-rep-sensenbrenner-urges-need-for-bipartisanship-in-restoring-voting-rights-act/

condemning Neo-Nazi's and other White supremacist groups who marched in Charlottesville.

While there are a few overlapping categories between White elected officials and African American elected officials, the groups differ in meaningful ways. Like White Republicans, African Americans are the most likely to speak about legislation in their racial outreach. However, unlike White Republicans, this discussion about racial legislation is generally not confined to a single piece of legislation. For example, African Americans spoke about the George Floyd Justice in Policing Act in fewer than 10 percent of their press releases tied to race. Instead, African Americans spoke about a wide variety of racially oriented legislation that they introduced. These press releases discuss bills that cover areas like increasing diversity in media,[10] gun violence,[11] and safety in childcare centers.[12] This diversity in how African American members of Congress speak about race and legislation further demonstrates the unique link between descriptive representation and *how* elected officials engage in Black-oriented rhetorical representation.

About one-tenth of African American elected officials' press releases are focused on Black public figures who have passed away or Black holidays, like Black History Month or Juneteenth. Whether these press releases are centered on former members of Congress like Elijah Cumming or Louis Stokes, Black celebrities like Muhammed Ali or Gwen Ifill, Civil Rights leaders like Julian Bond or Anne Moody, and Local African American leaders, like Bay Area Black Radio Host Ray Taliaferro or Ohio Bishop George Murry, African Americans dedicated much their outreach to recognizing individuals either in their passing or as part of their discussions around Black History Month.

Black elected officials also spent a significant amount of their outreach focusing on improving opportunities for people of color in education (8.5%) and in health-related issues (8.3%). Many of the former were tied to funding for HBCUs or discussions about improving opportunities for children of color in primary schools and high schools. For the latter, there was a wide diversity of issues that Black elected officials talked about with

---

[10] https://veasey.house.gov/media-center/press-releases/us-house-passes-bipartisan-veasey-led-media-diversity-act
[11] https://go.gale.com/ps/i.do?id=GALE%7CA598269416&sid=sitemap&v=2.1&it=r&p=AONE&sw=w&userGroupName=oregon_oweb&isGeoAuthType=true&aty=geo
[12] https://sewell.house.gov/2017/9/rep-sewell-child-care-center-amendment-adopted

regard to race and health. Some common discussions were centered on healthcare, COVID-19, AIDS, diabetes, and maternal health.

Latino/a elected officials appear to fall in between Black and White members of Congress with regard to their top five Black-centered topics. Latino/as' appeals to the Black community are largely centered around messages tied to Black Lives Matter, legislation, and Black celebrations. In fact, almost one out of every five (17.1%) racial appeal Latino/a elected officials made was tied to Black Lives Matter. Latino/a elected officials also devoted about 12.5 percent of their press releases to discussions around legislation. Like African Americans, these discussions tended to focus on a broader set of topics, many of which highlight shared interests between Latino/as and African Americans. For example, Rep. Ruben Gallego issued a press release highlighting a bill supporting a full-day kindergarten and noted, "Although studies show that enrollment in full-day Kindergarten improves children's short- and long-term academic outcomes, especially for low-income and *minority students*, an estimated 40 percent of Kindergarten-age students don't have access to such programs."[13] In this press release, he mentioned the benefits of a full-day kindergarten for communities of color. Similarly, Rep. Nannette Barragan spoke about the importance of representation for residents of Washington DC and noted that such an action would help enfranchise Black and Latino/a communities. "More than 700,000 Americans who live in the District of Columbia, the majority of whom are Black and Brown, should not be disenfranchised by our federal government."[14] Given Black and Brown communities' overlapping interests in several areas, it is not surprising that Latino/a elected officials highlight the benefits of their legislation for a broader community of color in their outreach.

Given their smaller size in the U.S. House of Representatives over our period of interest, Asian American members of Congress issued fewer press releases appealing to African Americans than to other groups in terms of absolute numbers. Thus, some caution should be taken with this analysis. With that said, Asian American members of Congress largely follow similar patterns as elected officials from other racial/ethnic groups in how they engage in racial rhetorical representation. Press releases tied

---

[13] https://rubengallego.house.gov/media-center/press-releases/rep-gallego-introduces-first-ever-bill-increase-access-full-day
[14] https://barragan.house.gov/2020/06/26/barragan-statement-in-support-of-washington-d-c-admission-act/

to White supremacy and Black Lives Matter were the most common topics that Asian Americans used to appeal to Black people. Similar to Latino/a elected officials, much of Asian Americans' discussions of racial legislation focuses broadly on advancing opportunities for communities of color, encompassing the interests of both co-racial individuals and African Americans.

The third most common form of racial outreach among Asian American legislators was mentions of the Congressional Black Caucus. This is likely driven by the fact that the Congressional Tri-Caucus, which consists of the Congressional Asian Pacific American Caucus (CAPAC), the Congressional Hispanic Caucus (CHC), and the Congressional Black Caucus, worked together to address a number of issues during our period of interest.

The review of the most common topics highlights important differences for legislators from different racial/ethnic groups. As discussed in previous chapters, the most high-profile issues are the most likely to be discussed by non-Black elected officials. Voting rights, White supremacy, Black Lives Matter, and police reform were the most common topics discussed by non-Black elected officials. In most cases, these topics were either the majority of Black outreach or close to the majority of Black outreach from non-Black elected officials. In contrast, Black elected officials seem to speak about less traversed topics. This is, again, consistent with the results in Chapter 4 that Black elected officials focus more on lower-profile topics in their outreach to African Americans.

Twitter Analysis

Table 6.3 presents the twenty-four most common racial topics discussed in tweets in the 116th Congress. For each racial/ethnic group, we take the average number of tweets with the highest probability of being in a particular topic and divide that by the total number of tweets that were coded as appealing to African Americans. Again, Table 6.3 shows that there is considerable overlap among elected officials in the most popular racial topics on Twitter.

Black Lives Matter, health (which is mostly tied to COVID-19), and discussions of John Lewis (which are mostly tied to his passing) were in the top five topics of racial rhetorical outreach discussed on Twitter for Black, White, Democratic, Latino/a, and Asian American elected officials. Discussions tied to Black Lives Matter were the most common form of racial outreach for White Democrats (23.43%), White Republicans

TABLE 6.3 *Proportion of Black-Centered Tweets in Each Topic for White, Black, Latino/a, and AAPI Members of Congress*

Topic	Black Mean	White Democrat Mean	White Republican Mean	Latino/a Mean	Asian American Mean
Announcements of Public Meetings	2.11%	1.62%	1.59%	2.16%	3.11%
Black Holidays/Black History Month	6.89%	6.89%	5.81%	5.32%	4.78%
Black Lives Matter	17.17%	**23.43%**	**25.66%**	**18.80%**	**25.34%**
Census	1.13%	0.53%	0.14%	1.51%	0.64%
Civil Rights Movement	4.80%	3.94%	2.16%	2.57%	2.87%
Courts	0.69%	0.50%	0.24%	0.65%	0.32%
Economy/Business	3.13%	1.64%	2.26%	2.13%	4.38%
Education	2.03%	1.30%	2.45%	1.27%	1.20%
Environment	1.05%	1.23%	0.00%	3.40%	1.20%
Facial Recognition	0.20%	0.23%	0.67%	0.31%	1.04%
Gender	3.54%	2.93%	0.43%	3.40%	3.03%
Health	**18.10%**	**10.03%**	2.50%	**14.51%**	**11.63%**
Honorees	1.16%	0.54%	2.11%	0.72%	0.32%
Immigration	0.38%	0.73%	0.38%	4.63%	0.64%
John Lewis	**7.84%**	**8.91%**	**15.38%**	**6.11%**	**7.49%**
Legislation	3.55%	4.91%	6.87%	3.91%	3.90%
LGBTQIA+	0.72%	0.98%	0.00%	1.06%	1.20%
Martin Luther King Jr.	3.45%	4.45%	**13.60%**	4.19%	2.31%
Military	0.92%	1.59%	0.19%	0.89%	1.91%
Organizations	2.38%	1.07%	1.25%	0.72%	0.56%
Passings/Deaths	0.39%	0.28%	0.53%	0.48%	0.40%
Trump	5.64%	**7.30%**	6.87%	**7.82%**	**8.84%**
Voting Rights	5.70%	6.69%	0.58%	5.15%	4.70%
White Supremacy	4.54%	6.81%	5.77%	**6.72%**	6.93%

Bold indicates the topic is in the Top 5 for the Racial/Ethnic Group. Black N=6,646, White Democrat N=8,638, White Republican N=2,081, Latino/a N=2,915, Asian American N=1,255

(25.66%), Latino/a elected officials (18.8%), and Asian Americans (25.34%). White Democratic, Latino/a, and Asian American elected officials mostly focused on discussions of fighting against systematic racism and changes to policing. For example, Representative Ann Kirkpatrick (D-AZ) used the hashtag Black Lives Matter to argue for changes to policing. "Facing calls for reform and accountability, the police are demonstrating why we need change. We've waited too long. #BlackLivesMatter." Republicans used the platform to argue for their version of the police reform bill, the JUSTICE Act, or combined sympathies for George Floyd and condemnations of the protestors. Representative Lee Zeldin (R-NY) fits this mold when he wrote, "There is so much going so wrong in Minneapolis right now. George Floyd is dead. Private property is being set on fire and looted." While some White Republicans responded similarly to other groups, they were unique in matching their support for George Floyd and some types of police reform with negative discussions of protestors.

African Americans also spoke a lot about Black Lives Matter issues on Twitter (17.17%). However, topics around Black healthcare were the top mode of racial outreach from Black elected officials (18.10%). This was the second most common racial topic discussed by White Democrats (10.03%), Latino/a elected officials (14.51%), and Asian American elected officials (11.63%). Many of these tweets were tied to COVID-19. For example, Representative Barbara Lee (D-CA) was coded as making a tweet in this category when she wrote, "We can't let COVID increase the fault lines in our society. We need to #ReleaseTheData on racial disparities so that Congress can get help to communities of color…" Similarly, Representative Tony Cárdenas' (D-CA) tweet, which stated that "Black and Latino Californians ages 18 to 64 are dying more frequently of COVID-19 than their White and Asian counterparts relative to their share of the population," also fits into this category. However, COVID-19 was not the only health-related issue that drove members of Congress to tweet about Black political interests. Topics in this category covered abortion, AIDS, diabetes, health care access, and maternal health.

While there were many similarities on Twitter, there were some differences. African American elected officials were unique in having Voting Rights as one of their top five topics in their racial outreach. Outside of African American elected officials, mentions of Trump, along with racial topics, were one of the top-five categories for non-Black Members of Congress. Unsurprisingly, these consisted of Democrats speaking about Trump's lack of care or outright racism toward people of color. For example, the following tweet issued by Representative Alan Lowenthal (D-CA) was classified into this category: "The president presided over a blatantly racist chant at his rally last night. He's stoking division and hate."

Republicans used tweets in this category to praise Trump's record with regard to the economy. For example, Representative Paul Gosar (R-AZ) reacted to Trump's 2020 State of the Union speech by highlighting Trump's economy and chastising Democrats for not being more supportive of his accomplishments directed at communities of color. "Disappointing to see so many Democrats at the #SOTU refusing to clap for millions of Americans being lifted from poverty and record low unemployment for women, African Americans, Hispanics, and disabled Americans." Along the same lines, Texas Representative Brian Babin posted a similar claim on Twitter: "If Dems cared about facts, they'd report on all of @realDonaldTrump's work to lift up Black Americans w/ policies that deliver historically-low Black unemployment."

DO BLACK ELECTED OFFICIALS SPEAK OUT IN MORE RACIAL CATEGORIES THAN NON-BLACK ELECTED OFFICIALS?

To assess whether there are differences in the average number of racial categories discussed in press releases and tweets among Black and non-Black elected officials, we gave scores of one to any of the twenty-three/twenty-four categories in which the elected official in question put out at least a single press release or tweet. For example, if a member of Congress put out one press release in the race and gender category, three press releases in the race and business category, and two press releases in the Martin Luther King Jr. category, and no press releases in any other category, they were given a score of 3 on our dependent variable. If a representative did not put out a racial press release during a particular Congress, they would be given a score of 0 on our dependent variable. For the press release data, we calculated the scores separately by Congress. As a result, members of Congress can have different scores in each congressional session (i.e., the 114th, 115th, or 116th Congress). We disaggregate our analysis by the race/ethnicity and party of the elected official.

Figure 6.1 presents the average number of Black outreach categories that Black, White Democratic, White Republican, Latino/a, and Asian American elected officials put out at least a single press release or tweet. The maximum number of categories among press releases is twenty-three,

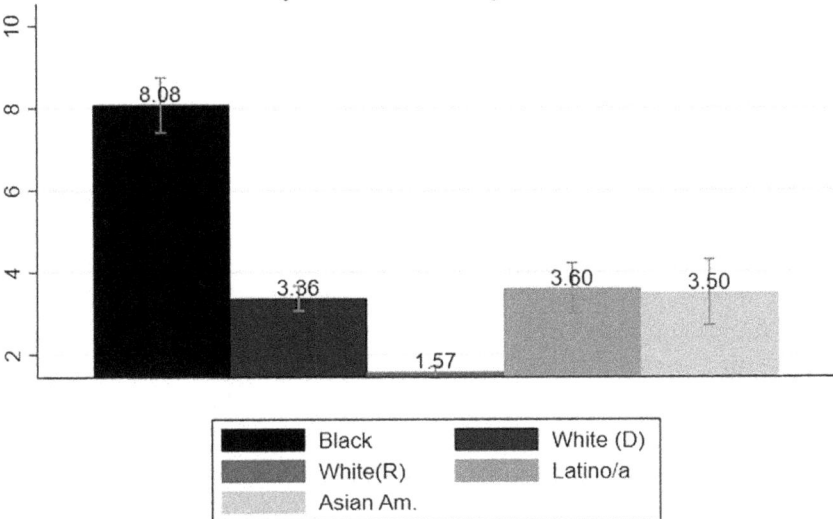

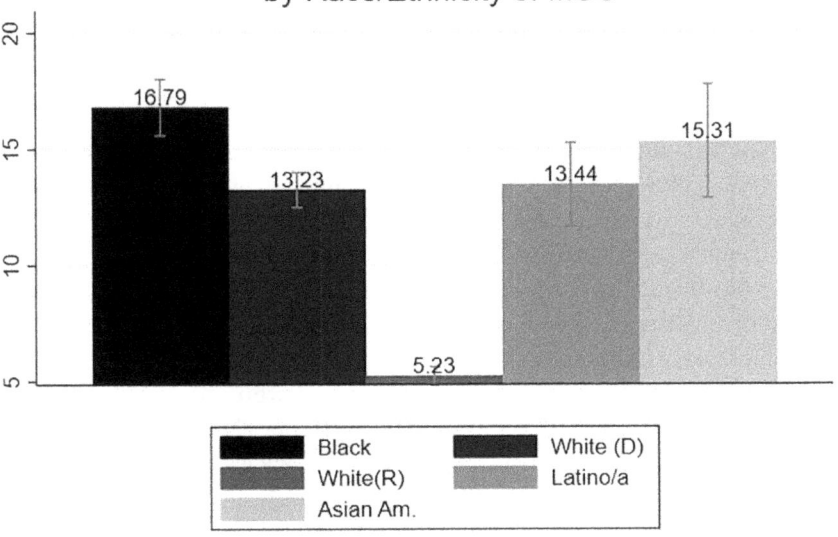

FIGURE 6.1 Average Number of Racial Topics Discussed in Press Releases and Tweets by Race/Ethnicity of Member of Congress W/ 95% Confidence Intervals T-tests are used for comparison.

and the maximum score for tweets is twenty-four. Figure 6.1 also includes 95% confidence intervals for each racial/ethnic group. African American elected officials not only engage in rhetorical representation more than other racial/ethnic groups (see Chapter 3), but they also speak out for Black political interests in a greater number of ways. In fact, on average, Black elected officials speak about co-racial political issues at least once in eight different topics in each congressional session. African American elected officials speak about a statistically significantly greater variety of issues than all other racial/ethnic groups.

White Democratic elected officials put out a single press release on about three-and-a-third different racial topics in each congressional session, while White Republicans only speak about Black-centered issues in one-and-a-half distinct racial topics on average in each Congress. The latter represents the fewest number of categories covered by the racial/ethnic groups in our analysis, and about 6.5 percent fewer topics than Black elected officials. Latino/a and Asian American elected officials issue racialized press releases in about three-and-a-half of the twenty-three categories in our analysis in each congressional session. While Black members of Congress speak out on more racial topics on average than other groups, White Democrats, Latino/a elected officials, and Asian American elected officials speak out a similar amount.

We find fewer differences tied to the racial/ethnic identity of the elected official when we examine the number of topics around racial issues covered on Twitter. Nonetheless, African American elected officials speak on average about more topics than any other racial group. On average, Black members of Congress touch on race at least once in almost seventeen of the twenty-four topics we identified in the 116th Congressional session on Twitter. This is over eleven more topics than White Republican elected officials (who speak about 5.23 topics on average), three more than White Democratic members of Congress (who speak about 13.23 topics on average), and three more than Latino/a elected officials (who speak about 13.44 topics on average). In fact, Black elected officials speak about significantly more topics than each of these groups based on a two-sample t-test. The difference between Asian American elected officials and Black elected officials is only about one and a half categories. This difference, however, is not statistically significant based on a two-sample t-test. These smaller differences on Twitter may be attributed to the ease with which elected officials can put out a tweet compared to a press release. The much larger volume of tweets being put out by members of

Congress compared to press releases may make it easier to touch on more topics, even superficially, on Twitter.

SUMMARY

In this chapter, we find more evidence that how elected officials engage in racial rhetorical representation differs by the race/ethnicity of the elected official. In addition to speaking out using more lower-profile and uncrystallized racial issues, as was discussed in the previous chapters, Black elected officials were also more likely to speak about race in a broader set of topics than all other racial/ethnic groups in press releases and, with the exception of Asian American elected officials, on Twitter.

As was discussed in our interviews with communication directors, Black members of Congress have a greater breadth in racial outreach due to their willingness to incorporate racial representation in different domains than non-Black elected officials. While racial biases in police interactions and voting rights continue to be a barrier to equal treatment for African Americans, racial discrimination is widespread in multiple facets of Americans' daily lives. African American legislators appear to be better able to speak to the many different ways that race plays an integral part in opportunities and challenges for African Americans. Black elected officials engaging in racial rhetorical outreach in a broader manner may create more personalized forms of racial outreach, which are likely meaningful to African Americans. Moreover, these broader discussions about race may make it so that African Americans with different intersectional identities have an ally in government who is working to raise awareness of their particular issues. For example, by speaking about Black people being promoted in the military at a lower rate than White officers, Black elected officials may make it so that Black soldiers have someone championing their specific concerns.

It is important to note that the differences in the breadth of racial discussions that we find in this chapter, while substantial, may be conservative estimates of how many more topics African Americans speak about in their rhetorical outreach than their non-Black counterparts. We found some evidence of this when exploring differences in press releases and tweets tied to race and legislation. Much of the discussion around racial legislation from non-Black members of Congress was tied to bills related to a single category, Black Lives Matter. In contrast, African American elected officials spoke about a whole host of racial legislation in their press releases and tweets. However, given that we confine these press releases and tweets to be categorized into a single topic, the results we present in this chapter may minimize the differences in discussions of a broader set of topics between Black and non-Black members of Congress.

We also find stronger evidence of differences in the variety of issues discussed by descriptive representatives in press releases than on Twitter. While Black elected officials still spoke about more topics on this platform, they were not statistically significantly different than Asian American elected officials in this regard. There are numerous reasons for the weaker relationship between the race/ethnicity of the elected official and the number of topics being discussed on Twitter in comparison to press releases. Some may be tied to the period under consideration, which had many high-profile racial incidents that elected officials would feel pressure to respond to, like the murder of George Floyd, the rise of the COVID-19 pandemic, and the deaths of prominent African American legislators, like John Lewis and Elijah Cummings. As a result, elected officials would feel in the environment of 2020 that they had to speak about race in different ways, leading to a ceiling effect where many groups spoke about race in most of the salient categories.

Another explanation may be features tied to the platform. The ease with which elected officials can put out a social media post may make it easier for them to speak about a wide variety of topics in any issue area. Overall, it does appear that Black elected officials engage in higher levels of proactive racial representation even on this platform, but social media may be more welcoming to more diverse forms of racial representation than traditional forms of outreach like press releases.

The breadth of discussion around racial topics is another important aspect of proactive rhetorical representation. Elected officials who use their public platform to ensure that the wide diversity of racial interests is highlighted, to ensure that intersectional identities are well represented in government. This is particularly important for marginalized groups within marginalized communities who are often overlooked by people in positions of power (Strolovich 2008). It also ensures that government officials are aware of the many ways in which our formal and informal structures may limit opportunities differently for people of color. In doing so, proactive rhetorical representation may further reinforce that marginalized groups are not homogenous and solving a single problem is not enough to address the broader set of inequalities tied to identity.

7

Not All Talk Is Cheap

The Link between Different Forms of Rhetorical Representation and Legislative Activity in Congress

Many African Americans feel let down by politicians who do not fulfill their promises to make progress toward racial equality despite rhetorical outreach to Black voters. LaTosha Brown, co-founder of Black Voters Matter, lamented, "Oftentimes when we're engaged in this process, it's a sense of urgency, of what we need when there's an election. But then once there's a result, it seems that our issues are always put to the back burner."[1] In an interview with the Washington Post, Dennisha Hayes, a 45-year-old African American, echoed the sentiment that politicians speak to Black voters when they need their vote, but don't follow through with substantive changes. "I don't think that they do enough...Some of the issues that we've raised as being top issues for us, they end up going further and further down the list of priorities for them as time goes on. And then they remember them at election time, then they come back up the list."[2] The disconnect between what politicians say they care about and what they are perceived to do in elected office can be a source of disappointment among African Americans, which depresses their levels of trust in government (Mangum 2003, Nunnally 2012, Bonilla 2022).

Racial rhetorical representation is premised on the idea that elected officials speak about issues that African Americans care about to ensure that they feel like their voice in Congress is heard. A key component of rhetorical outreach is to build trust with constituents (Eulau and Karp 1977). However, if elected officials who engage in racial rhetorical

---

[1] www.npr.org/2020/11/17/935886757/black-voters-say-they-will-hold-biden-to-his-promise-to-have-their-back
[2] www.washingtonpost.com/politics/interactive/2022/black-vote-elections-2022-democrats/

outreach in their communications do not take substantive actions in government to address racial inequality, then this form of representation may simply be cheap talk. Even worse, racial rhetorical representation, which is not tied to legislative action, can be misleading to the public, creating a situation where elected officials present themselves as fighting for African Americans but do very little to advance the goals of this community in government. This incongruence between talk and action can have negative consequences, which lead people to be less trusting of elected officials and feel disillusioned about the political process (Gillion 2016, Bonilla 2022).

This chapter will explore whether there is a link between racial rhetorical representation and legislative behavior. Previous research in this area has arrived at mixed findings on the relationship between campaign speech, floor speeches, newsletters, and legislative activities (Sulkin 2009, Gillion 2016, Cormack 2018). However, most find that elected officials who engage in public outreach on a particular issue also take legislative action around that topic. This chapter adds to these important studies in several ways. First, we take a more nuanced examination of the link between rhetorical outreach and legislative activity than previous research. Rather than treating all discussions about a topic as being the same, we differentiate whether certain types of rhetorical representation matter more in building trust with constituents than others. In particular, we explore whether proactive (as measured by low-profile racial outreach) and reactive (as measured by high-profile racial appeals) rhetorical representation differ in their correlation to legislative activity. This allows us to better understand whether some forms of rhetorical outreach provide more accurate information to voters about the member of Congress' legislative intent.

Second, we explore a wider range of legislative activities than previous research on this topic. Similar to previous studies in this area, we use rhetorical representation to predict legislative activities around the introduction/co-sponsorship of legislation and voting scores from civil rights organizations like the Leadership Conference on Civil and Human Rights (LCCR). In addition to these standard measures, we also explore whether public racial rhetorical representation correlates with speaking out for Black interests in committee hearings. This examination of congressional hearings, which receive little public attention and provide few electoral benefits (Minta 2011), allows us to better understand whether racial rhetorical outreach provides a more genuine commitment to advance Black political interests in the legislative process. In doing so, we can better assess whether elected officials can use different types of racial outreach to build stronger levels of trust with their constituents.

To examine the link between racial rhetorical outreach and legislative behavior, we combine our press release and Twitter data discussed in previous chapters with primary and co-sponsored legislation introduced during the 114th, 115th, and 116th Congresses, voting scores from the Leadership Conference on Civil and Human Rights (LCCR) over the same period and congressional hearing data from the 114th Congress. Using our rhetorical outreach data and 18,025 primary sponsored bills, 417,925 co-sponsored bills, 108,255 statements from hearings, and 1,300 unique voting scores, we find strong evidence that elected officials who engage in racial rhetorical outreach also engage in racial legislative actions across all substantive measures.

We also find that both high- and low-profile forms of racial rhetorical outreach are consistently significant correlates of legislative activity. However, elected officials who engage in lower-profile (i.e., proactive) forms of racial outreach are generally the most likely to advance Black political interests through the primary and co-sponsorship of legislation. Overall, racial rhetorical representation provides an accurate picture of how legislators behave in elected office. Rhetorical representation, and in particular proactive racial rhetorical representation, may be the most meaningful in building trust with constituents by having members of Congress actually follow through their rhetoric with action.

LINK BETWEEN SPEECH AND LEGISLATIVE ACTIVITIES

Previous research on the link between rhetorical outreach and legislative actions has been mixed. On one hand, Sulkin (2009, 2011) finds that elected officials who engage in television campaign appeals on a specific topic are more likely to follow through by sponsoring and co-sponsoring bills on that issue. For example, she finds that candidates who have commercials about environmental protections are significantly more likely to sponsor and/or co-sponsor bills about addressing climate change once in elected office. Campaign activity as a result can be extremely informative of the legislative priorities of elected officials (See also Cormack 2018).

On the other hand, Gillion (2016) and Haines et al. (2019) show that there is not always a link between rhetorical outreach and legislative activity. This appears to be particularly true for non-campaign speech from elected officials. Gillion (2016) finds that floor speeches are often weak predictors of voting records on issues tied to race. This is particularly true for Republican legislators who would speak about racial issues on the floor, but often vote against legislation that advances racial equality in Congress. Parties sometimes have rival bills, and legislators of opposing parties take to the floor to address the same issues. This incongruence in rhetorical outreach and legislative activity is also driven by Republicans and conservative legislators discussing race to ward off criticisms of racist attitudes. At the same time, these legislators do not actually support racially progressive legislation and so vote against it when given the opportunity.

Haines et al. (2019) and Gillespie (2020) find that in some cases, elected officials engage in stronger efforts to advance political interests substantively than they talk about. In their studies, they show that President Barack Obama did more behind the scenes to advance Black policy interests than he spoke about in his State of the Union speeches. Obama's lack of discussion on these issues, in spite of his work on Black-centered policy, is driven by fears of White voter backlash of public appeals toward African Americans (Orey and Ricks 2007, Gillespie 2010, Piston 2010, Stout 2015). Taken together, these studies demonstrate that there is not always a link between what elected officials say they are going to do on racial issues and what they actually do.

In spite of these mixed findings, we argue that there should be a strong correlation between racial rhetorical outreach and legislative activity. As described in previous chapters, one of the main goals of rhetorical outreach is to create a perceived area of specialization. To fully demonstrate this specialization, elected officials have to do more than just talk about the issues they care most about. They also have to engage in legislative actions around that issue. In fact, in some of our interviews, we found that politicians use rhetorical outreach so that party leaders will allow them to become major players in legislation in this area. By speaking about a particular issue and engaging in the legislative process around that area, elected officials may increase their territorial hold on a specific issue. This, in turn, should help them better reach out to targeted constituencies and increase their media attention when such issues are salient.

Additionally, previous research shows, and our interviews confirm, that elected officials often speak about specific issues because they are personally invested (Burden 2007, Minta 2011). This passion should lead legislators to speak about these issues publicly to ensure that they are on the political agenda and work to advance these goals legislatively in government. For example, a legislator who cares deeply about veterans' affairs is likely to speak more about this topic in their rhetorical outreach to the public (Cormack 2018). They are also likely to put forth bills and work with others on legislation that addresses problems that veterans face (Cormack 2018). These diverse efforts to advance goals around a single topic should lead to a strong correlation between rhetorical representation and legislative activities.

Legislators are very cautious about what they speak about publicly (Mayhew 1974, Grose 2013). They generally do not take a position on an issue they think may be incongruent with the preferences of their constituents (Milita et al. 2014, Piston et al. 2018, Brauninger and Giger 2018, Simas et al. 2021). When taking a position, elected officials generally know that speaking out will generate support from their voters (Milita et al. 2014, Piston et al. 2018, Brauninger and Giger 2018, Simas et al. 2021). Candidates who speak about voting rights or advancing opportunities for Black owned businesses do so because they know these topics are important to segments of their constituency who want to see these messages. Moreover, legislators who are reacting to events which may even be at odds with their policy preferences do so because they feel like silence on the topic could be electorally damaging (Militia et al. 2014, Piston et al. 2018). For example, given the national outrage over the murder of George Floyd and the widescale of demonstrations (Pressman et al. 2022), conservative elected officials who generally are unsupportive of the goals of Black Lives Matter may have felt it was safer to condemn police brutality in this instance than to stay quiet. As a result, racial rhetorical outreach is often a strategic decision that is meant to curry favor with the electorate.

Following the decision to engage in racial rhetorical outreach, there are also incentives to follow through with legislative actions. This is in large part because rhetorical outreach without substantive activity could increase the perception of disingenuity and pandering (Jacob and Shapiro 2000, Bonilla 2022, Zarate 2022). This could weaken connections with constituents that are needed for re-election. Voters generally expect that politicians will follow through on their promises (Kartick and Van Weelden 2019). Politicians who talk about a particular topic and do nothing in government to address it are generally viewed as less trustworthy and having weaker convictions (Simas et al. 2021, Bonilla 2022). This incongruent behavior can lead to lower levels of support for the elected official (Gillion 2016). In fact, Gillion (2016) found that the incongruence between racial rhetoric in floor speeches and voting is particularly damaging to members of Congress' approval ratings. Given these pitfalls, it benefits politicians to follow through on their rhetorical outreach with legislative activity to maintain trust with their constituents. Moreover, such actions prevent ambitious challengers from highlighting incongruencies between speeches and actions to paint incumbents as being "flip-floppers" (McTague 2015, McDonald et al. 2019).

In addition to avoiding attacks from their opponents, elected officials use public outreach as a form of credit claiming (Thomas and Grofman 1993, Dolan and Kropf 2004). It is unlikely that voters are paying attention to each action taken by their member of Congress. To ensure that their constituents are aware of their accomplishments, many legislators broadcast their legislative achievements and priorities through several communication channels. In fact, in our interviews with communications directors, many talked about using press releases, in particular, as a way to highlight what they've done for their constituents. For instance, one communications director talked about how they were very cautious not to issue too many press releases, but they always did when they were involved in sponsoring new legislation. And another said that they try to use press releases as a way to demonstrate to their constituents that "he's getting stuff done" for them. As an example, he noted that he just issued a press release highlighting the congress member's role in bringing grant funding into the district. These forms of communication lower the cost of learning for voters and, if the correct issue is highlighted by the elected official, endear the politician to their constituents. Thus, there may be an association between what elected officials say in their communications and their legislative activity because they are simply highlighting the latter with the former. For these reasons, we suspect that elected officials who engage in more racial rhetorical outreach will also be more active around race during the legislative process.

DIFFERENCES BY TYPE OF LEGISLATIVE ACTIVITY

Many elected officials and their opponents use congressional voting scores as shorthand for how they represent their constituents on a topic (Jackson and Kingdon 1992). Many elected officials will post their voting scores from prominent organizations, like the NRA, ACLU, or Planned Parenthood, on their websites or in communications via newsletters to summarize their strength on a particular issue (Dancey and Sheagley 2013). Similarly, opponents may call out incumbents for lower scores/

grades from prominent organizations to demonstrate a weakness in this area. Given the prominence of these summary scores with regard to elections, it is likely that elected officials who are the most vocal on racial issues should be likely to match that outreach with a strong voting record on that topic.

Moreover, party leaders are strategic about what legislation they bring up for a vote (Davidson et al. 2019). This strategy often leads bills around racial topics, which make it to the floor of the U.S. House to be more moderate and have broader support (Davidson et al. 2019). For example, in the 117th Congress, the U.S. House of Representatives voted on and passed the John R. Lewis Voting Rights Advancement Act of 2021 (H.R. 4), but did not have an opportunity to vote on the Commission to Study and Develop Reparation Proposals for African Americans Act (H.R.40). The latter is a much more controversial piece of legislation.[3] The consequence of this is that, generally, when one's party is in power, they are not forced to take votes on what may be perceived as a controversial issue. As a result, those speaking about racial issues in their press releases may feel safer about supporting bills on the same topic. In contrast, those who do not feel that voting for racially progressive legislation will benefit them will likely already remain silent on racial issues in their rhetorical outreach. The combination of which should lead to a strong correlation between speaking out about an issue in press releases and tweets and voting scores on that same topic.

Speech should also be strongly tied to bill sponsorship and co-sponsorship. In addition to this information being readily available to the public and potential challengers, the effort it takes to put forth a bill on a topic requires more active engagement on that issue. Rather than being asked to support a bill which comes up for a vote, bill introduction and co-sponsorship are more proactive actions. Members of Congress who want to address a particular problem central to their legislative identity and appeal to a subset of voters are likely to bring forth group-specific bills (Tate 2004, Hillygus and Shields 2008, Cormack 2018). We suspect that the same elected officials who are speaking in the public about racial topics will also be the legislators most likely to bring up such legislation. Given the few restrictions to introduce legislation and fears of perceptions of pandering, it is likely that members of Congress who speak

---

[3] https://fivethirtyeight.com/videos/why-house-democrats-probably-wont-pass-their-reparations-bill/

most vigorously about racial issues should have the greatest external incentives to introduce legislation on the topic.

This same logic may also be tied to co-sponsoring legislation. While co-sponsors generally play a much less significant role in the drafting of legislation than primary sponsors, the act of co-sponsorship allows elected officials to signal their policy priorities to their constituents at little cost (Davidson et al. 2019). When elected officials feel comfortable enough to engage in rhetorical racial outreach to appeal to their constituents, they are also as likely to feel comfortable enough to co-sponsor legislation about the topic. The ability to back up rhetorical outreach without much effort should make co-sponsoring racial legislation attractive to elected officials who speak about race in their public outreach. This should strengthen the link between racial rhetorical outreach and racial co-sponsorship.

Bills and voting records are easily searchable and accessible to the public. Moreover, in the minds of most voters, these actions are the most common and concrete parts of the legislative process. One often overlooked area of legislation is congressional hearings (Minta 2011, Ban et al. 2023). Committee hearings play an important role in shaping legislation through expert questioning and bill mark-ups (Davidson et al. 2019). While this information is readily available to the public through congressional transcripts, it is generally a lower-profile part of the legislative process. This should relieve some pressure for elected officials who speak about racial issues to follow through with discussions about race in congressional hearings. Moreover, it may be more difficult for opponents or voters to argue that an elected official engages in cheap talk if they do not fight for race-based changes to legislation in the committee hearings because of the inexact link between these discussions and the resulting legislation. This lack of electoral pressure to be consistent between speech and legislative action may make the link between racial rhetorical outreach and discussions of race in committee hearings murkier. Moreover, where the link exists, it may suggest a strong intrinsic motivation to advance Black political interests.

HIGH- AND LOW-PROFILE OUTREACH AND LEGISLATIVE ACTIVITY

We anticipate that the link between racial rhetorical representation and substantive behavior will be tied to *how* elected officials speak about racial topics in their public outreach. In particular, we suspect that elected officials who engage in more proactive rhetorical representation through the use of lower-profile racial appeals will be the most likely to engage in a diverse array of Black-centered legislative activities. As discussed in previous chapters, lower-profile forms of racial outreach likely signal a stronger commitment to racial progress. When elected officials speak out about lower-profile racial issues, they are less likely to be responding to a salient event that captures the nation's attention. Instead, the discussion of lower-profile racial issues is likely a self-motivated attempt to draw attention to that topic. This deeper interest in racial issues is likely most common among elected officials who are intrinsically motivated to advance racial progress. This inherent motivation to advance Black political interests should manifest itself in both more public racial outreach and more work within government around racial issues. As a result, the link between these forms of substantive representation should be stronger.

In contrast, the link between Black-centered outreach and substantive legislative actions may be weaker among representatives who engage in more reactive racial rhetorical representation. Elected officials who react to racially salient events by making statements around high-profile racial issues may not be as passionate about following through with actions within government. While many may try to back up their talk around racial issues with some action, the lack of inherent interest may lead their activities around racial issues to fall to the back burner as new concerns arise. As a result, elected officials whose primary form of rhetorical representation is reactive may provide weaker racial legislative representation.

Moreover, elected officials who speak out about race in a more reactive manner may not even recognize potential pitfalls around racial inequality, as we demonstrated in Chapter 5. As a result, they may be more silent in some parts of the legislative process around these topics than an elected official who demonstrates their concern through lower-profile racial outreach. This may be particularly true in congressional hearings, where less vigilant elected officials may miss opportunities to advocate for the interests of people of color. In contrast, elected officials who are speaking about lower-profile racial issues may be more cognizant and have more foresight of how discrimination may play out in legislation and be more vocal about these topics during congressional hearings.

Finally, members of Congress who speak about lower-profile forms of racial outreach may be motivated by carving out an area of specialization in the institution of Congress. Elected officials who put out only higher-profile racial appeals may not share this same motivation. The motivation to be perceived as a specialist on Black-oriented issues may manifest in elected officials speaking more about less popular forms of racial topics, as discussed in Chapter 4. In addition to defining oneself to the public as a specialist, elected officials may better demonstrate their specialized knowledge to their colleagues in Congress by discussing racial topics during committee hearings and introducing Black-related legislation. By demonstrating their knowledge to other members of Congress, elected officials may be better able to stake out a position on an issue amongst their colleagues. A strategy centered on cultivating perceptions of expertise to the public and other members of Congress may lead elected officials who use lower-profile forms of racial outreach to also be more active around racial topics in the legislative process.

DATA

We use several dependent variables to explore the correlation between racial rhetorical outreach and a diverse array of racial legislative actions. First, we use congressional voting scores from the LCCR. LCCR is a broad group of over 200 organizations focused on advancing Civil Rights in the United States and has been a major player in all Civil Rights legislation, starting with the 1957 Civil Rights Act.[4] The LCCR voting score is measured on a scale of 0 to 100. Higher scores on this measure indicate a stronger voting record on Civil Rights legislation. To create its measure, the LCCR selects twenty pieces of legislation that are tied to the goals of its organization during a particular Congress. They then give five points for each congruent vote. For example, in the 116th Congress, U.S. House members received five points for voting for statehood for the District of Columbia or supporting The FUTURE Act, which would provide more federal funding for Historically Black Colleges and Universities. While not all pieces of legislation covered by the LCCR are explicitly tied to Black political interests, this measure has been used as a shortcut for understanding racial representation in several studies (Grose 2005, Preuhs and Hero 2011, Gleason and Stout 2014). Moreover, it is collected more frequently than the NAACP's voting scores for the U.S. House of Representatives, which allows us to make comparisons across each of the three congressional sessions (114th, 115th, and 116th) covered in this study.

---

[4] https://civilrights.org/about/

To measure primary sponsorship and co-sponsorship of Black-centered legislation, we acquired the complete universe of bills, resolutions, concurrent resolutions, and joint resolutions from the 114th, 115th, and 116th Congress. This includes 18,025 pieces of legislation. We then use the same coding scheme outlined in the introduction to code for racial outreach in the legislative summaries of each bill. We gave scores of 1 if the legislative summary included Black-centered outreach and scores of 0 if it did not. We hand-coded 5,000 pieces of legislation using this coding scheme. We then used RTextTools to code the remaining 13,025 pieces of legislation. As was true with the press releases, this hand-coded and computer-coding content analysis did not perform well in a single iteration. To improve the intercoder reliability, we coded all pieces of legislation in which the computer-assisted program disagreed to determine whether it was a Black-centered piece of legislation or not (see Chapter 1 for more details on this strategy).

We then combined the hand coding of these additional 901 bill summaries with our original hand-coded 5,000 bill summaries to predict the remaining 12,124 pieces of legislation in a second iteration of computer-assisted content coding. While the additional pieces of hand-coding analyses improved the predictive capabilities of the computer, it still failed to predict symbolic racial legislation. This is in part because the naming of bills was done in a single case, and so the computer did not do well recognizing Black public figures without any context or prior coding. To circumvent this problem and make our scores more accurate, we hand-coded each piece of legislation that aimed to provide an honor, remembrance, or naming of a federal possession after a person. This allowed us to determine whether any of these pieces of legislation were tied to African Americans. Following this analysis, we achieved much better intercoder reliability scores. In fact, a comparison between our hand-coded/computer analysis and the hand-coding of a random set of 500 bill summaries from the complete corpus yielded over 99% agreement between the hand-coding/computer coding and the separate hand-coder and a Cohen's Kappa score of .82.

Following this coding procedure, we then created two dependent variables. The first is the percent of Black-oriented legislation that was primarily sponsored by members of Congress in each session. To create this measure, we divided the number of Black-centered legislation based on our coding by the total number of pieces of legislation introduced in each congressional session for each member of Congress. For example, if a member was the primary sponsor of two Black-centered pieces of legislation in the 116th Congress and they were the primary sponsor of twenty pieces of legislation overall, then they would be given a score of .10 for this dependent variable.

In addition to primary sponsorship, we examine the percent of Black-oriented legislation that is co-sponsored by members of Congress. Given the ease of co-sponsorship, this form of legislative activity is much more common. While the average U.S. House Representative will be the primary sponsor of about 14 bills in the three congressional sessions explored in our analysis, each representative will co-sponsor about 317 bills during the same period. Similar to the primary sponsor measure, we simply take the number of co-sponsored Black-related legislation and divide that by the total number of pieces of legislation the member was responsible for in each Congressional session.

Our final dependent variable is the percent of statements that are tied to a progressive racial agenda in congressional hearings. We rely on congressional committee hearing data collected by Park (2021).[5] Park's (2021) data looks at statements made by House committee members during public House committee hearings from the 105th to the 114th Congress that are available via the Government Publishing Office (GPO). Unfortunately, this data set only overlapped with our period of interest in the 114th Congress. As a result, our analysis of this dependent variable is confined to this congressional session. Furthermore, only hearing transcripts with greater than 20KB are included in the data, since anything less did not contain any statements. Procedural statements are also excluded from the data.[6] The hearing data is confined to single statements made by a member of Congress in each congressional hearing. This included 108,255 statements. We attempted to do a similar combination of hand-coding and computer-assisted coding for this data set as we did with the press release, Twitter, and legislation coding.

Unfortunately, there were too few cases of racial statements in our hand-coding to create guidelines for the computer to predict racial outreach in legislative hearings when we coded 5,000 of these statements. We increased the number to 7,000, but this did not improve the accuracy of the computer coding. To create our measure, we instead used a combination of a dictionary-based approach and hand-coding of each statement, which included a term from our dictionary. This dictionary (see

---

[5] The data is publicly available at: https://dataverse.harvard.edu/dataset.xhtml?persistent Id=doi:10.7910/DVN/GSMBFX

[6] See Park (2021) footnote 9 for the process of identifying procedural statements.

appendix) includes over 500 terms that we derived from our hand coding of press releases, legislation, and other forms of outreach. A more detailed description of the creation of our dictionary can be found in the appendix.

Following the application of the dictionary, we hand-coded all legislative statements with a score of one to ensure they were racially progressive and not using the term in a manner that was not consistent with Black-centered outreach. For example, in a hearing on poaching Massachusetts Representative William Keating (D) noted "Illicit trade in wildlife is a serious global environmental crime with significant negative impacts for endangered species protection, ecosystem stability, and bio-diversity conservation." The mention of diversity here would be coded by our dictionary as being a Black-centered appeal. To correct for this and similar mistakes, additional hand coding was used to ensure that the coded outreach is germane to our topic of interest. Following this combination of dictionary-based and hand-coding content analysis, we took the average number of Black-centered outreach in hearing statements by dividing the total number of statements we coded as being Black-related by the total number of statements the member made in congressional hearings during the 114th Congress.

We derive our independent variables from the press release and Twitter data discussed in previous chapters. For both the press releases and Twitter data, we disaggregate our measure of racial outreach into three parts. First, we measure the percentage of racial outreach in press releases in each congressional session between the 114th and 116th Congress and tweets for members in the 116th Congress. This measure is simply the percentage of racially related press releases or tweets that the member issued in a congressional session. Second, we look at the percentage of lower- and higher-profile racial outreach in each congressional session. Using the same coding scheme discussed in Chapter 4, we take the number of press releases or tweets from a particular member of Congress that included either a lower- or higher-profile form of racial outreach and divide that by the total number of press releases the member put out during that congressional session. This creates two separate measures of racial outreach and serves as our proxy for proactive (% of low-profile racial outreach) and reactive rhetorical representation (% of high-profile racial outreach).

RESULTS

Table 7.1 presents Pearson's R correlation coefficients.

Table 7.1 presents a correlation matrix between different forms of legislative activities, including the percent of primary and co-sponsored

TABLE 7.1 *Correlation Plot between Different Forms of Legislative Activity and Racial Rhetorical Representation as Measured Through Press Releases*

	Primary Sponsorship	Co-Sponsorship	LCCR
% Black Rhetorical Rep	0.437	0.568	0.411
% HP Black Rhetorical Rep	0.47	0.613	0.35
% LP Black Rhetorical Rep	0.576	0.655	0.398

legislation and LCCR scores against different forms of rhetorical representation. The rhetorical representation measures include the percent of all racial rhetorical representation in press releases, the percent of high-profile forms of racial rhetorical representation (% of HP Black Rhetorical Rep) in press releases, and the percent of low-profile forms of racial rhetorical representation (% of LP Black Rhetorical Rep) in press releases. As a reminder, we calculate these scores separately for each member of Congress and for each congressional session. As a result, it is possible that a single legislator has three distinct scores on each measure over our period of interest. Pearson's R scores range from -1 to +1. A positive score indicates that as racial rhetorical representation increases, so does the amount of supportive legislative activity around racial issues. A negative score reveals the opposite. The relationship between two variables is stronger as the Pearson's R coefficient approaches the absolute value of 1.

The results in Table 7.1 provide strong evidence that racial rhetorical outreach is not just cheap talk. Each of the Pearson's R scores presented in the correlation matrix are positive and statistically significant at .00. As a result, we find strong evidence that when elected officials engage in racial rhetorical representation in their press releases, they follow through by being the primary sponsor of racial legislation (Pearson's R=.437), co-sponsoring Black-oriented legislation (Pearson's R=.568) and voting on topics tied to civil rights (Pearson's R=.411). Each of these relationships is not only statistically significant, they are substantial.[7] Elected officials who speak about race are not pandering to the electorate, but instead are focused on ensuring that Black people are well represented in government. In doing so, they are following through on their rhetoric to build trust with constituents.

The correlations presented in Table 7.1 also reveal that there are substantial differences between the type of racial rhetorical representation

---

[7] In estimates in the appendix, we demonstrate that these relationships hold above and beyond other key predictors like the race of the elected official and their partisanship.

TABLE 7.2 *Correlation Plot between Different Forms of Legislative Activity and Racial Rhetorical Representation as Measured Through Tweets*

	Primary Sponsorship	Co-Sponsorship	LCCR
% Black Rhetorical Rep	0.339	0.741	0.597
% HP Black Rhetorical Rep	0.338	0.657	0.571
% LP Black Rhetorical Rep	0.407	0.734	0.562

and legislative activity around race. For all three measures of racial legislative activity presented in Table 7.1, we find that the percent of lower-profile racial outreach is more strongly correlated with the primary sponsorship of racial legislation (Pearson's $R=.576$), co-sponsorship of racial legislation (Pearson's $R=.655$) and voting on topics tied to civil rights (Pearson's $R=.398$) than higher-profile forms of racial outreach. Using a test of equality of two correlation coefficients, we find that the Pearson's R between low-profile racial appeals and primary sponsored legislation ($P=.02$) is significantly stronger than the same relationship with high-profile forms of racial outreach (Pearson's $R=.470$). The relationship between lower-profile racial outreach and the co-sponsorship of racial legislation is also marginally significantly stronger ($P=.075$) than the same relationship between higher-profile outreach and the co-sponsorship of racial legislation (Pearson's $R=.613$). The only area where there is not a statistically stronger correlation with low-profile racial outreach in comparison to high-profile racial outreach is with regard to LCCR scores. Given that the legislation that makes it to the floor of the U.S. House of Representatives is not determined solely by the legislator, it makes sense that a weaker relationship may exist in this area.

Table 7.2 presents Pearson's R scores for the relationship between the percent of Black-oriented primary and co-sponsored legislation introduced in a session, LCCR scores, and different forms of racial rhetorical outreach on Twitter. Similar to Table 7.1, each Pearson's R value in the matrix is statistically significant at .00. The results in Table 7.2 demonstrate that elected officials who engage in racial rhetorical representation on Twitter are also more likely to be the primary sponsor of race-related legislation (Pearson's $R=.399$), co-sponsor more Black-related legislation (Pearson's $R=.741$) and have higher LCCR scores (Pearson's $R=.613$).[8] Even on social media, which is a non-traditional form of communication

---

[8] Given that press releases and tweets are measured using different periods of time, caution should be taken when making any comparisons across correlations.

TABLE 7.3 *Correlation Plot between Racial Statements in Congressional Hearings and Racial Rhetorical Representation as Measured Through Press Releases*

	Black Appeal Hearing
% Black Rhetorical Rep	0.505
% HP Black Rhetorical Rep	0.387
% LP Black Rhetorical Rep	0.468

and is largely aimed at co-partisans, voters can be assured that elected officials who engage in racially rhetorical representation are also engaging in other legislative activities in Congress on that particular issue.

Again, there appear to be differences between the type of racial rhetorical outreach and the legislative activity of the member of Congress. The Pearson's R scores for low-profile forms of racial outreach and the primary sponsorship (Pearson's R=.407) and co-sponsorship (Pearson's R=.734) of legislation are greater than the Pearson's R scores for these activities and high-profile forms of racial rhetorical representation (.338 and .657, respectively). However, only the correlation between low-profile racial outreach and the co-sponsorship of legislation is significantly greater (P=.03) than the same relationship with high-profile forms of racial outreach based on a test of equality of two correlation coefficients. The Pearson's R between high- and low-profile forms of racial outreach and LCCR scores in the 116th Congress are both equally high (.571 and .562, respectively) and not statistically significantly different from each other.

Table 7.3 presents the Pearson's R correlation statistics between the percent of supportive racial statements in congressional hearings and different types of racial rhetorical representation in press releases for the 114th Congress. As is true with other forms of legislative activity, Table 7.3 shows that elected officials who speak about Black-centered issues in their press releases are also statistically significantly *(P<.00)* more likely to speak about race in a supportive manner in congressional hearings (Pearson's R=.505). The relationship between racial rhetorical representation in committee hearings is again stronger for lower-profile racial appeals (Pearson's R=.468) than higher-profile forms of racial outreach (Pearson's R=.387). However, these differences were not statistically significantly different based on a test of equality of two correlation coefficients.

SUMMARY

Over the past fifty years, there has been a decline in political trust in the United States (Nunnally 2011). This distrust is in part driven by large promises from politicians with little to show for it legislatively (Bonilla 2022). This possibility creates a strong concern about racial rhetorical representation's ability to build connections with constituents. In previous chapters, we made the argument that speaking out for Black interests likely has positive implications for racial representation. However, if such outreach is all talk and no action, it is possible that this form of representation could be misleading. Even worse, it could lead to more negative perceptions of politicians as pandering to Black voters without much substantive action.

In our analysis, we find that throughout the legislative process, this problem is largely absent. Members of Congress who speak about racial topics in press releases and tweets tend to be more likely to vote in support of racially progressive legislation, introduce and co-sponsor Black-related bills, and speak out in support of Black interests during congressional hearings. In this way, Black rhetorical representation is informative to a public who is unlikely to do a deep dive into the legislative activities of their representatives but may pay attention to the news every once in a while. Through this exposure to legislators' racial rhetoric, the public may gain an accurate picture of their elected officials' legislative priorities.

We find that this is especially true when it comes to lower-profile forms of racial outreach. When elected officials speak about lower-profile racial issues in their press releases, they are much more likely to be the primary sponsor of racial legislation and co-sponsor similar forms of legislation than when they engage in high-profile forms of racial rhetorical representation. This signifies that not all forms of racial rhetorical outreach are similar. While high-profile racial outreach is generally predictive of legislative activity, it is not as strong as racial outreach that is focused on less popular topics. Thus, individuals who are attempting to learn more about their elected officials' legislative priorities may gain more accurate information by focusing on more proactive forms of racial outreach.

There are a few important caveats to our findings. First, we do not make any causal claim that racial rhetorical representation *leads* to changes in legislative activity. Instead, we are interested in showing that the two are correlated. While it is possible that speaking about an issue is the first step that leads elected officials to engage in more racial representation in the legislative process, our interest in this chapter is simply exploring whether the two forms of representation are tied together. By showing this, we demonstrate that rhetorical representation is not divorced from policy representation.

Second, each member of the U.S. House of Representatives is one out of 435 voting members in their chamber and one out of 535 voting members in Congress as a whole. Additionally, even legislation passed through Congress faces challenges at the White House and through the Courts. As a result, even a legislator who is passionate about racial politics and introduces legislation around the topic may never see that legislation turn into a law. The outcome of which could lead citizens to care less about effort and more about results. While the former can be determined by the legislator, the latter is largely out of the hands of any individual member of Congress. So, while racial rhetorical representation can be informative about the legislator's activity, it may mean very little with regard to legislation becoming law. We explore the interactive effects of these structural barriers, expectations, and rhetorical representation on approval in the following chapters.

8

Can Racial Rhetorical Representation Improve Approval Ratings?

Communications directors are clear that, in addition to providing high-quality representation, they hope that rhetorical outreach is a powerful tool that members of Congress can use to connect with their constituents. One communications director from a Black Congressman's office said that when making communications decisions, her first priority is speaking directly to their constituents. She said her goal is to "show them what you're doing [in DC], [have them] understand the resources you received were because of the bills we passed, and make sure they know how to access resources." Another communications director from a Latino Democrat's office emphasized how they use communications as a means to show their commitment and responsiveness to their constituents. He said, "he knows his district. He was born and raised there. He's held elected office [at various levels] for over 20 years. If his constituents want something, he'll stick his head in it." Still another communications director said that her boss, a Latina Democrat, wanted to show women in her district that she "has their backs" and that this was particularly important to her after the Dobbs decision. For communications directors, regularly reaching out to their constituents was a central focus of their messaging efforts.

Building a connection with their constituents is essential in improving approval ratings and getting re-elected. While the first part of this book has explored how elected officials engage in racial rhetorical outreach, this and the next chapter will examine whether this at all matters to voters. Rhetorical representation is a well-intentioned form of outreach meant to connect the legislator to a specific population. However, it is possible that voters heavily discount what elected officials speak about and instead focus mostly on the legislation that they pass.

Moreover, in previous chapters, we have demonstrated that Black and non-Black elected officials tend to engage in rhetorical representation in different ways. One such difference was around the salience of an issue. Black elected officials were more likely to speak about issues that got less attention from the public than non-Black elected officials. This, we argued, demonstrated their willingness to provide proactive rhetorical representation by raising new issues that were not well known. Non-Black elected officials were more likely to focus on highly salient racial topics and provide Black constituents with reactive rhetorical representation. In addition to understanding whether rhetorical representation matters to voters, it is also important to understand whether either of these distinct forms of racial rhetorical outreach is more meaningful to constituents.

To answer these important questions around Black rhetorical representation, we begin this chapter by exploring why racially targeted discussions may matter to voters by reviewing research on racial campaign appeals. Through this review, we argue that African Americans should respond positively to Black rhetorical outreach, and this should manifest itself through expressions of approval for the elected official. This may be particularly true for lower-profile forms of outreach because they may demonstrate a perceived stronger commitment to Black voters. We also suspect that these forms of appeals will be less meaningful to the non-targeted group.

We take a multi-method approach to assess whether Black rhetorical representation matters and why. First, we use an experiment that was administered to a sizable sample of Black (N=600) and White (N=600) respondents. This experiment used a hypothetical politician and varied the race of the elected official (Black vs. White) and whether they focused on a non-racial liberal topic (climate change), a high-profile racial topic (police reform), or a low-profile racial topic (pay discrimination in manufacturing). We then assess whether Black and White voters respond differently to the race of the messenger, the forms of rhetorical outreach, and the interaction of the two factors. We find that for White elected officials, both forms of racial outreach matter, but the lower-profile form of racial outreach was more impactful in improving Blacks' perception of this hypothetical member of Congress. Black elected officials experienced an increase in support for both forms of racial rhetorical outreach from co-racial respondents, but not from White respondents.

We use qualitative measures by asking respondents to explain their reactions to the elected official to uncover *why* Black and White people respond differently to racial rhetorical representation. Differences in perceptions of ideological congruence and commitment explain much of why some forms of public outreach matter more to constituents than others. For example, Black people are more receptive to lower-profile forms of racial rhetorical representation from White elected officials because it is perceived to be a stronger commitment to African Americans than higher-profile racial rhetorical representation, which is more likely to be viewed as pandering. Overall, the results in this chapter demonstrate that racial rhetorical outreach is generally an effective way for elected officials to improve their standing with targeted populations. We also show that the messenger and the type of racial rhetorical outreach moderate this relationship.

ELECTED OFFICIAL APPROVAL RATINGS

Approval ratings are a powerful tool that elected officials can use to increase their likelihood of winning another term. Elected officials with higher levels of approval are more likely to ward off quality challengers (Highton 2008, Abramowitz 2006), have an easier time raising money (Henson et al. 2019, Currinder 2008), and ultimately have higher re-election rates (Jacobson 2021). Given the significance of approval ratings, members of Congress work hard to gain the support of their constituents throughout their term.

Members of Congress make numerous strategic decisions to draw in the support of those whom they represent (Mayhew 1974). First and foremost, members of Congress work to mirror the ideological and policy preferences of their constituents (Jones 2011, Pitkin 1967). A host of research demonstrates that voters are more approving of legislators who are ideologically similar to themselves (Ansolabehere and Jones 2010, Griffin and Flavin 2011, Łapiński et al. 2016, Langehennig et al. 2019). To demonstrate ideological congruence, elected officials will support public policies that matter to the electorate. For example, pro-life voters are going to be more supportive of an elected official who works hard to limit reproductive rights around abortion. Similarly, a constituent who is concerned about climate change is going to be more approving of an elected official who puts forth and advocates for legislation that invests in green energy. Knowing the policy preferences of constituents helps legislators stake out claims to different political positions.

One way that elected officials draw support from Black constituents is by demonstrating that they are concerned about similar topics around race. When studying campaigns, for example, numerous scholars show that Black voters are more supportive of candidates who speak about racial issues. Austin and Middleton (2004), Stout (2015, 2020), Wamble (2018), and Collingwood (2020), all show that Black people vote for candidates who engage in racial outreach at higher rates. These authors argue that racial outreach leads African American voters to feel that the candidate is ideologically similar to them. While we examine racial messaging in a non-electoral context, we suspect that racial rhetorical representation will lead Black voters to see political commonalities between themselves and their member of Congress. This should lead to higher levels of approval.

Beyond ideological and policy congruence, constituents tend to be more supportive of elected officials who make them feel heard (Costa 2020). For example, Serra and Moon (1994) show that when voters make requests to legislators that are fulfilled, they are more supportive of that legislator. Similarly, Costa (2020) found that how legislators respond to requests is important for approval ratings. Legislators who provided an automated or canned response were less likely to receive approval than elected officials who engaged in more tailored outreach.

While rhetorical representation, as we study it, is not direct legislator-to-constituent communication, we can gain some information from these studies to better understand how constituents may react to racial public outreach. When elected officials engage in Black-centered rhetorical representation, African Americans may feel heard by their elected officials. By speaking about issues which are often overlooked in American politics, Black constituents may feel that their elected official hears their concerns and is willing to amplify them to advance their political interests (Williams 2000). This public outreach may then lead to higher levels of approval among African American voters.

Along the same lines, a significant amount of research shows that voters are more approving of elected officials who they believe are empathetic to their group (DeSante and Smith 2020, McDonald 2021). With regards to African Americans, Stout (2015), Wamble (2018), and Garcia and Stout (2022) all show that when Black voters perceive candidates as being more likely to care about people like them, they are more supportive of that politician. These studies show that messaging is essential in cultivating perceptions of empathy among African Americans (Stout 2015, Wamble 2018, Garcia and Stout 2022). When candidates, regardless of their race, speak about issues that are tied to Black political interests, they are perceived as being more caring to African Americans. This perception of empathy is a strong predictor of support among African American voters (Stout 2018).

We anticipate that the rhetorical representation will be equally effective in generating perceptions of empathy from the targeted group. When elected officials speak about topics that are near and dear to African Americans in their public outreach, these voters may feel that the elected official is working for them. This may inspire perceptions that the elected official cares about their wellbeing and the wellbeing of their group. In turn, rhetorical representation may lead to an increase in approval ratings.

In contrast, these appeals may be less meaningful to non-Black constituents. While a growing number of White voters have displayed concerns about racial equality during the Black Lives Matter era (Stout 2020, Engelhardt 2023), they still tend to lag behind African Americans in their support for these issues. Moreover, there is a sizable number of White people who are unsupportive of policies that affirmatively address discrimination. The combination of factors should make it so that Black-centered rhetorical outreach may have a minimal effect on the support of White people. Studies looking at the campaign behavior of racial appeals on White political attitudes have largely been mixed. While some find that race-based appeals can improve support among White voters in the modern era (Stout 2020, Collingwood 2020), others find that Black-centered campaign outreach raises concerns of racial favoritism and leads to less electoral support among White people (Piston 2010, Gillespie 2010, Stephens-Dougan 2020, Reny et al. 2020, Hutchings et al. 2021). Overall, we anticipate that White people will not be as responsive to racial rhetorical representation as Black people.

THE CONTINGENT EFFECT OF THE RACE OF THE ELECTED OFFICIAL AND FORM OF RHETORICAL REPRESENTATION ON APPROVAL RATING

Elected Official Race

The aspect of rhetorical representation that makes it a unique form of substantive representation is that it alone does not move legislation forward. It is not the introduction of legislation, nor is it voting on legislation. As a result, when assessing rhetorical representation, constituents often have to make inferences about how serious the politician is about the issue that they are speaking about. If an elected official's position on any particular topic is seen as pandering, voters may reject the outreach. The effect of rhetorical representation on approval ratings is likely contingent on perceptions of the elected official's commitment to the issue, honesty, and genuineness.

There are several factors that may influence the faith that the average voter has in politicians' ability to follow their rhetoric with action. First, it is likely that the race of the elected official matters in the efficacy of racial rhetorical outreach. Numerous studies demonstrate that African American elected officials are perceived to be the most passionate about advancing a racial agenda (Tate 2004, Minta 2011, Hayes and Hibbing 2017). The fact that African American elected officials are consistent champions of Black political issues will likely make fewer Black constituents question the motives of co-racial elected officials engaging in racial rhetorical representation. This should make this form of outreach from descriptive representatives more likely to have the intended effect.

Moreover, African Americans' racial identity often leads voters to infer a sense of empathy and commitment to advancing racial justice in the United States (Harris 2012, Stout 2018). For example, even though President Obama did not speak about race publicly much (Haines et al. 2019), many African Americans expected that Obama would work behind the scenes to advance opportunities for African Americans (Harris 2012). This belief that African Americans will advance Black political interests is often driven by perceptions that co-racial individuals care about others who share their identity (Stout 2018). This perception of genuine concern, combined with the historic systematic exclusion of African American legislators, may lead African Americans to perceive racial rhetorical representation as being more genuine when it comes from co-racial elected officials.

The link between racial rhetorical representation and Black approval may be less clear for non-Black elected officials. On one hand, most people expect that elected officials will speak out for those who share their identity (Jones 2016). So, when non-Black elected officials speak out in support of racial equality, they may be seen as particularly unselfish. This may improve levels of approval for these individuals. Garcia and Stout (2022), for example, show that Black-centered campaign outreach from White candidates can erase African Americans' enthusiasm gap for co-racial politicians. They show that when White political candidates engage in racial outreach on a hypothetical website, potential Black voters viewed them as being as caring as co-racial elected officials (Garcia and Stout 2022). Based on this work, it is possible that non-Black elected officials who speak about racial topics in their routine public outreach will be viewed as being more caring for African Americans. This perception of empathy could make this outreach effective in improving White politician's positions among the Black population.

On the other hand, skeptics of White politicians' racial rhetorical representation may perceive any racial outreach as a form of political pandering. Given that White elected officials are rarely on the forefront of racial issues in Congress, many may question the commitment of White elected officials to follow through on their racial outreach with action. In this way, White elected officials who engage in racial rhetorical representation may have to show that it is more than cheap talk with a longer record of activism to demonstrate that their public outreach to Black voters is genuine. In absence of this, many Black constituents may perceive White racial outreach as being driven more by political pressure to speak out rather than a genuine concern to improve the lives of African Americans. This may create a murkier link between racial rhetorical outreach and Black approval for White politicians.

Political Messaging

Beyond the race of the elected official, we anticipate that the message of the appeal should also matter. We anticipate that higher-profile forms of racial rhetorical outreach will be less meaningful than lower-profile forms of outreach to African Americans. The former may be the most likely to be perceived as elected officials being pressured to speak out given high-profile events. For example, an elected official who condemned George Floyd's murder in 2020 during periods of protest and a general consensus that Derek Chauvin was in the wrong may not appear as being particularly committed to racial justice. Instead, given the national attention on the issue, voters may expect that this is the bare minimum a politician could do to show that they are paying attention. This reactive form of racial outreach may then be seen as a less genuine commitment to advancing Black political interests and may be dismissed.

Additionally, the fact that politicians have long spoken out about racial injustices in areas like policing and voting rights and very little has been accomplished may leave many Black constituents skeptical that anything can get done. Returning to our policing example, the fact that Black Lives Matter has made significant inroads into federal politics without much federal legislative action may lead voters to perceive discussions on these issues as cheap talk.

As discussed in previous chapters, lower-profile forms of racial outreach may lead voters to view the members of Congress as being aware of the many places where racial discrimination occurs. Moreover, elected officials' willingness to speak out about lower-profile racial topics may lead African Americans to view them as not just following the trends, but as being proactive in addressing racial inequality. This perceived unsolicited outreach may make the elected official appear as being more genuine in their efforts to advance Black political interests. Proactive racial rhetorical representation may be particularly important in connecting Black voters with White elected officials. White politicians may be perceived as being more committed to racial equality when they speak about lower-profile issues which provide few electoral benefits.

EXPERIMENTAL DATA

To explore how Black rhetorical representation shapes approval ratings of elected officials from different backgrounds, we administered an experiment through the survey vendor Prolific.[1]

Our experiment required respondents to review the website of a hypothetical member of the U.S. House of Representatives who we mentioned to be in their area. We randomly varied the race of the elected official by describing him as being Black or White. By explicitly mentioning the race of the elected official we do not leave it up to the discretion of the respondents to make guesses about the hypothetical elected official's race. Our hypothetical representative's name was Mark Harris and was described using the following vignette...

Representative Mark Harris is a **Black/White** elected official in your area. Representative Harris has served in Congress for 6 years. Below is a statement pulled from his website.

---

[1] Peer et al (2021) explored different survey platforms across four measures including attention, comprehension, honesty, and reliability. They found that only Prolific respondents scored high in each one of these measures, indicating that Prolific provides high quality data. In fact, in our own sample, only 9 percent of respondents failed attention checks. While we do not remove individuals who failed the attention checks, in the supplemental appendix we arrive at the same results if we do. We worked with Prolific to administer our experiment to 600 White and 600 Black respondents for a total sample of 1,200 respondents. We selected 600 respondents for each racial group to ensure that we had at least 100 respondents in each experimental group. The experiment was administered in the Summer of 2023 and took about 6 minutes to complete.

Following this prompt, respondents were asked to review one of three randomly selected websites. The headlines of each website are as follows...

1. Mark Harris Joins Environmental Justice Caucus in Support of Legislation to Combat Climate Change *(Non-Racial-Baseline Category)*
2. Mark Harris Joins Congressional Black Caucus in Support of Legislation to Combat Police Discrimination *(Racial-High-Profile Category)*
3. Mark Harris Joins Congressional Black Caucus in Support of Legislation to Combat Manufacturing Employment Discrimination *(Racial-Low-Profile Category)*

These headlines were followed by a full press release which can be read in Figure 8.1.

We modeled our headlines after those from actual members of Congress' websites. As is common with members of Congress, we highlight the organizations that the member worked with to further signal to the respondent that the representative is advancing environmental or racial policies. For example, David Trone (D-MD), who is a White member of Congress, signaled that he was working with the Congressional Black Caucus on the Justice in Police Act in a press release entitled "Rep. Trone Joins Congressional Black Caucus in Cosponsoring the Justice in Policing Act."[2] While some may be unfamiliar with the legislation, the fact that Representative Trone is coordinating with the Congressional Black Caucus signals that he is working on Black issues. Similarly, Adam Schiff (D-CA), who is a male, highlighted his support for women's causes by mentioning his work with the Democratic Women's Caucus; "Rep. Schiff Joins Democratic Women's Caucus in Demanding Health Insurers Fully Cover Birth Control."[3] We hope that connecting the topic with a caucus focusing on addressing group-specific issues, we provide a stronger signal to respondents that the elected official is making a racial or environmental appeal.

The websites for the hypothetical member of Congress had the same exact design and the same language, other than a few phrases. Thus, the

---

[2] https://trone.house.gov/2020/06/08/rep-trone-joins-congressional-black-caucus-cosponsoring-justice-policing-act/
[3] https://schiff.house.gov/news/press-releases/rep-schiff-joins-democratic-womens-caucus-in-demanding-health-insurers-fully-cover-birth-control

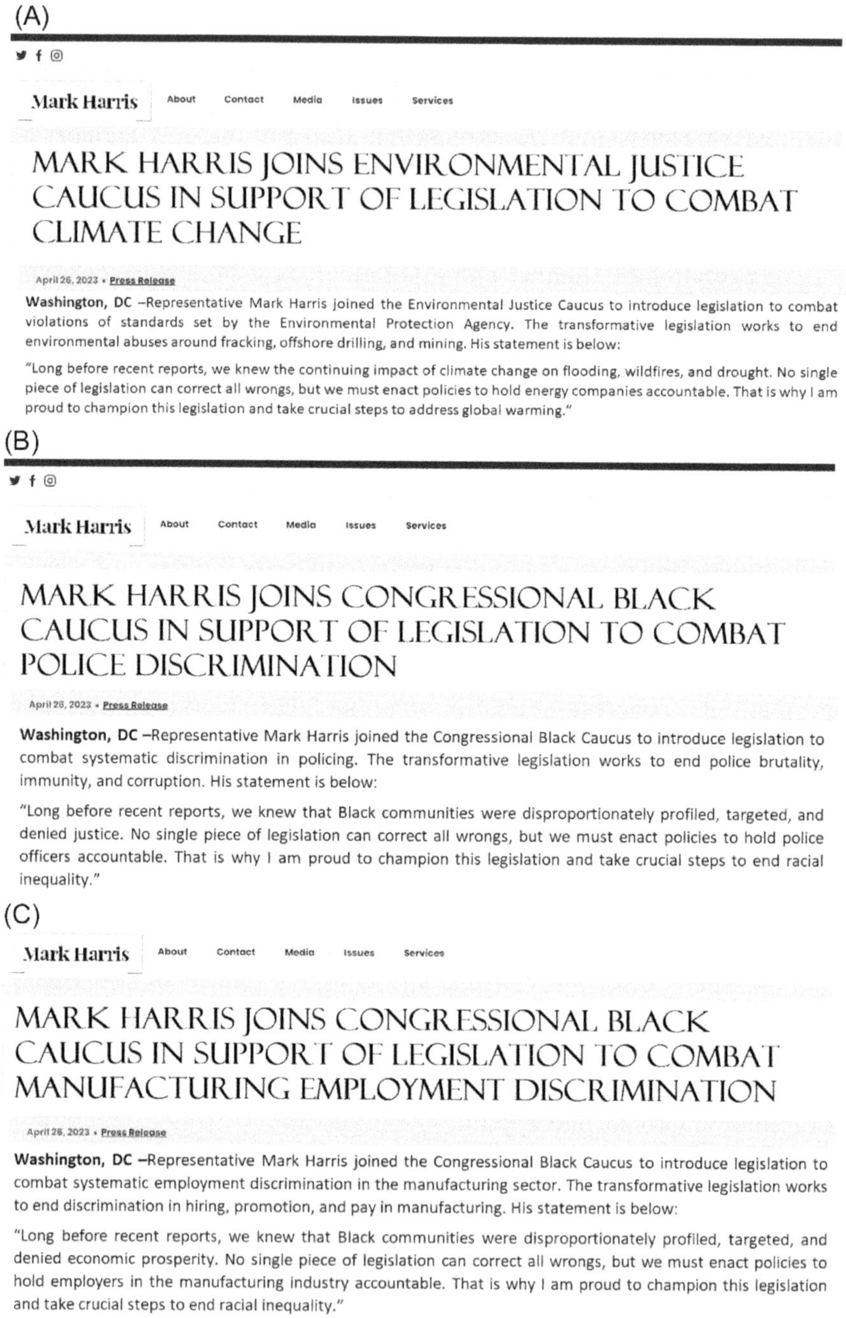

(A)

Mark Harris About Contact Media Issues Services

MARK HARRIS JOINS ENVIRONMENTAL JUSTICE CAUCUS IN SUPPORT OF LEGISLATION TO COMBAT CLIMATE CHANGE

April 26, 2023 • Press Release

Washington, DC –Representative Mark Harris joined the Environmental Justice Caucus to introduce legislation to combat violations of standards set by the Environmental Protection Agency. The transformative legislation works to end environmental abuses around fracking, offshore drilling, and mining. His statement is below:

"Long before recent reports, we knew the continuing impact of climate change on flooding, wildfires, and drought. No single piece of legislation can correct all wrongs, but we must enact policies to hold energy companies accountable. That is why I am proud to champion this legislation and take crucial steps to address global warming."

(B)

Mark Harris About Contact Media Issues Services

MARK HARRIS JOINS CONGRESSIONAL BLACK CAUCUS IN SUPPORT OF LEGISLATION TO COMBAT POLICE DISCRIMINATION

April 26, 2023 • Press Release

Washington, DC –Representative Mark Harris joined the Congressional Black Caucus to introduce legislation to combat systematic discrimination in policing. The transformative legislation works to end police brutality, immunity, and corruption. His statement is below:

"Long before recent reports, we knew that Black communities were disproportionately profiled, targeted, and denied justice. No single piece of legislation can correct all wrongs, but we must enact policies to hold police officers accountable. That is why I am proud to champion this legislation and take crucial steps to end racial inequality."

(C)

Mark Harris About Contact Media Issues Services

MARK HARRIS JOINS CONGRESSIONAL BLACK CAUCUS IN SUPPORT OF LEGISLATION TO COMBAT MANUFACTURING EMPLOYMENT DISCRIMINATION

April 26, 2023 • Press Release

Washington, DC –Representative Mark Harris joined the Congressional Black Caucus to introduce legislation to combat systematic employment discrimination in the manufacturing sector. The transformative legislation works to end discrimination in hiring, promotion, and pay in manufacturing. His statement is below:

"Long before recent reports, we knew that Black communities were disproportionately profiled, targeted, and denied economic prosperity. No single piece of legislation can correct all wrongs, but we must enact policies to hold employers in the manufacturing industry accountable. That is why I am proud to champion this legislation and take crucial steps to end racial inequality."

FIGURE 8.1 Websites of Hypothetical U.S. House Representative by Treatment Type
Non-Racial-Baseline Category
Racial-High-Profile Category
Racial-Low-Profile Category

only change that should influence respondents' assessments of the politician is the issues highlighted on the website and the caucus with which they align themselves. While some experiments use just a description of the elected official as the baseline category, we felt a more realistic comparison would be someone who took a liberal position on a non-racial issue. This position, environmental justice, allows a more similar and direct comparison to an elected official who focuses on equally progressive issues. This allows us to better determine whether a change in support is based on racial rhetorical representation and not simply support for a liberal policy position.

In addition to creating a baseline/comparison category, we also compare two forms of racial rhetorical representation. The first is based on a high-profile and well-known Black-centered issue: police reform. Over the past few years, there have been large numbers of protests, significant media coverage, and numerous politicians speaking about the need for police reform. Moreover, as is shown in previous chapters, more people search for terms related to police reform than for most other racial issues. The fact that this issue is well known to the population makes it an ideal representative for reactive rhetorical representation.

Our second racial issue, employment discrimination in manufacturing, represents a low-profile issue. Given that this topic is not well traversed in the news and receives few searches on Google, we felt that it may be a good comparison to police discrimination. Moreover, we believe that this press release is realistic given that Black elected officials' lower-profile press releases often come in the form of calling out specific industries for racial discrimination. The lack of public clamoring to address this specific issue leads any such press release to represent a proactive rhetorical representation. Given that we vary the race of the elected official (1-Black, 2-White) and the type of press release the respondent receives (1-Non-Racial-Baseline, 2-Racial-High-Profile, 3-Racial-Low-Profile), we have a 2 by 3 experiment.

Following the presentations of these press releases, we then asked respondents to rate the politician using the following question: "How much do you approve of Mark Harris as a member of Congress?" Respondents were given scores which ranged from 1-"Strongly Disapprove" to 3- "Neither Approve nor Disapprove" to 5-"Strongly Approve." As a result, our dependent variable is measured on a five-point scale. This experimental approach is similar to the work of Dietrich and Hayes (2023), who are interested in exploring whether

Black people judge the use of issue-based symbolism differently when it comes from descriptive representatives. While these authors focus on mentions of civil rights symbols in discussions of policy, our focus is on differences tied to higher and lower-profile racial issues.

RESULTS

African American Respondents

Figure 8.2 presents the average levels of approval with 95% confidence intervals for the hypothetical politician Mark Harris by his described race and the press release condition. Figure 8.2 *only* includes responses from African American respondents. Before delving into differences across elected official types, it should be noted that the average level of approval for the hypothetical politician Mark Harris is high regardless of his race or message. More Black respondents approve of Mark Harris regardless of his position than disapprove. The high levels of support for even the non-racial position mean that our study provides a conservative test of the

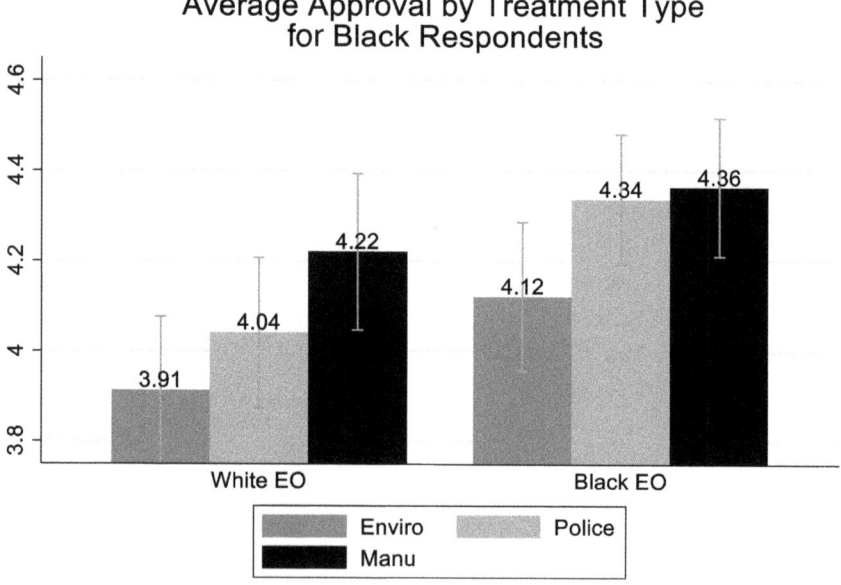

FIGURE 8.2 Average Approval Rates for Hypothetical Politician by Treatment Type for Black Respondents W/ 95% Confidence Intervals
T-tests are used for comparison.

effect of reactive and proactive racial outreach on approval rating, given the high starting position of our baseline categories.

With that said, there are key differences in approval ratings by message type. For White elected officials, not all forms of racial rhetorical representation improve their standing among African Americans. While Black respondents rated the White elected official as being about .13 points more favorable when they spoke about police reform compared to environmental justice, this difference was statistically insignificant. However, Black respondents rated the White elected officials about a third of a point more favorably when they spoke about a low-profile form of racial outreach than the environmental justice message. This difference was statistically significant at .05.

Black elected officials in all but the case of manufacturing are rated significantly more highly than their White counterparts when discussing the same issue. This indicates that Black voters continue to place a premium on descriptive representation, but that lower-profile forms of racial outreach may close this gap. Figure 8.2 also shows that even among descriptive representatives, Black respondents favor those who provide racial rhetorical representation. Black elected officials who engaged in either low- or high-profile racial rhetorical representation received higher levels of average approval than Black elected officials who spoke about a non-racial progressive issue. Black respondents rated the hypothetical Black elected officials as being about a quarter of a point more favorable when they used either a high- or low-profile form of racial rhetorical representation than when they discussed a similarly liberal non-racial issue. This magnitude of the increase in support is impressive given the high levels of approval for the baseline Black elected official, leaving little room for growth. The combination of results for both Black and White elected officials signals that racial rhetorical representation matters to Black people. Those who engage in this form of substantive representation generally receive higher levels of Black support.

White Liberal Respondents

Given that we expect differences based on the political preferences of White Respondents, we disaggregate our sample by White liberal respondents (N=355) and White non-liberal respondents (N=247). The greater variance in White respondents' political preferences and our smaller sample when disaggregating these respondents warrants some caution in interpreting the results of our analysis. Figure 8.3 presents

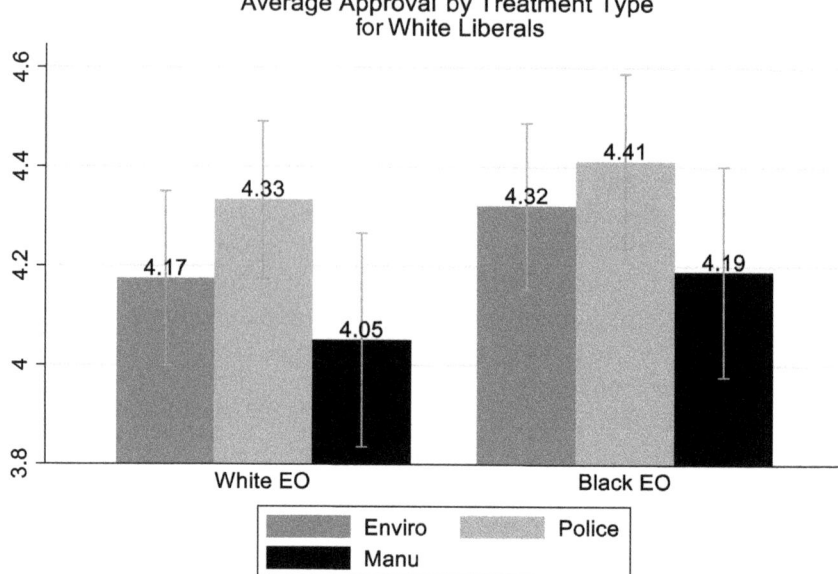

FIGURE 8.3 Average Approval Rates for Hypothetical Politician by Treatment Type for White Liberal Respondents W/ 95% Confidence Intervals
T-tests are used for comparison.

the average level of approval on a five-point scale for White liberal respondents by the race of the elected official and press release treatment. Liberal respondents are those who identified in our sample as being "very liberal" or "liberal." Figure 8.3 also presents 95% confidence intervals. It is worth noting that White liberal respondents provide high levels of approval for the hypothetical politician in all treatment types. However, unlike African Americans, there does not appear to be a strong preference based on the race of the elected official. There are no significant differences between White respondents' ratings of Black or White elected officials when they present the same message.

There are also no significant differences between White liberal respondents' ratings of the non-racially liberal message and the different forms of racial rhetorical representation for the Black elected official. The only statistically significant difference that does exist is among White liberals' ratings of the different types of racial rhetorical representation for White elected officials. White liberals approve of the White elected officials who discussed police reform (i.e., the high-profile of racial rhetorical representation) a quarter of a point more than the White elected officials who discussed inequality in manufacturing (i.e., the low-profile of racial rhetorical representation). This difference was statistically significant at .05 based on a two-sample t-test. In contrast with our findings for Black respondents, White liberals appear to respond more to police reform than to calls to address inequality in manufacturing.

White Non-Liberal Respondents

Given the lack of White moderate and conservative respondents in our data set, we combine these groups for our analysis of approval. Figure 8.4 presents the average level of approval for the hypothetical elected official based on race and issue type. Figure 8.4 also contains 95% confidence intervals. White non-liberals tend to be less approving of the hypothetical politicians than Black respondents and White liberal respondents. Like White liberal respondents, however, there are few statistically significant differences based on message and/or the politician's race.

While White non-liberal respondents slightly approve of the White hypothetical politician more when they speak about police reform

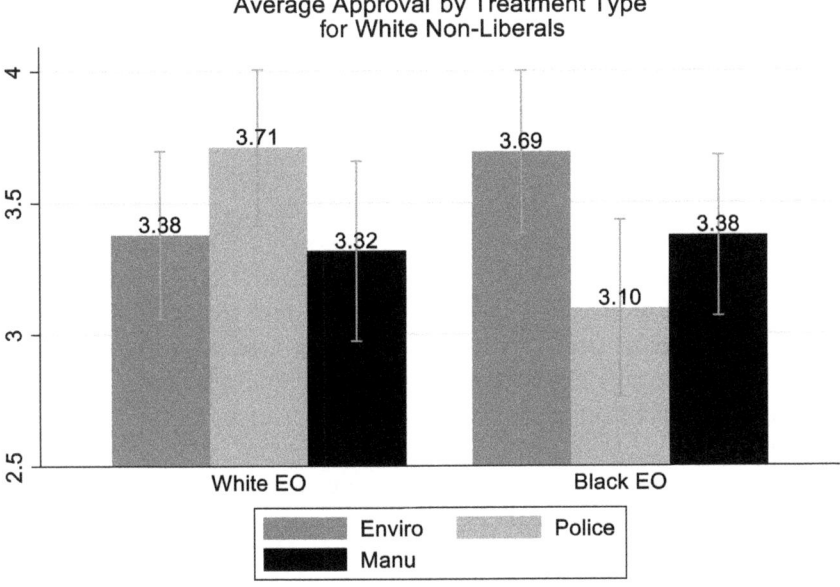

FIGURE 8.4 Average Approval Rates for Hypothetical Politician by Treatment Type for White Moderate/Conservative Respondents W/ 95% Confidence Intervals
T-tests are used for comparison.

compared to the environment, this difference is not statistically significant. In large part because of the small number of non-liberal White respondents in our sample. In fact, White non-liberal respondents rate the hypothetical White politician statistically equal, regardless of their message.

They do, however, rate the Black elected official who does not engage in racial rhetorical representation more positively than the same elected official who speaks about police reform. White non-liberal respondents approved of the Black elected official who speaks about the environment in their press release, over half a point more than the Black elected official who speaks about police reform. While they also approve of the elected officials who speak about the environment more than inequality in manufacturing, this difference is not statistically significant. Overall, the findings suggest that while Black respondents reward White and co-racial elected officials for engaging in racial rhetorical representation, the link between Black-centered outreach and approval ratings for White respondents is less consistent.

QUALITATIVE RESULTS

So why did Black respondents rate Black elected officials more positively than White elected officials who engaged in the same messaging? Why did Black respondents also respond more positively to different forms of racial rhetorical representation than non-racialized messaging? Why were White respondents largely unmoved in their attitudes about co-racial politicians, regardless of their messaging?

To answer these and other questions, we asked respondents on our survey to explain why they approved of or disapproved of the hypothetical member of Congress they reviewed in a few sentences. The vast majority of respondents (>95%) left some pertinent information about how they arrived at their assessments of the hypothetical politician. We content-coded the 1,200 responses into three categories: policy/ideological congruence, skepticism of follow-through, and finally, whether the respondents made negative comments about the politician or the policy presented. *Respondents could mention more than one theme in each statement or none of these themes.*

For policy/ideological congruence, we simply looked for whether the respondent mentioned liking, supporting, or approving of the message put out by the elected official. For example, one Black respondent who received the White-police reform elected official mentioned, "Mark

Harris has the same ideology as I do, which is why I would support him." Another White respondent who received the White environmental justice message wrote, "I approve [of] his efforts to introduce legislation that'll help fight climate change. Climate change is one of the most, if not THE most, pressing issues our world faces." Statements like these, which mentioned the policy or alluded to a favorable view of the policy, were coded as being policy/ideologically congruent.

We coded skepticism as any comment that questioned whether the elected official would follow through on their promise. These could be general statements about politicians overall or comments specific to Mark Harris, our hypothetical politician. A Black respondent's comment expressing concern about Mark Harris when he was described as White and discussed inequality in manufacturing fits our skeptical category. "I don't believe he is sincere in his statements about why he joined the caucus. His words sound like something he memorized from a script." Another Black respondent described their skepticism of Mark Harris' follow-through when he was described as White, and his message was centered on police reform. "I am neutral on Mark because oftentimes [W]hite politicians make promises to [B]lack constituents that they never actually follow through with."

Finally, we coded general negative statements about Mark Harris, if the person disagreed with the policy put forth or expressed negative opinions about the hypothetical politician. A White respondent who described their disapproval of a White elected official who supported climate change was coded as making a negative statement when they wrote, "I do not believe in climate change and I would not support someone who does." Similarly, a White respondent who disapproved of a Black member of Congress who discussed police reform by arguing that the elected official was injecting race into the debate was also coded as making a negative statement. "I feel like he is trying to make race a huge issue, and he is anti-police." Table 8.1 presents the average percent of responses in each of these three categories. Table 8.1 is also disaggregated by the race of the respondent, the race of the elected official, and the issue presented in the press release.

Black Respondents

Policy/ideological congruence was the most common explanation for why Black respondents approved or disapproved of Mark Harris. However, there were some differences based on the type of message presented in the press release. Fifty-three percent of Black respondents in the White

TABLE 8.1 *Average Responses in Four Categories Detailing Approval for Hypothetical Elected Official by Race and Issue Type*

Race of R	Race of MoC	PR Issue	Policy Congruence	Negative Comments	Skepticism
Black	White	Environment	53%	8%	2%
Black	White	Police	54%	6%	12%
Black	White	Manufacturing	72%	2%	7%
Black	Black	Environment	63%	9%	2%
Black	Black	Police	67%	1%	2%
Black	Black	Manufacturing	80%	2%	3%
White	White	Environment	77%	8%	4%
White	White	Police	66%	9%	8%
White	White	Manufacturing	70%	16%	4%
White	Black	Environment	80%	6%	5%
White	Black	Police	66%	16%	5%
White	Black	Manufacturing	75%	15%	1%

politician treatment group and 63 percent of respondents in the Black-treatment group mentioned policy as at least one of the reasons they supported the politician who spoke about the environment in their press releases. Black respondents were slightly more likely to mention policy congruence from the same race elected official (54%-White Politician, 67%-Black politician) who spoke about police reform. This difference in discussions about policy congruence was not significantly more for the police reform message than the environmental message. However, Black respondents did speak more about policy congruence for both the Black (80%) and White elected officials (72%) when they spoke about discrimination in manufacturing. This difference was not statistically different from the police reform message but was statistically significantly greater than the environmental message. This higher level of support, at least qualitatively, may partially explain why Black respondents were more approving of the White elected official when they discussed this issue.

We find similar results when we explore the percent of negative comments about the politician by race and message type. Both White (8%) and Black (9%) politicians who spoke about the environment received the highest number of negative comments. Black respondents also wrote a statistically similar percentage of negative comments about the White politician who supported police reform (6%) as about environmental justice. Black respondents wrote the least negative comments about White elected officials when they spoke about racial inequality in manufacturing (2%), which was statistically significantly lower than the percent of comments for the same race member of Congress who spoke about environmental justice or police reform. For the hypothetical Black elected official, negative comments about those who engaged in racial rhetorical representation was rare (1% for police reform, and 2% for racial inequality in manufacturing). Both of these sets of negative comments were significantly lower for the Black politician who engaged in racial rhetorical representation than for the same politician who spoke about a non-racial issue in their press release.

We also explore the percent of skepticism about the commitment to the issue based on the elected official's race and message. Black respondents appeared to be the most skeptical of White politicians' willingness to follow through on racial issues. While only 2 percent of Black respondents mentioned being concerned about the link between statements and actions for White politicians who spoke about the environment in their comments, 12 percent of Black respondents showed the same concern when the elected official spoke about police reform and 7 percent were concerned about follow through when the elected official spoke about racial inequality in manufacturing. The former was statistically significantly greater than the levels of skepticism in the comments for White elected officials who spoke about environmental justice. This provides some support for the idea that Black people are skeptical of White elected officials who speak about high-profile racial issues.

In contrast to White politicians, Black respondents were generally confident that Black politicians would follow through on their rhetoric with action. Only about 2 percent of comments in each of the messages express skepticism that the elected official would follow through. This greater belief in Black politicians may explain why they were more approving of them. Black constituents believe that descriptive representatives are less likely to engage in cheap talk. This appears to be particularly true for high-profile forms of racial rhetorical representation.

White Respondents

When discussing the quantitative results, we disaggregated by the ideology of the respondent, in this section, we refrain from this disaggregation to better understand how White respondents reacted to non-racial and racial rhetorical representation. White respondents mentioned policy and/or ideological congruence in discussing their support for the hypothetical elected official who spoke about environmental issues in 77 percent of their responses for the White elected official and 80 percent of their responses for the Black elected official. This was a = "a dozen" about dozen percentage points greater than mentions of policy support or ideological congruence in comments from those who received the police reform message from either the Black (66%) or White (66%) politician and seven (in the case of the White politician) to 5 percent greater (in the case of the Black politician) than those who received the manufacturing message. The former is statistically significant.

When disaggregating by the race of the elected official, White respondents wrote the most negative comments about the racial inequality in manufacturing message for both the Black (15%) and White (16%) politicians. Many expressed concern that racism was not actually occurring in this industry. One White respondent noted, "Going by his statement from the article, I feel he may be a little out of touch with hiring practices in various industries. I have worked at a variety of places (with and without manufacturing) for many years, and I have not seen any discrimination in hiring practices."[4] Another noted, "Discrimination is already outlawed so I don't think there are many widespread cases." The percentage of statements with negative comments about this issue was statistically significantly greater than the percent of negative comments in statements about politicians who spoke about the environment (8% for the White politician, 6% for the Black politician). Additionally, the Black politicians who spoke about police reform were described negatively in 16 percent of comments made by White respondents. Again, several felt that pleas for racial justice in policing were uncalled for. This negativity toward Black elected officials who engage in racial representation in some ways explains lower levels of approval for these politicians.

Beyond the approval of the issues and/or negative views of politicians who engage in different types of messaging, White respondents appear to be equally as likely to discuss Black and White politicians as being committed to the issues they speak about and also display low levels of skepticism that they will follow through regardless of their message.

SUMMARY

One of the main goals of rhetorical representation is to ensure that the targeted group feels seen and heard by their representative. If this is done

---

[4] While anecdotal, a Black respondent wrote that they faced this type of discrimination in this industry in their comments. "I approve [of] this [message] because discrimination in the workplace is true. I've experienced it firsthand, and I felt like crap afterwards."

successfully, it should lead to higher levels of approval for elected officials. Our findings in this chapter corroborate this expectation. Black voters tend to be more supportive of elected officials who speak about racial issues in their public outreach. This was generally true regardless of the race of the elected official. In this way, our work is in line with previous research, which has explored racialized campaign messaging and changes in voting behavior (Austin Wright and Middleton 2004, Gillespie 2010, Stout 2015, Wamble 2018, Dietrich and Hayes 2023). Targeted discussions of issues that concern African Americans are viewed as appealing to this racial group. Moreover, Black respondents reward politicians who provide racial rhetorical representation with higher levels of approval.

However, similar to some work in racialized campaigning, racial rhetorical representation may not be costless. This is particularly true for Black politicians. Non-progressive White respondents rated Black elected officials who spoke about racial issues more negatively than those who spoke about a liberal non-racial policy, environmental justice. This was even true when we combined all White respondents into a single category. White politicians did not face the same backlash for this type of racial rhetorical representation. In fact, White politicians who spoke about police reform received a significantly greater boost in approval ratings from co-racial respondents compared to the same candidate who spoke about environmental issues. Black politicians who speak about race may face greater perceptions of racial favoritism and may be punished with lower approval from White people as a result. Nonetheless, Black politicians may take some comfort in the fact that racial rhetorical representation did not statistically significantly hurt their standing with White liberals, a group who is more likely to be in their electoral coalition.

In addition to finding differences by the race of the respondent, we also found key differences based on the interaction of the race and the message of the hypothetical politician. Black people tended to be more approving of White politicians when they discussed lower-profile racial issues. Our qualitative data analysis revealed that this preference was driven by a combination of factors such as perceptions of ideological congruence and the belief that the politician is committed to the issue. This finding suggests that proactive forms of racial rhetorical representation may be the most effective in demonstrating a connection between White politicians and Black voters. When White elected officials engage in rhetorical representation in a reactive manner, some Black people may question their commitment to advancing their political interests. This may dampen the link between approval ratings and rhetorical representation. This conclusion is similar to the analysis of Dietrich and Hayes (2023), who show that Black people are more skeptical of White politicians who invoke civil rights symbols in issue-based appeals. Dietrich and Hayes (2023) argue that such appeals are often perceived as being pandering rather than genuine. In combination with our research, it appears that White elected officials have to demonstrate a stronger sense of commitment for racial rhetorical representation to be an effective tool to draw support from Black voters.

We also found that Black respondents were more approving of co-racial members of Congress when they spoke about racial issues. However, unlike White politicians, both proactive and reactive forms of racial rhetorical representation elicited positive responses from Black people. Black respondents appear to view those who share their identity as being the most committed to racial issues. Thus, regardless of the topic being discussed, Black people seem to have more confidence in their co-racial counterparts to follow through with their outreach with action.

9

What If It Fails? Is Rhetorical Representation without Legislation Valuable in the Eyes of the Constituents

Through our interviews with communication directors in Congress, we learned that U.S. House Representatives and their staff use rhetorical representation to outline their priorities and ensure that their constituents know what they are fighting for in government. In Chapter 7, we showed that racial rhetorical representation was not hollow. Elected officials who spoke about racial topics in their press releases and tweets followed this talk up with substantive legislative actions. Regardless of effort, several communication directors lamented that the arduous legislative process makes it so that rhetorical representation is often the only thing they can accomplish, particularly when their party is in the minority. Emphasizing this point, a communications director for a Democratic legislator said, "so much of what you do [when] in the minority is messaging."

In Chapter 8, we showed that Black-centered rhetorical representation is an effective way for elected officials to gain the support of targeted communities. However, our qualitative responses also revealed a potential risk to this communicative strategy. Namely, regardless of the effort or intent of the legislator, some voters fear that elected officials who engage in racially rhetorical outreach are simply pandering to the electorate without the realistic intention of getting anything done. If this is the case, then rhetorical representation may lead to an increase in support in the moment, which may return to the mean or worsen if nothing actually gets accomplished. Given that 95 percent of bills introduced in Congress fail to become law, most racial rhetorical outreach discussing legislative intent is going to be tied to an unsuccessful endeavor.

While a significant amount of research has explored whether there is a link between what representatives say in their public outreach and what they do as legislators, less is known about how individuals respond to legislators when there is a disconnect between their speech and the outcome of legislation. Given that most bills fail to become law, the question arises of whether rhetorical representation is adequate to potential supporters. Or, do constituents' views of elected officials sour when they speak about advancing a group's interest and fail to show results?

We answer these questions by exploring whether potential supporters' views of politicians change when the issues they advocate for in their outreach fail to become law. We begin this chapter by reviewing literature on legislative performance and approval at both the aggregate and individual levels. From this review, we argue that voters will reward members of Congress when bills they advocate for publicly make it through the legislative process. However, voters may not punish these elected officials with lower levels of support for stating a position on legislation that stalls in the process.

To examine whether the connection or disconnection between racial rhetorical representation and the success of legislation matters in altering approval ratings, we return to our experimental analysis of Black and White respondents from Prolific. Following the presentation of different messages (See Chapter 8), we let the respondent know that the bill discussed in the press release either passed and became law or failed to advance in the legislative process. We then ask respondents whether this outcome changes their opinions of the elected official, both quantitatively through a scale and qualitatively through an open response. We find that there are no significant declines in approval ratings for elected officials who advocate for a policy that fails to become law. Instead, our qualitative responses reveal that most voters build this expectation into their initial evaluations of members of Congress. Respondents also seem to be very aware that each member of Congress is only a single actor in a larger political system and are grateful for them taking action (if they supported the policy). Thus, rhetorical representation without resulting legislation does not lead to a backlash towards the elected official.

However, when legislators speak about an issue in their press release and that legislation becomes law, they receive an increase in support. In large part, this is because voters give credit to individual legislators when bills make it through the process. Overall, the results show that rhetorical representation matters in generating approval regardless of the outcome of legislation. Nonetheless, members of Congress who speak about legislation and then are able to succeed in this political process improve their approval ratings from the public.

Legislative Performance and Approval

Numerous studies demonstrate that when elected officials are inconsistent in their public outreach and legislative activity, they receive lower levels of support. For example, Sulkin (2011) shows that legislators who fail to follow through on campaign promises perform worse in subsequent elections. Similarly, Simas et al. (2021) show that voters punished elected officials with lower levels of support when elected officials spoke about an issue but voted in a different way than they promised (see also Tomz and Van Houweling 2009). Inconsistency in position taking and legislative activity often leads to lower levels of trust for the elected official. This decline in trust raises questions about how genuinely concerned the elected official is about the issues they champion and whether the elected official is simply pandering to receive votes when speaking out.

While different from flip-flopping, the inability of legislators to follow through on their promises with tangible policies may raise concerns about commitment from legislators to succeed in the policymaking process. Elected officials who speak passionately about an issue but are not able to follow through with action may raise concerns from the public that their representative is overpromising for electoral gains. Voters may also question whether their elected official is realistic about what can be done in the legislative process. This may lead voters to be less supportive of a politician who speaks strongly about an issue in their outreach but is unable to convert a bill into a law.

Moreover, if a legislator simply speaks about the issues the constituent cares about, but does not get anything done, the constituent may become disillusioned with the legislator (Svolik 2013). This may manifest itself in constituents becoming more skeptical about the elected official's effectiveness. Along these lines, Treul et al. (2022) show that voters are more supportive of candidates who are able to follow through on their speech with legislative action in the primary than legislators who are generally ineffective policy makers. On the one hand, legislators who are unable to follow their rhetorical outreach with policy may receive lower levels of support.

On the other hand, voters are often aware of the limitations of a single legislator in the policy process and may not blame them for being unable to deliver on their promises. One prominent example of this is that voters tend to strongly disapprove of Congress, but generally re-elect their representative. In June of 2023, only one in five Americans strongly approved or approved of Congress' job performance, according to

Gallup.[1] However, reelection rates for individual members of Congress remained high. In the preceding 2022 Midterm elections, over 90 percent of incumbents to the U.S. House of Representatives were reelected.[2] The inconsistency of high levels of support for individuals but disdain for the institution is often driven by perceptions that one's legislator represents their values and wants to work in their interest. However, these well-intentioned legislators are stifled by an unresponsive political process. Moreover, many constituents view their ideologically congruent representative as being in touch with what the population wants, even when Congress is out of step with the country's preferences. In a 2014 Gallup Poll, 81 percent of respondents viewed Congress as a whole to be out of step with the political preferences of the nation. However, 47 percent, a minority, viewed their individual legislator as being out of touch.[3]

African Americans may have particularly high levels of faith in elected officials who take strong stands on issues that never progress legislatively, given their experiences of being overlooked in the policy process. While advocates for Black interests, like the Congressional Black Caucus (CBC), often put forth legislation and budgets that appear symbolic given their low likelihood of passage (Tate 2014, Nelson 2022), Black voters support the CBC at high rates. In fact, according to the 2020 Collaborative Multiracial Post-Election Survey, fewer than 9 percent of Black voters disapproved of the work of the CBC.

Additionally, African Americans' experience with Congress often leads them to perceive the institution as being systematically biased against their political preference (Higginbotham 1998, Williams 2000). Even when there is strong support for racial progress, tactics such as filibusters have long been used to water down or completely block racial legislation (Ray 2021). Moreover, many Black people blame a lack of diversity in the institution for a lack of racial progress. For example, a 2020 Pew poll showed that 68 percent of Black respondents felt that if Congress were more diverse, there would be more progress toward racial equality in the United States.

For all of the aforementioned reasons, voters may be particularly forgiving of legislators who engage in racial rhetorical representation, which does not lead to tangible policies in the current era. In recent years, Black people have experienced significant declines in voting rights and a

---

[1] https://news.gallup.com/poll/1600/congress-public.aspx
[2] https://ballotpedia.org/Election_results,_2022:_Incumbent_win_rates_by_state
[3] https://news.gallup.com/poll/178487/americans-member-congress-not.aspx

lack of success at the federal level for police reform. Nonetheless, they are able to see prominent voices in Congress speak about these issues and protest in support of this legislation.

African Americans are keenly aware that racial change happens incrementally in Congress and needs constant champions to make progress in this area. Black people may be hopeful that racial rhetorical representation can lay the groundwork for eventual change. As a result, they may be especially understanding when legislators who speak about racial topics are not able to see this discussion turn into legislation. Instead, they may be grateful that their representative is starting the process toward improving opportunities for African Americans, which may take a longer period to become law. Overall, it is possible that constituents will not hold negative views of legislators who provide racial rhetorical representation but are unable to enact the legislation they are advocating for.

While there are competing expectations for whether voters will punish or ignore rhetorical representation that does not lead to tangible policy, the question remains about whether constituents will be more approving of elected officials who can show that their rhetorical representation is realized with legislation. Previous studies have demonstrated that members of Congress are rewarded with higher approval ratings when they are effective legislators. (Sulkin et al. 2015, Grimmer et al. 2015, Butler et al. 2023). Volden and Wiseman (2014) show that in Congress, there are vast differences in legislative effectiveness. As expected, legislators who are in leadership positions and have longer tenures tend to be more effective in Congress than others. In spite of these differences, voters are often in the dark about legislative effectiveness (Butler et al. 2023).

However, when constituents are presented with evidence that their legislator is able to implement their legislative priorities, voters tend to be more supportive of these elected officials. Butler et al. (2023) in an experiment find that when presented with evidence that their legislator is effective, voters are more approving of their job performance. Hargrave and Smith (2023) corroborate this finding and show that, regardless of a legislator's identity, voters tend to reward members of Congress with higher approval ratings when they are presented with evidence of legislative effectiveness. Consistent with these findings, several studies show that voters are more approving of legislators who are able to do more for their districts. Grimmer et al. (2014) and Gerber et al. (2022) both show that legislators who are able to bring back more money to their districts receive higher levels of support from their constituents. Grimmer et al.

(2014) show that legislators who engage in public credit claiming do not actually have to be active in the process of bringing pork to the district as long as they take credit. The key to these studies appears to be that the legislator must publicize their successes through their rhetorical outreach.

Why are voters more supportive of legislators who are able to enact the policies they speak about? Politicians who can point to legislative successes may present themselves as better able to navigate the policy process in the face of insurmountable hurdles. The savviness of the politician may lead similar ideological constituents to view the elected official as not just sharing their preferences, but also as having the ability and connections to turn their promises into legislation. This may result in increased trust in the politician and higher approval ratings. Constituents may not blame politicians for their inability to get laws passed. However, they may give extra credit to politicians who are able to get their bills through the legislative process.

Given the difficulty of gaining ground in racial equality, supportive respondents may be particularly astonished by elected officials who are able to make progress on racial legislation. Voters may view elected officials who are able to break through a political system that they perceive as being biased against African Americans as being particularly skillful in building important coalitions. The recent lack of federal legislation around racial issues may lead constituents to be hopeful about a legislator who is able to both speak about racial inequality and address it with legislation. As a result, we anticipate that Black voters and allies will be especially supportive of a legislator who is able to link racial rhetorical representation with tangible policy progress.

TESTING THE LINK BETWEEN RHETORICAL REPRESENTATION AND LEGISLATION

To understand whether voters feel differently about elected officials who engage in rhetorical representation and see their legislation fail or succeed, we return to our experiment discussed in Chapter 8. As a reminder, we administered a survey to 600 White and 600 Black respondents through Prolific. We then randomly presented respondents with a hypothetical press release that varied in discussing policies around climate change, police reform, and employment discrimination. In each of these press releases, the hypothetical member of Congress spoke about working with a larger caucus to introduce legislation around these topics. We also varied the race of the politician to be either Black or White. Following this presentation of our treatments, we asked respondents to rate the elected official and explain their ratings. The results of this portion of the experiment are reported in Chapter 8.

Then, after a few more questions, we presented the respondents with updated information about the legislation discussed in the press release. Respondents were randomly presented with one of two updates.

1. Bill Passes Condition: The bill that Mark Harris advocated for in the press release you read became law in the past few weeks.
2. Bill Fails Condition: There was not enough support from others for the legislation that Mark Harris advocated for in the press release you read. As a result, the bill will not become law in this Congress.

Following this additional information, we asked respondents on a five-point scale. "Does this information change your levels of approval for Mark Harris?" Responses ranged from 1-"Yes, leads me to disapprove of him a lot more," 2-"Yes, leads me to disapprove of him a little more," 3-"No," 4-"Yes, leads me to approve of him a little more," and 5-"Yes, leads me to approve of him a lot more." We then asked respondents to write, in a few sentences, how this information influenced their opinion about Mark Harris. In particular, we asked respondents, "Please write in one to three sentences how or whether your views of Mark Harris have changed as a result of the legislation they spoke about becoming law/ failing to become law."

RESULTS

Figure 9.1 presents Black respondents average change in support after learning a bill has passed or failed. The results are disaggregated by the race of the elected official and the type of legislation they are advocating for. Figure 9.1 includes average scores on the five-point scale along with 95% Confidence Intervals.

Two things are immediately apparent when reviewing Figure 9.1. First, neither Black nor White elected officials who champion racially or non-racially liberal policies in their rhetorical representation see a decrease in support when the bill they focus on does not become law. In fact, given that the averages are all above three regardless of treatment type, these elected officials saw their support increase when they engaged in rhetorical representation, even when such outreach was tied to failed legislation. There are, however, differences based on the types of policy the elected official is advocating for and the race of the elected official. For

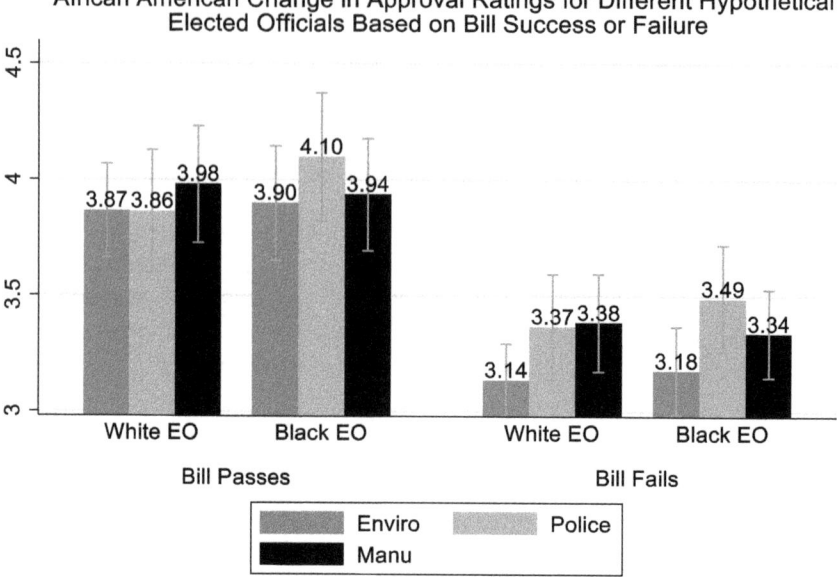

FIGURE 9.1 Change in African American Support for Hypothetical Candidate When Bill They Advocated for Became Law/Failed to Become Law by Treatment Type W/ 95% Confidence Intervals
T-tests are used for comparison.

White elected officials, they receive marginally significantly more support ($P<.10$) when they advocated for policies around employment discrimination (3.38) and the bill failed than when they supported environmental policies (3.14) and the bill failed. These higher levels of support may be tied to the belief that White elected officials who engage in proactive racial rhetorical representation care about them more than co-racial elected officials who speak about a non-racial issue. Black respondents may be more forgiving of a legislator who opens the discussion around a topic that has not received a lot of attention, even if this outreach is linked to legislation that fails to become law.

Similarly, Black respondents provided a statistically significantly greater increase in support for Black legislators who fought for police reform (3.49), but failed than the same race legislator who was unable to see their legislation around the environment become enacted (3.18). The combination of factors suggests that Black respondents think about the inability of legislators to connect their rhetorical representation to legislation differently. They tend to be more understanding of policy failures

Results 179

when they are tied to racial rhetorical representation. This may be driven by the fact that Black-centered issues may appear as being particularly difficult to move through the legislative process.

Second, Figure 9.1 shows that when racial rhetorical representation is tied to the passage of legislation, positive feelings toward the elected officials significantly increase. On average, racial rhetorical representation that is tied to legislation that passes leads Black respondents to improve their perceptions of the elected official by about half a point more than when the same outreach is tied to a bill failing. In all treatment types, Black respondents are significantly more approving of the legislator when the bill passes than the same legislator in the same condition when the legislation fails. There are also no significant differences in the amount of approval based on the race of the elected official or the issues they stand for when the legislation succeeds. Overall, Figure 9.1 indicates that while Black people do not punish elected officials when the topics they discuss fail to become law, they do reward them when their public statements are tied to successful legislation.

White respondents in many ways follow the same patterns as their Black counterparts. Figure 9.2 presents White respondets' changes in views about the hypothetical elected official when the legislation in the press releases passes or fails. Figure 9.2 presents the average scores about whether the updated information about the legislation's fate changed respondents' levels of support for the elected official with 95% confidence intervals. Figure 9.2 is also disaggregated based on the treatment types. As a reminder, scores above 3 indicate that voters became more supportive of the legislator after being presented the second part of the treatment (i.e., the bill passes or fails). Scores below this average reveal the opposite.

Like African Americans, White respondents do not punish elected officials who engage in progressive non-racial or racial representation and are unable to see that legislation becomes law. In contrast to Black respondents, there was no significant variance regardless of the treatment type. White respondents did not rate Black or White elected officials differently when they spoke about different legislation in their press releases, and then did not see those bills become law.

However, White respondents did become more supportive of both Black and White elected officials when the topics they spoke about in their press releases made it through the legislative process than they were of the same legislator when their press releases were tied to a failing bill. It appears that White Respondents, like Black respondents, reward effective legislators. With that said, there are differences based on the type of legislation that

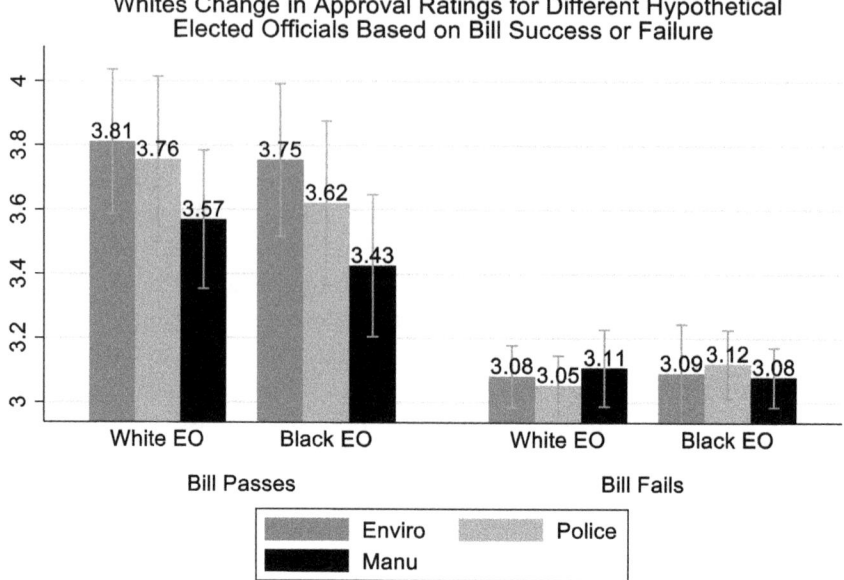

FIGURE 9.2 Change in White Support for Hypothetical Candidate When Bill They Advocated for Became Law/Failed to Become Law by Treatment Type W/ 95% Confidence Intervals
T-tests are used for comparison.

passes. Whites were generally more supportive of both the Black (3.75) and White (3.81) legislators whose advocacy for environmental legislation was tied to a bill that was successful than they were of the successful advocacy of a policy tied to employment discrimination for Black (3.43) and White elected officials (3.57). As was detailed in Chapter 8, this finding may be driven by White respondents' lower levels of support for the government becoming involved in employment discrimination issues. As a result, the bill they dislike most succeeding may depress their support for the elected official. The results in Figures 9.1 and 9.2 suggest that respondents reward success but do not blame politicians for speaking out in support of legislation that fails to make it through the legislative process. To understand why this relationship occurs, we turn to our qualitative data.

Why Do Respondents Reward Success but Not Punish Failure?

To better understand how Black and White people responded to information about rhetorical representation being tied to successful or unsuccessful legislation, we asked respondents to write a few sentences explaining how information about the bill's fate changed their approval rating for the hypothetical candidate Mark Harris. The vast majority of respondents (>95%) left some meaningful comments explaining their decision. We then coded these responses into four commonly occurring topics. Similar to our content analysis in Chapter 8, responses to this question could be coded as appearing in multiple categories or in none of the following categories.

First, we coded respondents into a category that mentioned that the treatment did not change their views of the politician. Many respondents left comments that would be coded into this category including, "It has not changed because he still has his core beliefs that line up with mine," "My views about him have not really changed. This just shows that my intuition was correct and that he was the right man for the job," or "I can't get any lower of an opinion, so no change." All of these comments, in one way or another, explicitly mention that the fate of the legislation did not really change their opinion of the elected official.

Second, we coded for whether respondents spoke positively about the legislator's actions. This positive valence category includes any defense of the legislator's inability to get the bill passed, praises of his effort or conviction, or comments that complement his ability to move legislation through a byzantine political system. Comments like the following were coded in this category; "I think it's good he at least tried to make [environmental legislation] happen [it is] better than what most people do," "My approval has increased a bit. At least he is trying and I don't see anyone else taking a stand. I hope he comes back bigger and better and gets it passed this time," and "It shows that Mark Harris is actually making moves, and that his actions are performing well. He is aware that there is no easy fix, and he is doing stuff to gradually fix the problems facing the black community."

Third, we coded comments for whether respondents wrote negative things about Mark Harris. Comments in this category most often came in blaming the hypothetical elected official for the failure of the bill, and comments that disparaged Mark Harris. Examples of comments in this category included, "I believe Harris is someone that isn't trustworthy," "He did not try hard enough. He should still keep fighting," and "It is unfortunate that Mark Harris was not able to succeed. I still believe in him...but less."

Finally, we coded responses that attributed the legislation's fate to political forces outside of the legislator, such as Congress as an institution, the political environment, or other members of Congress. This could include either blame for the bill failing or credit for the bill succeeding. Statements about the latter were rare. As a result, the vast majority of comments we coded in this category explicitly blamed outside political forces for the failure of the bill. Statements in this category include, "[Mark Harris] can't control what other people do. If not enough people support it, it isn't going to go anywhere. That's the way it goes, at least he tried and went on the record saying he's concerned," and "I don't think this is Mark Harris's fault at all, the current political climate around climate change is contentious at best."

Qualitative Responses Results

Table 9.1 presents the percent of mentions of each of our four categories by the race of the respondent and treatment types (race of elected official, issue type, and fate of the legislation). The overall results help us understand why rhetorical representation without legislation did not depress political support for our hypothetical elected official. It also provides clues about why speaking out in support of legislation before it passes enhances approval for Mark Harris. When the bill failed, the modal response across most treatment types was that the legislation's fate did not change the respondent's level of support for the politician. Across all categories, a majority of respondents (52.6%) mentioned that learning that the legislation failed did not influence their levels of support for Harris.

Moreover, in all cases, the respondents who received the "bill failing" treatment were more likely to make comments that fit into the positive category than the category encompassing negativity about the hypothetical politician. Only about 8 percent of responses mentioned the candidate in a negative manner when the bill failed. Instead, many of these comments mentioned that Harris speaking out for the bill led them to believe that he was fighting for legislation even if it did not pass. One White respondent wrote about a co-racial elected official who supported a failed police reform bill, saying, "...He's on record supporting a cause I believe in and made an effort to push and advocate for change."

Others wrote comments arguing that rhetorical representation was key to getting the process moving forward, even if the bill failed in this session. A Black respondent speaking about a White elected official praised his effort for a failed bill around race and manufacturing said, "The effort is the important bit, whether or not something is legislatively possible is another matter. You have to at least *try* to move the ball forward..." Another Black respondent wrote about a co-racial elected

TABLE 9.1 *Percent of Mentions of Whether Information About Bill Fate Shapes Approval of Hypothetical Elected Official or EO*

Respondent Race	Race of MoC	Issue	Bill Fate	No Change in Support	Positive Statements	Negative Statements	Others' Fault/Credit
Black	White EO	Environment	Bill Fails	35%	22%	12%	22%
Black	White EO	Police	Bill Fails	33%	33%	8%	27%
Black	White EO	Manu	Bill Fails	38%	30%	8%	40%
Black	Black EO	Environment	Bill Fails	38%	28%	2%	19%
Black	Black EO	Police	Bill Fails	29%	31%	10%	31%
Black	Black EO	Manu	Bill Fails	30%	36%	2%	21%
White	White EO	Environment	Bill Fails	40%	33%	4%	42%
White	White EO	Police	Bill Fails	43%	29%	6%	57%
White	White EO	Manu	Bill Fails	57%	15%	7%	36%
White	Black EO	Environment	Bill Fails	46%	21%	5%	41%
White	Black EO	Police	Bill Fails	60%	33%	8%	33%
White	Black EO	Manu	Bill Fails	63%	20%	2%	49%
Black	White EO	Environment	Bill Passes	67%	48%	4%	4%
Black	White EO	Police	Bill Passes	35%	48%	12%	6%
Black	White EO	Manu	Bill Passes	38%	48%	0%	2%
Black	Black EO	Environment	Bill Passes	66%	40%	0%	0%
Black	Black EO	Police	Bill Passes	39%	44%	4%	2%
Black	Black EO	Manu	Bill Passes	49%	61%	2%	0%
White	White EO	Environment	Bill Passes	38%	54%	4%	2%
White	White EO	Police	Bill Passes	49%	43%	5%	5%
White	White EO	Manu	Bill Passes	78%	38%	2%	5%
White	Black EO	Environment	Bill Passes	38%	50%	5%	7%
White	Black EO	Police	Bill Passes	52%	34%	5%	5%
White	Black EO	Manu	Bill Passes	50%	40%	2%	2%

official who supported a failed police reform bill, "I believe there is time for everything and Mark Harris['] time will one day come." Even when the bill fails, many respondents viewed the elected official as moving the topic forward in a positive manner.

While part of this may come from our treatment, which mentioned that the bill failed because of a lack of support, many respondents argued that the bill's fate was not the fault of the hypothetical member of Congress. As a result, the fact that respondents recognize that a single legislator is only a small part of the overall process may be a reason why rhetorical representation without results did not lead to a decrease in support for the elected official. This view is particularly true for Black people around racialized legislation. Black people are marginally significantly ($P<.10$) more likely to blame the fate of the bill on the policy process in their qualitative responses when it is a racial bill (29%) than when the press release spoke of a non-racial piece of legislation (20%). This difference is likely tied to Black people's recognition of biases against legislation tied to racial issues.

Significantly fewer respondents said their opinions about the elected official did not change when the bill passed (39%) than when the bill failed (53%). Instead, many more respondents sing the praises of the elected official when the bill discussed in the press release becomes law. In all treatment types, more of the respondents gave credit to the hypothetical candidate for the bill passing and spoke positively of them than they did for the same elected official when the bill failed. In many cases, respondents were twice as likely to write positive comments about the legislator when the bill made it through the complete process as the same legislator who publicly supported failed legislation.

When elected officials engage in rhetorical representation around legislation that makes it through the process, many voters view them as being more skillful and better at building coalitions. A Black respondent who received the Black elected official-police reform treatment mentioned the following when told that the legislation passed, "I have more confidence in Mr. Harris's ability to accomplish goals as a politician. He seems to be skilled in this regard." In a few cases, it made people skeptical of the sincerity of the politician's rhetorical outreach to become believers that the elected official was earnest in their efforts. A Black respondent speaking of a hypothetical White elected official who advocated for an employment discrimination bill that passed wrote, "It's good to know my trust in the representative was not misplaced. He promised to face the issue head on and made good on his promise. That makes him a great representative." The results demonstrate that when a bill passes, potential voters impute more positive characteristics to the elected official, and this, in some cases, improves their levels of support for them.

While respondents are more likely to blame a bill's failure on factors outside of the elected official, very few respondents gave credit to Congress as a whole for the legislation's success. In fact, only 3 percent of respondents said that the legislation's passage was not the work of the legislator who advocated for it in their rhetorical representation. Moreover, respondents were much less likely to make negative comments about the elected official when the bill succeeded (.037) than when it failed (.062). Overall, the qualitative responses reveal that when rhetorical representation is tied to failed legislation, respondents do not blame the representative for the fate of the bill. Instead, they praise them for their effort. When a bill succeeds, they tend to attribute success to the effort of the individual rather than a supportive system. This positive framing about a single person's capabilities improves their standing among the electorate.

SUMMARY

This chapter explores empirically whether racial rhetorical representation has any value in the eyes of voters if it does not ultimately lead to a bill becoming law. Both quantitative and qualitative assessments of our hypothetical elected officials demonstrate that it does. For the former, people did not feel more negatively toward the hypothetical member of Congress when he spoke about advancing racial progress, but were unable to see it through with actual legislation. Even without this success, most of our respondents, both Black and White, do not perceive racial rhetorical representation as cheap talk. Instead, they are savvy enough to know that a single legislator is not always able to move legislation forward without allies.

For the latter point, respondents appear to see real value in racial rhetorical representation even if it does not ultimately lead to legislation. Many voters felt supportive of the hypothetical elected official when he spoke about racial issues because they felt that the political process is long, and they viewed it as important that elected officials raise new concerns. Many viewed rhetorical representation as a way to do this, even if the bill did not succeed in one session. Moreover, many were appreciative of the effort that the hypothetical elected official put forth when speaking about issues they too were concerned about.

The results indicate that elected officials who have few opportunities to move racially progressive legislation forward should not refrain from speaking out about issues that matter to underrepresented groups. This outreach not only improves the standing of the elected official with their constituents, but it also provides hope to people of color that someone is speaking about the issues that they care about. Racial rhetorical representation by itself is important to voters.

Based on our qualitative analysis, the reason why rhetorical representation did not lead to a drop in support was the expectation that the elected official would continue to fight for the topics they spoke about. In fact, it was clear from many of the qualitative statements that voters expect that the legislator will not give up in his efforts even if the bill initially fails. Several mentioned that the only way that rhetorical representation without legislation would lead to a decrease in support is if the elected official stopped trying.

An additional incentive to not simply engage in cheap talk is that the interaction of racial rhetorical representation and bill passage generally yields more positive feelings about the elected official and the system overall. The most consistent finding across racial groups, the elected official's race, and issue type is that voters' assessments of elected officials improved when the issue they championed in their press release became law. In fact, many viewed these elected officials as being especially effective legislators. One participant in our study wrote this about the hypothetical candidate when they were tied to the passage of an employment discrimination bill stating, "My views of Mark Harris [have] changed in a very positive manner because he singlehandedly helped the legislation become law. His efforts have helped the black community tremendously." While in reality the political process is out of the control of any single legislator, many gave much of the credit for a bill's success to the legislator who engaged in racial rhetorical representation. As a result, the findings in our chapter do not signal that elected officials can make a statement and stop working toward a goal. Instead, elected officials receive a significant bonus in approval by combining rhetorical representation with tangible legislation.

10

Conclusion

Is Racial Advocacy Enough?

George Floyd became a household name in the summer of 2020. A seven minute and forty-six second video of his detention and murder was watched over a billion times worldwide.[1] In the month following his murder, there were over 4,500 protests around the world including one in every single congressional district in the United States. During the summer of 2020, one in ten Americans took to the streets to express their support for Black Lives Matter.[2] Many Americans spoke about the topic of police violence and racism candidly with others and some thought deeply about these issues for the first times in their lives.[3] Others took to social media to express their support for police reform. #Blacklivesmatter was used in over 150,000 tweets each day in the summer of 2020 and peaked at over a million tweets containing this popular hashtag.[4]

Rank-and-file citizens were not the only ones using this hashtag and speaking about police violence. As we noted at several points in this book, elected officials too became much more vocal in support of the Black Lives Matter movement following the murder of George Floyd. While Black elected officials led this charge, White, Latino/a, and Asian American members of Congress also spoke out about this issue. Moreover, it wasn't

---

[1] https://advancementproject.org/george-floyd-one-year-later/#:~:text=According%20to%20Pex%2C%20Twitter%20shows,the%20Chauvin%20Trial%20in%202021.

[2] www.nytimes.com/interactive/2020/07/03/us/george-floyd-protests-crowd-size.html

[3] www.pewresearch.org/social-trends/2020/06/12/amid-protests-majorities-across-racial-and-ethnic-groups-express-support-for-the-black-lives-matter-movement/

[4] www.pewresearch.org/internet/2023/06/29/ten-years-of-blacklivesmatter-on-twitter/#:~:text=But%20the%20most%20active%20period,uses%20in%20a%20single%20day.

just Democrats, White Republicans condemned the murder of George Floyd and issued press releases and tweets about racial bias in policing. This outcry represents a significant increase in Black rhetorical representation in the summer of 2020.

A decade before the Black Lives Matter movement was starting to gain momentum, a Black Minnesota Woman, Brittany Clardy, was abducted and killed by Alberto Palmer. Clardy was a sex worker, and Palmer had contacted her through a website. This could be one of the reasons why her case was initially ignored by the police when her family called for help. While women of color are kidnapped and murdered at a much higher rate than their White counterparts, this topic rarely receives attention from the media.

The late journalist Gwen Ifill once referred to this as "Missing White Women Syndrome" in which the media becomes fascinated with the abduction and disappearance of White women, but women of color are often ignored. Unlike the murder of George Floyd, violence against Black women and girls is often overlooked (Slakoff 2013, Crenshaw et al. 2015). There are no large-scale protests, no trending hashtags, and names like Brittany Clardy are confined to the family and the activists who worked to bring her justice.

Given the lack of media attention, it is not surprising that most elected officials stay silent on the disproportionate kidnapping and murder of women of color. In spite of its need for an urgent solution, this is not a topic that the population is clamoring to have addressed. As a result, there are significantly fewer electoral incentives to speak out. With that said, there are some elected officials who use their public platform to bring attention to these often-undervalued problems in society. U.S. House Representative Robin Kelly (D-IL) worked with the Congressional Caucus on Black Women and Girls to host a roundtable discussion about missing Black girls and women from Chicago. In hosting this forum, she notes, "For too long, the cases of missing Black women and girls and other women of color have not received the attention they deserve. Our girls are at greater risk of interpersonal violence and human trafficking. I am hosting this event to help educate our community about the issue and to discuss what we can do to save our girls."[5] Representative Bobby Rush (D-IL) hosted a similar event. In promoting the event, Representative Rush put out a press release which highlighted the lack of attention

---

[5] https://robinkelly.house.gov/media-center/press-releases/rep-kelly-congressional-caucus-black-women-and-girls-host-event

violence against Black women receives, stating that "The erasure, silence, and lack of collective attention resounds as profoundly violent and yet another example of the vast chasm between who does and who doesn't care about the lives and livelihoods of Black girls and women."[6] Press releases are not the only platform where attention to this problem has been raised. In a Tweet, Rep. Bonnie Watson Coleman (D-NJ) noted, "In 2020, 34% of missing females were Black, though they make up only 15% of the female population. Their lives matter."[7]

These examples show that while there has been a growth in racial rhetorical representation, not all forms of outreach are equal. A wider variety of elected officials provides racial rhetorical representation around higher-profile topics, where public pressure often necessitates some sort of public outreach. This was the case with the murder of George Floyd. However, we see descriptive representatives being the most likely to speak about racial issues that fly under the radar, as was the case with bringing attention to the disproportionate amount of violence that Black girls and women face. While Black elected officials provide racial rhetorical representation at a greater rate than non-Black elected officials, they also do so by raising awareness about overlooked racial topics. As a result, many descriptive representatives use their public platform to not only build connections with constituents, but also to alter the policy landscape to be more responsive to marginalized groups.

In this, the concluding chapter, we explore questions about the importance of descriptive representation in the current political climate which has seen the growing acceptance of racial outreach. While more elected officials feel comfortable speaking about Black politics, we argue that descriptive representatives play a vital role in shaping this discussion and ensuring that the diversity of Black interests receive adequate attention. We also discuss the significance of descriptive representation and rhetorical representation in advancing the goals of the most marginalized groups in society.

After recapping the strong link between descriptive and rhetorical representation for Black people, we highlight the growing significance of rhetorical representation in the current political atmosphere where partisan polarization and gridlock reign. We argue that as voters become increasingly disillusioned with a federal government, which is unable to

---

[6] https://blockclubchicago.org/2021/07/29/bobby-rush-calls-for-special-task-force-to-find-missing-black-women-and-girls/
[7] https://twitter.com/RepBonnie/status/1704598210591981797

bring change to pressing problems, rhetorical representation may be an important tool that legislators can use to let voters know they are thinking about them and that they are continuously working to advance policy. As a result, we argue that rhetorical representation is an essential part of legislators' jobs which deserves further attention from political scholars. We conclude the chapter by discussing how Black elected officials engaging in racial rhetorical representation is necessary for the full and equal representation of Black people.

The End of Black Politics?...

A continuing debate among political scientists and practitioners is the significance of Black representation in advancing Black people's substantive political interests (Swain 1995, Whitby 1997, Lublin 1999, Canon 1999, Tate 2003). While many early studies around this topic argued that descriptive representation was necessary for Black people to have a voice in government, in recent years skeptics raise concerns about the necessity of Black elected officials to advance Black political interests. Despite Barack Obama's ascension to the White House and record increases in the number of Black politicians elected to the U.S. Congress over the last two decades, some claim that Blacks have gained little. In fact, during this period, the wealth gap for Black and White Americans has increased as have attacks on Black people's constitutional rights (Seamster and Charron-Cheneir 2017, Hasen 2020, Shah and Smith 2021).

Notably, Obama's election symbolized the peak growth of Black politics with him at the head of government, but Black people in his administration lacked the ability to set the national agenda (Harris 2014). Obama himself was outwardly perceived as not working to advance Black politics from his position of power (Harris 2012, Haines et al. 2019). This was in large part because Obama and similar politicians refrained from engaging in rhetorical representation in fear of being labeled as favoring their racial group over others (Gillion 2016, Haines et al. 2019). The wave of mass demonstrations over police violence and anti-Black racism in 2020 established the dissatisfaction Black people have with the political system. Some contend that more than electing Black politicians, Black people should engage in a progressive social movement to fight for racial change and uplift (Dawson 2011).

Beyond Obama, there are broad critiques of Black political leadership. These critiques are centered on the idea that Black leaders may no longer be the key to advancing Black political progress. Robert C. Smith (1996) contends that Black elected officials have become too accommodating of mainstream politics. They are less insurgent and as a result are largely indistinguishable from their liberal White counterparts. This is consistent with the work of Tate (2010, 2014) which finds that Black Democrats in the U.S. House have moved closer to the Democratic Party overall. Black members of Congress are less likely to challenge the Democratic Party from the left, she concludes, and sees their integration in the political system as having moderated their politics.

Political analyst Matt Bai (2008) published a piece in The New York Times Magazine called "The End of Black Politics." He describes Obama's ascent as the Democratic presidential candidate as the end of a long struggle to win political power by Blacks. Martin Luther King's "I Have a Dream" was delivered in 1963 when Obama was two. Black people would win most of their House seats in the South in 1992. Obama represented the new type of Black leader who entered politics after the civil rights movement (Gillespie 2010). These are Black politicians who speak as easily to White voters as they do to Black voters, in large part because they had abandoned their racial outreach (Gillion 2016, Haines et al. 2019). This change in rhetoric, according to critics, signified the end of descriptive elected officials as being necessary to carry on Black politics.

...Not Yet: Descriptive Representation, Rhetorical Representation, and Black-Centered Policy

This book contests "The End of Black Politics" narratives, which argue that Black politicians no longer take unique actions to advance Black political interests. One of the key findings of this book is that Black elected officials provide the highest levels of racial rhetorical representation. Moreover, they are more likely to engage in proactive racial rhetorical representation than their non-Black counterparts. This form of rhetorical representation was most strongly tied to other forms of substantive representation in government and was the preferred form of rhetorical representation among African Americans in the population.

Black elected officials worked more consistently to speak out about the interests of their co-racial constituents than non-Black elected officials. In doing so, they did not just wait for public pressure to highlight racial inequality in different areas or to highlight Black achievement. Instead, they described this as a core part of their mission in some of our interviews with communication directors. By being proactive in their outreach, Black elected officials spoke about topics that received little attention from other legislators.

This unique take on race in America is one of the core reasons why descriptive representation is necessary. As described in Chapter 6, African Americans have multiple intersecting identities that create specific forms of discrimination (Cohen 1999, Greer 2013). For example, Black women face different barriers to normalcy compared to their co-racial male counterparts (Simien 2005, Junn and Brown 2008, Ford Dowe 2023). Similarly, poorer African Americans face a different set of challenges than Black people in the middle and upper classes (Wilson 1980; 1987). In a one-size-fits-all model of racial outreach, those with more resources tend to receive the most attention (Robnett 1997, Cohen 1999, Strolovitch 2008). As a result, a model of rhetorical representation that is more responsive to public pressures will likely further exacerbate intersectional inequalities. The most marginalized groups who are not able to get their issue into the mainstream due to a lack of resources and social connections will be overlooked without vigilant elected officials being willing to take up their cause. Having Black elected officials speak out about lower-profile topics (See Chapter 4) and a greater variety of topics (see Chapter 6) increases the likelihood that a broader swath of Black people feel heard and have a voice in government.

Proactive rhetorical representation also provides solutions to problems that have not yet made it into the political mainstream. With regards to policing, Black elected officials have long spoken about problems around racial biases in law enforcement. These topics were generally ignored by non-Black elected officials because those with the most contact with police officers tended to have the fewest resources. However, when social movements and the media highlighted racial biases in policing through the Black Lives Matter movement, politicians took notice (Gillion 2012, Gause 2022). They then looked to Black elected officials who had long been speaking about this problem and offering solutions.

Through proactive rhetorical representation, Black elected officials frame the debate and provide solutions for elected officials who want to demonstrate an awareness of a particular problem when it becomes salient. In this way, proactive rhetorical representation shapes the discussions that occur under reactive rhetorical representation. If the former did not exist, elected officials would be slower to respond to critical moments as they would be looking for potential palatable solutions. The fact that Black elected officials speak about intersectional racial inequality provides a playbook for other elected officials who want to respond to critical moments but would otherwise not know what to say. By providing this framework, Black politicians' proactive rhetorical representation speeds up the ability of other elected officials to signal empathy to African Americans and creates a smoother legislative process by providing solutions.

Black elected officials' use of proactive rhetorical representation also matters because it identifies the racial interests in emerging policy debates. In Chapter 5, we demonstrated that Black elected officials were more likely to speak about nascent problems around racial inequality. One example of this was with regard to the COVID-19 pandemic. Having Black elected officials in positions of power increased attention to racial biases in potential solutions to this crisis. As Mansbridge (1999) argues, having descriptive representatives in the decision-making arena provides a unique perspective and vigilance about the impact of policies for those who share their identity. We find this to be true even in the current political era, where there is more attention being paid to racial inequality. Black elected officials were more likely to discuss race in their outreach around the COVID-19 pandemic than non-Black members of Congress. In doing so, Black representatives continue to use rhetorical representation to highlight the needs of their group in policies that are ostensibly race-neutral. This is yet another way in which rhetorical representation can shape policy solutions to be more favorable to Black people.

Descriptive Representation, Rhetorical Representation, and Black Political Empowerment

Beyond advancing policy, proactive rhetorical representation increases the likelihood that Black people feel heard by their elected officials. Racial talk is an important aspect of Black and minority politics (Harris-Perry 2004). It establishes that elected representatives care about the problems of racial injustice and inequality. Finding that Black legislators are more likely to engage in racial rhetorical outreach shows how co-racial elected officials have improved the quality of representation for minority citizens. When Martin Luther King Jr. was assassinated in 1968, minority elected officials were few. King's death led to major riots across the nation. Blacks who rioted felt that there was no one left to continue Dr. King's work. Today's legislators can convey sympathies to aggrieved communities through social media and press releases. These legislators are not only talking to voters but to their colleagues.

As was discussed in our interviews with communication directors, congressional offices are intentional in their outreach to ensure that specific communities, like African Americans, feel heard by their elected officials. This rhetorical outreach is particularly important when paths to legislative success are closed because of numerical or institutional barriers. Rhetorical representation, particularly proactive rhetorical representation that targets overlooked groups, may increase perceptions that they are not being ignored by elected officials. Through rhetorical representation, legislators make emotional connections to their constituents, standing for their interests, values, and identities.

In fact, in our experiment covered in Chapters 8 and 9, we asked respondents after reading the randomly selected press release how much they believed the hypothetical politician Mark Harris cared about them on a five-point scale. Black respondents were significantly and substantially more likely to believe that Harris cared about them when he spoke about racial issues, as compared to the environment. This was true both when Harris was described as being White or Black. While rhetorical representation matters in the policy debate, one of the key findings of this book is that it also matters in the eyes of the voters. Having someone speak out in support of their political interests helps underrepresented groups feel heard.

Why the Voting Rights Act Is as Necessary as Ever

The 1965 Voting Rights Act (VRA) was a landmark piece of legislation aimed at addressing discrimination in voting practices. It also allowed for the creation of majority-minority districts in which minority voters have a better chance of electing minority candidates, thereby increasing minority representation in government. Section 5 of the VRA required jurisdictions covered under the Act to obtain federal approval before making any change to election laws and maps. In 2013, the Supreme Court struck down Section 4, which provided the formula used to determine which states and counties were covered under the Act, thereby undercutting Section 5's preclearance requirement. Already, there are fewer majority-Black districts than in the past.

There has been significant litigation under the Act, and most recently, in 2023, the Supreme Court, in a surprising move, ruled in favor of the plaintiffs suing Alabama for racially discriminatory maps. This was a 5-4 decision where Alabama now needed to draw two majority-Black districts instead of one. The Alabama legislature refused to do this, and a federal court has designated a special master to draw the new map. The legislature appealed to the Supreme Court again, hoping that Justice Kavanaugh, who had joined the majority, might change sides. The Supreme Court refused to hear this appeal. The Alabama case has implications for other southern states, like Florida and Louisiana, where the number of majority-minority districts could increase.

Racially polarized voting is extreme in the South, and Republicans could gerrymander out majority-Black districts to form partisan maps to elect only Republicans. Republicans have taken advantage of the lack of federal preclearance by cracking Black communities in cities such as Nashville to merge with suburban communities. There is a bill to restore Section 4 by providing a new formula to determine which jurisdictions are covered, but today's Republicans are hostile to efforts to repair the Act. It is expected that without strong Democratic majorities controlling the House and Senate, the VRA will expire in 2032.

Our study shows that the diversity of elected officials made possible by the VRA brings different perspectives and priorities to the decision-making process in government. This is important to obtain the equal representation of all citizens. In speaking out for topics which receive less attention and being able to articulate Black interests around uncrystallized issues, Black elected officials provide unique benefits for a group fighting for equal rights. While studies that simply focus on the end products of the legislative process may conclude that descriptive representation is no longer necessary for Black people to receive an adequate voice in government, our work shows that Black elected officials often do the little things to ensure that Black people enjoy full citizenship in our democracy.

WHY RHETORICAL REPRESENTATION IS MORE IMPORTANT THAN EVER

In the preceding section, we argued that descriptive representatives are essential for African Americans to receive rhetorical representation. Moreover, Black elected officials were unique in the levels of proactive rhetorical representation they provided to individuals who share their race. In this section, we outline why rhetorical representation is more important than ever.

Growing Gridlock in Congress and the Disconnect between Public Opinion and Legislation

A common way that representation scholars assess the quality of substantive representation is by focusing on what representatives deliver to their communities through the passage of pertinent legislation or by measuring how much financial resources members of Congress bring back to their district (Preuhs 2005, Haider-Markel 2007, Evans 2011). Unfortunately, in the current political climate, it has become more difficult for elected officials to provide either of these forms of substantive representation because of changes in institutional norms and growing political divisions. For the former, the use of the procedural filibuster has made it so that even legislation and ideas with overwhelming political support are able to be blocked by a few legislators. The use of this filibuster has grown significantly since Obama's election to the White House. While there have been over 2,000 filibusters over the last 100 years, more than half have occurred since 2008.[8]

One possible explanation for the increased use of the filibuster is growing partisan polarization in society (Jones 2001, Burden 2011, Barber et al. 2015). For a host of reasons, Americans have become more politically divided on a variety of political issues, from cultural topics around the rights of underrepresented groups, abortion, and speech to economic issues like student loan forgiveness, taxation, and investment in green energy (Grossman and Hopkins 2016, Simas 2018). This growing political polarization in the public is mirrored in Congress (Levendusky 2009). Members of Congress are vote maximizers and want to ensure that they win the next election by as large a margin as possible. As the American electorate becomes more divided in politics, compromise has become a four-letter word. Elected officials who reach across the aisle face punishment from their co-partisans (Anderson et al. 2020).

As a result, outside of a few landmark pieces of legislation, which are passed through the reconciliation process and a growing number of symbolic pieces of legislation, most legislation fails to make it through the complete process, even when public opinion is in support of a particular issue. For example, following the murder of George Floyd in May of 2020, there was overwhelming support among both Democrats and Republicans for federal police reform. According to a Gallup poll collected a month after Floyd's death, 94 percent of Americans believed that there needed to be either major or minor changes to policing in the United States. A vast majority, 58 percent, argued that there needed to be major changes. Support for specific changes was also high. Seventy-six percent of Americans believed that management changes needed to occur to make sure that police involved in misconduct where properly punished, 77 percent supported providing resources so that officers could build better relations with the communities they serve, and 98 percent of Americans

---

[8] https://www.brennancenter.org/our-work/research-reports/filibuster-explained

agreed that police officers with multiple incidents of abuse should not be allowed to serve again.[9]

Congress initially appeared to follow public opinion on this topic, introducing two competing police reform bills. The Democrats introduced the George Floyd Justice in Policing Act, and Republicans introduced the Just and Unifying Solutions to Invigorate Communities Everywhere (JUSTICE) Act. In spite of overwhelming public support, both bills failed to become law (as of the writing of this book). The former passed the Democratic led U.S. House of Representatives but was not given a vote in the U.S. Senate, which at the time was controlled by Republicans.[10] However, in the following Congress, where Democrats made up the majority in both the U.S. House and U.S. Senate, the bill failed because it was blocked via filibuster in the U.S. Senate.[11] The JUSTICE Act was never even taken up in the U.S. Senate because of a filibuster.[12]

The lack of anything to show around police reform in spite of the massive protests and support from Americans left many confused and angry that nothing was accomplished. In a statement, NAACP President Derrick Johnson blamed Congress for its inability to pass meaningful legislation. "In a year unlike any other, when the American people spoke up, marched, and demanded reforms in policing, law enforcement unions and partisan politicians chose to stand on the wrong side of history. They have chosen to stand with those who have lynched the very people they are meant to protect and serve."[13]

While the example of police reform is pertinent given our focus on race in this study, the lack of action in Congress around political problems with high levels of support is numerous. For example, in several public opinion polls, Americans express concerns about the large amount of money in politics, and many support placing limits on campaign spending.[14] Public support for some gun control measures and the lack of action by Congress also demonstrate the disconnect between public opinion and the passage

---

[9] https://news.gallup.com/poll/315962/americans-say-policing-needs-major-changes.aspx
[10] www.congress.gov/bill/116th-congress/house-bill/7120/all-actions?overview=closed&q=%7B%22roll-call-vote%22%3A%22all%22%7D
[11] www.congress.gov/bill/117th-congress/house-bill/1280
[12] www.congress.gov/bill/116th-congress/senate-bill/3985/all-actions?overview=closed&q=%7B%22roll-call-vote%22%3A%22all%22%7D
[13] https://naacp.org/articles/naacp-president-and-ceo-derrick-johnson-releases-statement-bipartisan-police-overhaul
[14] https://assets.pewresearch.org/wp-content/uploads/sites/5/2018/04/26140617/4-26-2018-Democracy-release.pdf

of legislation. In fact, in a 2023 AP-NORC Poll, 63 percent of Americans think that U.S. laws and policies reflect what Americans think about gun control not too well or not well at all. In fact, only 10 percent of Americans think that U.S. laws and policies reflect Americans' opinions extremely well or very well.[15]

The overall disconnect between what Americans support and legislative outcomes is one reason why most Americans disapprove of the institution of Congress as a whole.[16] It also has the potential to leave individuals feeling powerless over a political system which does not address their interests. This is likely especially concerning for African Americans who have historically and even in recent years been unable to translate their political activism into tangible legislation (Hajnal 2009).

How Rhetorical Representation May Close Perceptions of Inattentiveness in Government

How can individual legislators let their constituents know that they care about them and their interests in a political system built for slow change? How can they demonstrate that they are working to be responsive even in the absence of legislation? Members of the U.S. House of Representatives are only 1 of 435 voting members in their chamber and 1 of 535 voting members in Congress overall. As a result, their individual efforts may not yield success in a hyper-partisan environment with significant competition to get things done. The ability to get legislation to the political finish line is even more difficult when a legislator is in the minority. Legislators acknowledge this problem, and in our qualitative results discussed in Chapters 8 and 9, rank-and-file Americans appear to also be aware of these limitations.

One of the simplest ways that legislators can let their constituents know that they are paying attention to them and are working for their interests in government is by telling them. Members of Congress engage in multiple activities on behalf of their constituents that often fall under the radar including introducing legislation, speaking in committee hearings, and/or constituent services. While the end results of the legislative process receive the most attention, whether it be the bill succeeding or failing, the work that legislators do on behalf of their constituents is numerous and may go undetected if legislators are not vocal about it. The lack of

---

[15] https://apnorc.org/projects/most-adults-feel-the-interests-of-people-like-them-are-not-well-represented-2/
[16] https://news.gallup.com/poll/1600/congress-public.aspx

progress with tangible legislation to some may seem like nothing is being done on behalf of one's group. This may lead to a lower sense of efficacy and approval for their representatives.

Rhetorical representation can dispel the myth that individuals' pleas for assistance are falling on deaf ears among those in positions of power. As one communications director said in an interview, she viewed her primary job as explaining to their constituents what her boss has done in Congress and what he's brought back to the district. It can lead voters to feel that even if the complete legislative process is unresponsive, they have an ally in government. This ally and others like them over time may help move progress forward.

For example, in the aforementioned press release from NAACP president Derrick Johnson where he expressed anger in the inability of Congress to pass meaningful police reform legislation, he speaks positively of two members who heavily publicized their actions toward addressing police violence in Congress. "Senator [Cory] Booker and Congresswoman [Karen] Bass heard those demands and took the responsibility of ushering in a new vision for policing...They attempted to work across the aisle to ensure a sustainable solution could be reached... Without their efforts, we would not have made the inroads that we have."

This statement embodies the large number of comments from our qualitative analysis in Chapters 8 and 9. In these chapters, Black respondents spoke positively about the hypothetical elected official who worked to advance racial issues in Congress even when the effort fell short. Like NAACP President Johnson, Black respondents praised the hypothetical elected official for creating a vision of what could be accomplished in the future and were grateful that the elected official worked toward an important goal. Racial rhetorical representation informs voters that legislators are working on their behalf to make progress. This display of support may provide a sense of hope that pressing issues are not being ignored even if legislation is not moving forward. As demonstrated in our qualitative analysis, the sense of responsiveness that comes from rhetorical representation matters in how voters feel about their representatives.

Rhetorical Representation and Keeping an Issue on the Agenda in a Fast-Paced Society

The proliferation of news sources in the current media environment and competition for viewers has increased the speed of the present-day news cycle (Rosenberg and Feldman 2008). As a result, a news story which grips the attention of the public in one week quickly dissipates in the next.

In fact, a study by Lorenz-Spreen et al. (2019) of global attention spans demonstrated that people are increasingly likely to move from one topic to another rather quickly. For example, in 2013 a popular hashtag on Twitter would remain in the top-50 for an average of 17.5 hours. Just three years later, popular hashtags on Twitter would remain in the top 50 for about two-thirds that time (11.9 hours) (Lorenz-Spreen et al. 2019).

This means that political and social crises which would dominate the news cycle for a longer period of time in the past, fade more quickly. This has important policy implications. Namely, numerous studies demonstrate that critical events play a key role in the policy process (Smooth 2013). Moments which capture the nation's attention place pressure on legislators to respond with legislation. For example, following a high-profile instance of police violence, public attentiveness and support provide members of Congress more momentum to pass legislation around police reform. However, after a period of time, attention and support for legislation regresses to the mean. Thus, elected officials have a policy window to address the most pressing issues and this window is closing more quickly in the current political era.

Rhetorical representation can work to keep an issue on the political agenda even when the news cycle is focused elsewhere. By continuously speaking about a particular issue, legislators can ensure that even if there is not activity in Congress and the media has moved on, the plight of individuals still afflicted by this problem are not forgotten. In a period with a fast-moving news cycle, elected officials who engage in rhetorical representation, and in particular, proactive rhetorical representation, can work to elongate the policy window and ensure that their colleagues do not forget about pressing issues.

The policy process is long and as mentioned throughout this book often filled with failure. While it is unlikely that any given bill will pass in a particular session, keeping the topic on the agenda through proactive rhetorical representation improves its chances of success when the right opportunity arises. Some of the largest changes around racial equality in United States history occurred with the passage of the post-Civil War Amendments (13th, 14th, and 15th Amendments to the U.S. Constitution) and the 1964 Civil Rights Act and 1965 Voting Rights Act. While each of these periods of legislative success occurred in a relatively short time frame, they were preceded by decades of activism both within and outside of government. The brave activists and elected officials who continued to speak about the horrors of slavery and Jim Crow fought to bring attention to issues that were convenient for the average person to ignore. By keeping these topics on the agenda, they were able to take advantage of an opportunity for change under the right political environments. While these are more ambitious examples, proactive rhetorical representation and the continued fight around topics that elected officials care about provides the framing for potential solutions when the political system is confronted with pressure to change.

Rhetorical Representation and Getting Issues on the Agenda

While the segmented media presents challenges in terms of keeping the public's attention focused, it also provides important opportunities. In particular, social media democratizes information and allows for discussions around novel ideas. Social movements from groups with fewer resources have been able to get their issues on the political agenda through the use of social media. From the Arab Spring, to #Blacklivesmatter, to the #MeToo movement, social media has played a vital role in providing a platform for marginalized groups to disseminate messages and frame political and social debates. Social media sites like Twitter have provided underrepresented groups like African Americans a particularly powerful arena to discuss issues of concern to their group that are generally ignored by other forms of media (Tillery 2019, Bonilla and Tillery 2020).

Black people have used Twitter to shape discussions around culture and politics in a sub-space of the platform colloquially labeled as "Black Twitter" (Graham and Smith 2016). Black Twitter has been instrumental in sharing Black ideas to the broader public (Sharma 2013). While Black Lives Matter is certainly the largest movement sparked by the platform, Black Twitter was also responsible for several other important discussions which moved our politics. "#Sayhername," "#Oscarssowhite," "#Blackgirlmagic," and "#Bringbackourgirls" were all popular hashtags which pushed the population and political elites to make change and recognize groups which were overlooked in society. The ability for Twitter to allow unfiltered communication between rank-and-file members of the community, the media, and political elites, makes the platform a powerful tool to build important connections.

Twitter has also been used by elected officials to amplify the topics that underrepresented groups speak about on the platform. This is particularly true for members of Congress from marginalized groups who often echo the concerns of those who share their identity (Stout et al. 2017, Bonilla and Tiller 2020). By doing so, elected officials who engage in proactive rhetorical representation are able to place the messages of groups who would otherwise be overlooked in front of decision makers.

Additionally, social media provides an unfiltered way for elected officials to raise new ideas and provide information to the population. Before Juneteenth became a national holiday in 2021, many Black elected officials would put out tweets about the topic. While Juneteenth was recognizable to a smaller subset of individuals with knowledge of Black History, having Black elected officials use their public platforms to highlight this holiday likely broadened its reach. Following the murder of George Floyd and the Democratic takeover of Congress and the White House in the 2020 election, legislation on Juneteenth passed to make this celebration of the unofficial end of slavery in the United States a national holiday. By raising issues which may be overlooked, elected officials are able to make salient different ideas which can lead to the passage of legislation under the right environment.

The growing number of channels that elected officials can use to connect with constituents means that rhetorical representation does not just have to be a reaction to what is publicly salient. Instead, entrepreneurial legislators can use rhetorical representation to educate the public on key issues which affect their group and frame the debate around policy solutions. In doing so, elected officials can use proactive rhetorical representation to educate the public about accomplishments of individuals within a particular group, highlight group disparities and raise novel policy solutions.

Challenges Ahead
While new forms of communication provide opportunities for rhetorical representation, they also bring challenges. Some have argued the social media can be a significant source of misinformation and can create echo chambers (Chen et al. 2023, Nyhan et al. 2023). Twitter, which played a significant role in Black political life in recent years, is rapidly going through changes. The most prominent is the sale of the platform to Elon Musk who recently rebranded the social media site to X and overturned bans based on conspiratorial postings often tied to racially biased speech (Hickey et al. 2023).

These changes have led to some dramatic changes among users of the platform. For example, in a 2023 Pew research survey, a majority of Americans stated that they took a break from the platform a year after it was acquired. Moreover, Black people and Democrats were more likely to report taking a break from the platform in comparison to White people and Republicans respectively.[17] Democrats also became much more pessimistic about the site in comparison to Republicans.[18] This may explain why followers of Democratic politicians left the site at a greater rate than followers of Republican elected officials.[19]

These changes to the platform raise interesting questions about racial rhetorical representation on Twitter. While the base of the platform has changed with disproportionately more African Americans leaving Twitter, there have not been large changes to the partisan and racial composition of members of Congress on the site. In fact, all members maintain a Twitter account even after Musk's takeover.[20]

We asked nine Black communication directors how changes on X following Musk's acquisition of the site altered their levels of rhetorical representation on the platform. They largely stated that the change in ownership did not modify their behavior on the platform. One communications director talked about how when Musk initially took over there was a time when some key players, like other legislators and non-profit organizations and interest groups, left the platform. However, she described this time as relatively short and one that is no longer present. She said everyone's back on the platform now, and some are even willing to go so far as to pay to be authenticated with the blue check mark by X. As a result, she views it important for her legislator to maintain an active presence on X. Another communications director said, "honestly, I think everyone's still trying to figure it [what Musk's takeover of Twitter] out. Things are constantly changing, but we try to stay pretty consistent in our message."

Many of the communications directors said that their overall approach to Twitter hasn't significantly changed. However, many did mention that they receive more negative engagement since Musk's takeover. One communications director said that under the old Twitter rules, some of the responses they get to their tweets would be flagged and removed. Now that those guidelines aren't there, negative responses are much more prevalent. However, this same communications director said that this "really hasn't influenced [his] decision to post" on the platform.

---

[17] www.pewresearch.org/short-reads/2023/05/17/majority-of-us-twitter-users-say-theyve-taken-a-break-from-the-platform-in-the-past-year/
[18] www.pewresearch.org/short-reads/2023/05/01/after-musks-takeover-big-shifts-in-how-republican-and-democratic-twitter-users-view-the-platform/
[19] www.washingtonpost.com/technology/2022/11/27/musk-followers-bernie-cruz/
[20] https://pressgallery.house.gov/member-data/members-official-twitter-handles

He said, "my thing is, I don't want to let others determine what we say." Another communications director said, "we're seeing more negative engagement with what we put out," but this hasn't really impacted what they post. The communications director said that "we stand our ground. We have our priorities and we stick with them." Still another communications director reiterated that while the volume of negative engagements with their posts has increased, her overall approach to the platform hasn't really changed much. However, when she posts she often finds herself thinking about if and how she's going to respond to the negative posts. She said that with most of the negative engagement it's "so off the wall" that she doesn't feel any need to respond.

CONCLUSION

The COVID-19 pandemic wreaked havoc on lower class Americans and in particular people of color. One area in which people of color felt the economic pinch was with rising rents during a period where many were laid off or furloughed. According to a January 2021 report from the Joint Center for Housing Studies at Harvard University, one in ten Black Americans felt that they would likely be evicted when a Center for Disease Control moratorium on evictions was lifted.[21] When this issue was lost in the panoply of topics related to COVID-19 in the summer of 2021, including fights around vaccine access and masking, the CDC was quietly going to let the moratorium expire on July 31, 2021. With little fanfare about the issue, most members of Congress left for the August recess.

One, U.S. House Representative Cori Bush (D-MO), stayed behind and used her public platform to bring attention to this issue. As a Black woman, who herself had been homeless at multiple points in her life, Representative Bush in a CNN op-ed argued that it was especially important for her to bring attention to the expiration of the moratorium.

> I've lived out of my car for months with my two babies. I've seen my belongings in trash bags along my backseat. I know what that notice on the door means. Cold from the elements or wondering where I could find a bathroom, *I've wondered who was speaking up in DC for people in my situation.* I never knew who had the resources to make this situation end. Now that I was in Congress myself, a

---

[21] www.jchs.harvard.edu/blog/black-and-hispanic-renters-face-greatest-threat-eviction-pandemic

member of one of the three branches of our government in a position to act, I knew we couldn't leave.[22]

Bush's activism and voice around this topic made it a national news story. Soon other legislators including then Speaker of the House Nancy Pelosi and Senate Majority Leader Chuck Schumer praised Cori Bush for bringing attention to this issue.[23] Other members of Congress joined her on the steps of the Capitol to highlight the plight of people who would be evicted when the moratorium ended.[24] This outreach was effective as soon after, President Biden extended the CDC's eviction moratorium. Bush's advocacy was mentioned as a motivating factor in the White House's decision according to Press Secretary Jen Psaki.[25]

Elected officials were not the only ones who took notice of Cori Bush's actions. Strategic communication consultant Anat Shenker-Osorio tweeted in response to Cori Bush's actions. "We turned out in record numbers for new leaders who would make this a place where freedom, fairness and a better future are for all, no exceptions...Your voice makes change."[26] Similarly, community organizer Arti Walker-Peddakotla wrote on Twitter that Cori Bush's actions should set an example for all elected officials. "The tears, the sweat, the raw emotion she put into this-I am in awe. That she showed up unapologetically, bravely, and fiercely is what every elected official must do."

This example demonstrates that descriptive representation continues to matter for Black people and particularly those with fewer resources. Cori Bush's activism and the response exemplifies Black elected official's willingness to use their public platform to advance Black politics. This outreach not only moves a racially progressive agenda forward, but it ensures that Black people feel like they have a champion in government. Representative Bush's passion for speaking out about a topic which is easy to ignore came from her personal experiences with being unhoused. These experiences created a sense of urgency that led her to speak out in support of a large group of people, including a disproportionate number

---

[22] www.cnn.com/2021/08/06/opinions/sleep-on-capitol-steps-for-eviction-moratorium-motivation-cori-bush/index.html
[23] www.nbcnews.com/politics/congress/democrats-cheer-rep-cori-bush-s-eviction-moratorium-win-even-n1276243
[24] www.thecut.com/2021/08/cori-bush-capitol-protest-wins-eviction-moratorium-extension.html
[25] https://fox2now.com/news/white-house-praises-rep-cori-bush-on-eviction-awareness-more-work-needed-for-long-term-solution/
[26] https://twitter.com/anatosaurus/status/1422664947599921175

of African Americans, who would face harsh realities without some sort of government intervention. The same passion was not felt by many others who had left Washington DC for the August recess.

This example also speaks to the significance of rhetorical outreach in improving the lives of others. When a legislative path was not available to address this problem, Representative Bush used her public platform to get this topic on the agenda and put pressure on decision makers to make a change. Rhetorical representation does not always lead to such direct changes within government. However, this form of outreach can bring much needed attention to societal and political problems which are easy to disregard. While there are many actions that elected officials take in government to advance the goals of their constituents, this book demonstrates the value of speaking out.

Moreover, our book demonstrates that what elected officials use their public platform to highlight matters. While it is important that elected officials speak about racial topics which are in the public eye, elected officials who speak out on a greater variety of topics have a higher likelihood of reaching people who most politicians keep at a distance. In the case of Cori Bush, she used a campaign attack[27] against her to be a source of strength to speak out for the unhoused population. In the introduction of this chapter, we discussed Black elected officials speaking out for a sex worker, Brittany Clardy, to highlight the threats that some Black women face. Given stereotypes about homeless people and sex workers, such outreach is rare in Congress. However, Black elected officials' greater willingness to use their public platform to advance the diversity of Black political interests not only moves this agenda forward, but it ensures that *all* Black people, even those who are most marginalized, feel like they have a voice in the halls of power.

---

[27] https://theintercept.com/2021/08/06/deconstructed-cori-bush-eviction-poverty/

Data and Methods Appendix

The arguments and analyses in this book were derived from a wide variety of independently collected sources, including interviews with political elites, press releases, tweets, and survey experiments. To examine this diverse set of data, we used a mixed methods approach, which covered a wide variety of both quantitative and qualitative analyses. Throughout the book, we provided a brief summary of the different data sources we used in each chapter. We also provided cursory information about coding and validity checks used in that chapter. However, to ensure that our theoretical contribution was not getting lost in the technical details of each of our analyses, we created this data and methods appendix.

In this appendix, we provide a more detailed summary of the decisions we made in the book, along with more information about our validity checks. In particular, this data and methods appendix provides information about how we collected our interviews with political communication directors, including who was targeted, our response rates, and the questions we used in the interviews. The appendix also provides more details about the press release and Twitter data that we used in this book, outlines our coding scheme, and provides information about how we used machine learning to classify press releases and tweets as being Black-related or not. Along these lines, the appendix covers the decisions we made to increase intercoder reliability, along with the statistics we use to check the validity of our analyses.

We hope that this information will be useful for others who want to conduct similar studies around racial outreach in the future.

INTERVIEW DATA COLLECTION: SAMPLING STRATEGIES AND INTERVIEW QUESTIONS (AS DISCUSSED IN CHAPTER 2)

To build our theory around who engages in racial rhetorical outreach, we interviewed twenty-nine communications directors in the U.S. House of Representatives during the 118th Congress. The interviews were semi-structured and took place via phone or Zoom. The first round of interviews occurred between February and April 2023. We reached out via email (see below) to all communications directors whose legislator identifies as Black or Latino/a.[1] We also reached out to a random sample of fifty Democratic and fifty Republican offices. To increase the number of respondents from Black U.S. House offices, a second round of interviews was conducted between May and June 2024. The recruitment email read...

SUBJECT: OBERLIN COLLEGE PROFESSOR INQUIRY – PARTICIPATING IN STUDY

Dear Mr./Ms. XXXXX,

My name is Jennifer Garcia, and I am a professor of political science at Oberlin College. My co-authors (Dr. Katherine Tate, Brown University, and Dr. Christopher Stout, Oregon State University) and I are working on a research project that is interested in better understanding the decisions that go into the issuing of press releases and posting on social media by House members' offices. We would like to ask you a few questions in your capacity as a communications director. It should take no more than twenty minutes, and we can speak over Zoom or the phone, whichever is best for you. Do let me know when would be a good time to speak.

I appreciate your consideration and hope to hear from you soon.

Best,
Jennifer

We did not guarantee confidentiality, but we did agree not to disclose the name of the communications directors or their legislators. We also committed to not using any information they gave in their interviews that may identify their office. This project was cleared by Oberlin College's Internal Review Board.

In total, we spoke with communications directors from the offices of seven Latino Democrats, two Latina Democrats, four Black Democratic

---

[1] Legislator identities were determined based upon information provided by the US House of Representatives. https://history.house.gov/Exhibitions-and-Publications/

TABLE A1 *Response Rates for the Communications Directors We Asked to Interview*

Communications Directors' Interview Response Rate		
	Respondents/Total Emailed	Response Rate
Black	13/59	22.03%
Latino/a	9/53	16.98%
White Democrat	5/50	10%
White Republican	2/50	4%

Congressmen, nine Black Democratic Congresswomen, three white Democratic Congressmen, two white Democratic Congresswomen, and two Republican males. Table A1 presents the response rates for the different categories.

During our Interviews, we asked the following questions:
(1) Do you begin the Congressional session with a communications strategy/plan, or is it something that evolves over time?
(2) Do you ever feel pressure to speak out? Explain.
(3) How involved is your legislator in the issuing of communications?
(4) How do you decide when to issue a press release? How do you decide when to post to social media?
(5) Who are you trying to speak to in your press releases? Social media posts? Are there differences in your postings to Twitter vs. Facebook?
(6) Is there a difference in your communications strategy when you're in the majority versus when you're in the minority?
(7) Is there a difference in your approach to Twitter before and after Elon Musk's takeover?
(8) What role, if any, does your legislator's identity have on the communications your office issues?
(9) Is there anything else you'd like to add or that you think we've missed in our questions?

PRESS RELEASES AND TWITTER DATA (AS DISCUSSED IN CHAPTERS 3, 4, 5, 6, AND 7)

Beyond the interview data, we are interested in exploring elected officials' communication to better understand how they engaged in racial rhetorical outreach. We draw from two separate data sets to determine levels of Black-oriented outreach in Congress. This includes almost the complete universe of press releases for members of the U.S. House of Representatives in the 114th (2015–2017), 115th (2017–2019), and 116th (2019–2021) Congresses. We collected this data from members' webpages at the beginning of every year for each year in the six-year period. Given these time intervals, we would only miss press releases that elected officials had deleted from their webpages. Our cursory analysis of a few members' press release sections using the Wayback Machine reveals that elected officials rarely, if ever, delete press releases from their webpage within a year.

Overall, our press release data set includes 204,806 individual press releases from 401 members in the 114th Congress, 403 members of the 115th Congress, and 407 members in the 116th Congress. Our dataset represents over 92 percent of the membership in each of the Congresses we examine.

Our Twitter data are confined to the 116th Congress (2019–2021). This data set includes 601,303 individual tweets from 411 members of the 116th U.S. House of Representatives. This includes the universe of members of Congress who put out a tweet during our period of interest (January 3, 2019, and January 2, 2021) and/or had an active Twitter account. However, it is possible that deleted tweets were not included in this analysis, as we only collected the data at a single point in time in early 2021.

Unfortunately, we only have Twitter data for a single congress, given the time at which we collected this data. However, since we find relative consistency around racial appeals across congressional sessions with press release data, we have no reason to believe the same pattern would not hold among Twitter users if we obtained the data for the social media site over the complete six-year span.

Why We Focus on Outreach Between 2015 and 2021

One key decision we made was the period that we wanted to center our analysis on. Practically, we focused on the period that occurred between January 3, 2015, and January 2, 2021 because we had been continuously collecting press releases over this span. Moreover, starting in the period of the 116th Congress, we were able to collect Twitter data. This provided us with a multi-year period of data, which allowed us to examine how elected officials put out public statements in a variety of different situations, including both responses to crises and outreach during more routine periods.

Additionally, the period we examine has many ideal properties to test our hypotheses. This period is a crucial one for the examination of racial outreach, given some of the dramatic shifts in American politics that occurred during these dates. One of the most important of these shifts was with regard to discussions of race among politicians and the electorate. The increasing attention to racial disparities was in part driven by racial protests tied to Black Lives Matter and the presidential campaign and presidency of Donald Trump.

Just five months before the start of the 114th Congress (2015–2017), racial protests around the country erupted following the death of Michael Brown in Ferguson, MO. In the month following his death, tens of thousands of protesters across the United States began speaking out against police violence toward Black people (Freelon et al. 2016). It was also during this period that the hashtag that would define the next decade in American Politics, #Blacklivesmatter, went from being rarely used on social media to being used over a million times in the days following Brown's death (Freelon et al. 2016). Our period of examination would include several other high-profile events tied to Black Lives Matter including the 2015 racial terrorist attack of Black Parishioners at the AME Emanual Church in Charleston, South Carolina, the unrest around the murders of Philando Castile and Alton Sterling in the Summer of 2016, and the racial protests around the murders of George Floyd, Breonna Taylor, and Ahmaud Arbery in 2020. These events and the attention they drew placed pressure on elected officials to speak out, which provided us with good opportunities to explore who engages in reactive racial rhetorical representation.

While Black Lives Matter drew attention to race and provided a context for elected officials to respond, the shift from the first Black President, Barack Obama, to the Presidency of Donald Trump and events surrounding his tenure also amplified the significance of race. Our period of examination occurs between the end of Obama's second term and the years in which Trump occupied the White House. For the former, Obama's first years in office led many to believe that we had entered a period of post-racial politics (Tesler and Sears 2010, Price 2016).

Obama's 2008 election signified that a Black man could overcome the history of racism in the country and be elected to the highest office in the United States. Eight years later, racist attacks against the president (Parker and Barreto 2013) and racial unrest tied to the Black Lives Matter movement led some to question whether race relations had worsened over his tenure. When Obama was asked by ABC journalist George Stephanopoulos whether race relations had improved during his tenure,

Obama responded, "I am absolutely convinced that race relations on the whole are actually better now than they were 20 years [because] we have greater awareness of where we're falling short than we used to."[2] Obama's comment highlighted that in the past, discussions of race were taboo and, as a result, were rarely part of the public dialogue. However, his election and the growing awareness of racial divisions gave license for more elected officials to openly speak about racial inequality.

Awareness of racial inequality and continued racism was highlighted during the presidency of Donald Trump. Trump made several racially insensitive comments during his campaign and time in office including questioning whether President Barack Obama was born in the United States, calling African countries "shitholes," and calling Black players who were boycotting the national anthem "thugs."[3] Trump also engaged in racially biased rhetoric in his disputes with Black members of Congress. A common theme was saying that Black majority districts were "hell holes" and/or "rat-infested."[4] Trump also famously responded to a gathering of White Supremacists in Charlottesville, VA, and counterprotests, stating that there were fine people on both sides.[5]

The rapid pace at which national events tied to race occurred made keeping quiet on racial issues difficult for elected officials. Moreover, the vast number of racial topics that arose during this period allows us to better understand *how* and *when* elected officials engaged in racial rhetorical representation.

While there were numerous nationally salient events that would lead a broader swath of elected officials to discuss race, there were also a number of lower-profile racial issues that occurred during our period of interest. For example, while individuals like George Floyd, Breonna Taylor, and Philando Castile gained attention, there were over 100 other protests tied to lower-profile cases of police and vigilante violence across the country.[6] Similarly, while issues like voting rights and the removal of Confederate symbols demanded national attention, Black maternal death rates grew precipitously[7] during our period of interest, and issues tied to

---

[2] www.presidency.ucsb.edu/documents/interview-with-george-stephanopoulos-abc-news-this-week-15
[3] www.theatlantic.com/magazine/archive/2019/06/trump-racism-comments/588067/
[4] www.cnn.com/2019/07/27/politics/elijah-cummings-trump-baltimore/index.html
[5] www.congress.gov/118/meeting/house/116973/documents/HHRG-118-ED00-20240417-SD006.pdf
[6] https://countlove.org
[7] Unequal weighting of US maternal mortality [Infographic] - Business News (crast.net)

climate change's disproportionate effect on communities of color were much less remarked on. The vast number of both higher and lower profile challenges and opportunities that Black people faced during our period of interest provides us a unique lens to explore where differences between Black and non-Black elected officials' use of racial rhetorical representation existed.

Our period under examination is also a period in which new issues arose. The most prominent of these issues was the COVID-19 pandemic. As we discuss in more detail in Chapter 5, the COVID-19 pandemic raised a host of concerns that, without rhetorical representation, had the potential to further exacerbate racial divisions. The challenge that COVID-19 presented provided a unique opportunity to explore how elected officials spoke about race in burgeoning issue areas.

While a wide variety of time periods could be used in our exploration of racial rhetorical representation, we believe that the period under examination has several advantages. It provides a period in which high-profile racial issues put pressure on a wide variety of elected officials to respond, which allows us to explore nuances in how elected officials speak about race. It also occurs during a period when politicians feel more comfortable speaking about race. Whether it be in support of people of color (Stout 2020) or to engage in racist appeals (Valentino et al. 2018). While we are only interested in the former, the latter played a role in sparking defensive responses to racially insensitive outreach. Finally, the evolving political landscape during this period provided opportunities for proactive elected officials to use rhetoric to help define new racial issues. No period of interest may be perfect, but the period from 2015 to 2021 provides a useful context to understand racial rhetorical representation.

With that said, it is also important to detail some of the shortcomings of our focus on the latter half of 2020. While the growth in racial discussions grew during this period of time, the year 2020 was certainly an outlier. Not only did the COVID-19 pandemic occur during this period, but the Black Lives Matter protests were the largest recorded in history (Pressman et al. 2022). Moreover, public opinion toward racial issues improved significantly, with White people displaying substantially more racially progressive attitudes in the days after the murder of Floyd (Pew 2020, Reny and Newman 2021). This period creates the perfect conditions for studying racial rhetorical representation because the volume of outreach allows us to explore nuance in discussions of Black-oriented topics.

However, this era of support for Black people quickly receded to the mean in the years following the summer of 2020. Discussions about race by elected officials and the public in the summer of 2021, for example, are met with anti-DEI efforts around the country and the passage of legislation at the state level to curtail discussions of racial topics in education. While our results hold outside of the summer of 2020, indicating that the period of interest is not an outlier, it is important to be cognizant about how shifting discussions of race over time may enhance or diminish the magnitude of our effects of descriptive representation and racial rhetorical representation in this study.

Coding for Racialized Content

We use press releases and social media posts to determine levels of Black-oriented rhetorical representation. We consider Black-related rhetorical representation to be any discussion of an issue, topic, public figure, event, institution, or organization that is explicitly tied to Black political interests. Additionally, these discussions must frame Black political interests in a positive or supportive manner.

Unfortunately, there is no established measure of Black-oriented outreach, so we inductively and deductively created our own codebook for Black political appeals by using a comprehensive review of both our own communication data (i.e., press releases and tweets) and the work of scholars in this area (Metz and Tate 1995, Reeves 1997, McIlwain and Caliendo 2011, Minta 2011, Grose 2011, Gillespie 2010, 2012, Stout 2015, Wamble 2018, Arora 2019, Stephens-Dougan 2020, 2021, Crowder 2023). We supplement this review with an additional audit of Black-centered organizations' websites. This review allowed us to broaden the number of potential topics being covered and ensure that we would not miss key issues. For example, there are several names tied to Black Lives Matter that received low coverage in the media, and several Historically Black Colleges and Universities (HBCUs) that may not be recognizable to the average coder. By including each of the names associated with Black Lives Matter, through a review of the organization's website along with databases tied to political protest like countlove.org and ephrame.com, and each HBCU, we cast a wider net to ensure we are not missing lower-profile cases of Black outreach.

Finally, we coded all bill summaries that were issued in the U.S. House of Representatives during our period of interest (2015–2021), which recognized an individual or proposed naming a place after an individual. We then searched Google.com for biographies and photos of each individual named in the summary. While this is an inexact science, we were able to find several individuals who are African American who would not have been included in our initial coding scheme. For example, Kira Johnson was a Black woman who died during childbirth due to prejudiced health care. In recognition of her and all Black mothers who face greater risks during pregnancy, Alma Adams (D-NC) introduced the Kira Johnson Act. While not initially on our coding scheme, the inclusion of this name and people like her increases the probability that a Tweet or press release highlighting this legislation would be appropriately coded as appealing to African Americans.

From our review of research and an exploratory coding analysis of the data that we had available, we created a coding scheme that highlighted fifteen broad themes and over 500 words and names tied to Black political outreach. These themes varied from outreach focusing on advancing racial diversity or fighting against racial inequality in several domains, advancing civil and voting rights, condemnations of hate crimes, bigotry of other forms of racial discrimination, addressing police misconduct and showing support for Black Lives Matter, supporting criminal justice reform, celebrating Black focused holidays (Black History Month, Martin Luther King Jr. Day, Juneteenth, etc.), recognizing Black leaders or members of the Civil Rights Movement or Abolitionist movement, supporting HBCUs and Black focused fraternities and sororities, condemning white nationalism and racism, mentions of Black organizations like the National Association for the Advancement of Colored People (NAACP) or the Congressional Black Caucus, Black healthcare (i.e., sickle cell anemia or Black maternal care) and/or connecting any issue explicitly to Black political interests.

This list is not meant to be exhaustive, simply illustrative of the words and topics used in a vast majority of racial appeals to assist coders to more quickly identify Black outreach and improve intercoder reliability where confusion may exist. By creating this codebook and dictionary, we hope to have developed the broadest and most detailed measure of Black political outreach available. We also hope that this comprehensive list of racial outreach can be used as a guide for further research on Black appeals.[8]

We focus on explicit Black outreach because press releases and tweets around these topics demonstrate the most direct and recognizable appeals to African Americans. Moreover, race is a central part of American

---

[8] See the book appendix for these coding themes as well as the dictionary we used for coding.

politics and spillovers into many different domains such as healthcare (Tesler 2016), welfare (Gilens 2000), crime (Mendelberg 2001), and gun control (Filindra and Kaplan 2016). To ensure that the appeals we focus on are made directly to African Americans and are not simply racially tinged, we confine our coding to issues explicitly tied to race.

Moreover, we are not interested in racial outreach, which is meant to harm Black political interests. For example, several posts on Twitter following the murder of George Floyd accused Black Lives Matter of being a violent movement that encouraged rioting. While these forms of outreach make race a salient issue, they do so in a way that harms African Americans. For example, tweets like "The radical #Antifa and #BLM groups rampaging in the streets are only the foot soldiers of this domestic terror threat," issued by Representative Ken Buck, would not be coded as an appeal to African Americans. While it mentions Black Lives Matter (#BLM), it does so in a derogatory manner. While it was rare for members of Congress to be so antagonistic towards Black groups (in fact, all instances that we found in our coding were centered around BLM), we did not code negative outreach as a Black appeal. Given that racial rhetorical representation is not simply discussing race, but means doing so in a way that advances Black politics, we do not code attacks on African Americans as a form of rhetorical representation in our analysis.

For our purposes, we used the aforementioned codebook and dictionary as a guide to hand-code press releases and tweets. We use a hand-coding approach rather than a dictionary-based approach because the latter would not be able to identify the direction of the outreach, nor would it be able to ensure that the document is Black-related or not. As mentioned above, on Twitter, a few posts from Republican elected officials condemned Black Lives Matter or spoke in opposition to the George Floyd Justice in Policing Act. A dictionary-based approach would mistakenly identify these texts as being Black appeals. However, with human coders and later computer-assisted coding,[9] we could better distinguish how mentions of Black-related issues are discussed in the text to

---

[9] The computer largely performed well in distinguishing positive appeals from negative mentions of Black groups. This was in large part because negative mentions of Black-centered groups were tied to Black Lives Matter and used words like "violent," "riots," "radical," and/or "antifa" which helped the computer, based on our coding, distinguish supportive text from oppositional text. Moreover, we did not find instances where Republican members attacked groups like the NAACP. Moreover, they used different terms to describe policy issues. For example, they would not use voting rights or voter suppression, but instead discuss voter fraud when discussing topics around voting.

ensure they are supportive. Moreover, just mentions of keywords like "Black" or "diversity" may be tied to topics that are not related to African Americans. For example, a legislator may mention the Black Hills National Forest or biodiversity in their outreach. A dictionary-based approach would code these words as being Black-related when they have nothing to do with racial outreach. A hand-coded and computer-coded content analysis better identifies whether mentions of words like these are Black-related or not. Given these advantages, we opt not to use a dictionary-based approach in our coding.

It should be noted that we consider any outreach to African Americans in a positive way to be a Black-related appeal. For example, if a press release about poverty mentioned Martin Luther King Jr. as an illustrative example of someone who fought against poverty or mentioned Shirley Chisholm in a larger press release about reproductive rights, we considered the complete press release to be a Black appeal. While the central topic of these press releases or tweets may be a non-racial issue, we consider the invoking of Black leaders to be at the very least a nod to the Black community by recognizing the work of individuals who share their race. By mentioning the work of Black leaders, the elected officials are tying themselves to high-profile African Americans and thus are making a Black appeal.[10] Beyond this illustrative example, we believe that anything that is flagged as an appeal to African Americans, either through the recognition of Black leaders or through policy outreach, is a form of rhetorical representation.[11]

It should also be noted that appeals to broader communities of color can also be considered as Black-related. For example, if a press release condemned changes in voting rules because they would harm communities of color, or support investments in minority-owned businesses, or

---

[10] A similar example of this would be if a Democratic candidate invoked Ronald Reagan in a larger discussion about immigration reform. While the topic has little to do with Republican interests, the discussion of Ronald Reagan is at least in part meant to attract individuals who viewed Reagan favorably.

[11] For theoretical and practical reasons tied to intercoder consistency, we coded all forms of Black outreach as being present or not. As a result, we treat a press release that makes at least a passing mention of Black-related outreach the same as a press release or tweet that only speaks about Black political interest. Future research may want to consider a spectrum around the strength of Black outreach in the text. The advantage of such an approach would be to provide more nuance into how strongly a press release or tweet is written to speak out in support of Black interests. The disadvantage of such an approach is that finding consistency in coding across human coders and computer coding would be challenging.

argued that colleges provide more opportunities to individuals from underrepresented groups, we would code it as Black-related. While such a press release would appeal to a broader group of people, if African Americans were included in this appeal, we coded it as being tied to Black interests. We recognize the overlapping interest that African Americans have with other groups in the United States and account for that in our coding.

EXTENDING OUR HAND-CODING OF RACIAL OUTREACH IN PRESS RELEASES AND TWITTER TO MACHINE LEARNING TO COVER A WIDER VARIETY OF CASES: AN ITERATIVE APPROACH

Given the large number of press releases and tweets, it would be extremely time-consuming and cumbersome to code each one individually. To circumvent this problem, we use a combination of hand-coding and computer-assisted content coding using RTextTools (Jurka et al. 2012). While much has been written about machine learning content analysis (see Grimmer and Stewart 2013, Barbera et al. 2016), recent research demonstrates that it performs better than dictionary coding approaches and, with the proper environment, as well as manual coding (Barbera et al. 2016).

RTextTools combines multiple machine learning algorithms to assist in the content coding of different documents. In essence, RTextTools uses an ensemble approach where it predicts the scores of each uncoded press release or tweet based on a set of hand-coded texts. RTextTools estimates the scores of each press release or tweet six separate times. Each estimation is disaggregated using the following estimators: support vector machine (SVM), Scaled Linear Discriminant Analysis (SLDA), bagging analysis, boosting analysis, random forest, and decision tree (see Jurka et al. 2013 and description below for how each estimator classifies documents).

These estimators are commonly used individually by computational social scientists to predict scores on uncoded text (Collingwood and Wilkerson 2011, Jurka et al 2013). Each model has some advantages and disadvantages that, by themselves, may make it difficult to correctly identify uncoded press releases or tweets as having instances of Black outreach. For example, SVM performs worse with data sets in which the classes of text have many overlapping qualities. Moreover, the decision tree model is most accurate when a few words distinguish the classes of text. The strengths and weaknesses of each coding algorithm in isolation could lead the choice of machine learning techniques to play a large role in the accuracy of our estimations (Collingwood and Wilkerson 2011). In our own case, while some algorithms performed better than others, none were foolproof.

However, by using an ensemble approach in which the different algorithms code the same text and provide unique scores on each document, we gain a more holistic understanding of the classification process. When all of the algorithms agree in their estimations, we can be more confident that they, as a group, got it right. When they disagree, we have the opportunity to further explore these texts.

In general, the models agree much more often than they disagree. In the few instances in which they disagree, we are able to review the cases by hand to correctly classify the press releases or tweets as being Black-related or not. By winnowing down the number of cases in which the coding algorithms are confused to a manageable number, we are able to more effectively use a combination of hand-coding and computer coding to more accurately classify texts as being Black-related or not.

For each of these estimators, we use a bag-of-words approach. The bag-of-words approach assumes that the words themselves, rather than the order of the words, matter in the classification of text. So, for example, our models would treat the words "African American" and "American African" similarly because they would only look for the presence of each word rather than the ordering of each term. In most cases, Bag of Words performs well as a classifying approach and is also computationally efficient. By introducing n-gram terms, the time to classify text skyrockets. Moreover, as Dietrich and Hayes (2023) note, Black elected officials speak about racial topics differently than non-Black elected officials. As a result, if we accounted more for the structure of outreach rather than the terms themselves, we may bias our results towards different racial groups.

We used an iterative coding approach, which began with the hand-coding of a random sample of 5,000 press releases and 5,000 tweets. While we coded tweets in their entirety, we only coded the first 100 words of each press release. We use a 100-word cutoff to ensure the racial outreach was at least somewhat central to the main argument of the press release and not an off-the-cuff remark 800 words into a 1,500-word press release. By having the racial discussions in the first few sentences, we better ensure that the message is received by the reader and is at least part of what the elected official was trying to get across. A large percentage of readers rarely read past the first few paragraphs of any article (Manjoo

2013), so to ensure that the message is received by the intended audience, we focus on the first 100 words of each press release in our coding.

Following our initial coding, we used RTextTools to code the remaining 199,806 press releases and 596,303 Tweets using our hand-coding mechanism as a guide. To assess the computer's performance, we used 5,000 press releases and tweets that we hand-coded. We designated 4,000 to be the training set (i.e., the set the computer learns from) and the other 1,000 to be the tester set. These initial tests for both the press releases and tweets performed poorly. The Cohen's Kappa scores (A measure of intercoder reliability) comparing our coding and the computer's coding of the same 1,000 press releases or tweets were less than .6, indicating substantial disagreement.

The low levels of intercoder reliability were almost all tied to the computer's inability to identify Black-related appeals when they were present. While there were no false positives in our analysis of the 1,000 press releases and very few in our 1,000 tweets, the false negative rate for the former was 3.5 percent and the latter was 2.8 percent. For press releases, in our initial iteration, the program had more false negatives than correct positives.

Why did the algorithms fail to recognize the Black-related outreach when it was present? Large imbalances in classes of categories can lead to poorer fits for machine learning. Even though we coded a large corpus of press releases and tweets, racial outreach is often relatively rare. In fact, Black outreach was present in only about 3.4 percent of press releases and 5.4 percent of tweets. These low numbers in the initial trial meant that the algorithms may not have had enough information to properly distinguish racial and non-racial outreach. Moreover, since some coding algorithms account for the baseline probability of being a Black-related text or not in their coding of different documents, the algorithms' starting position would be biased toward coding for no Black-related texts. This would underestimate the percent of Black outreach in press releases and tweets. The combination of factors would lead to more false negatives.

Fortunately, RTextTools' inability to identify Black-focused text when it is present is in part driven by disagreement among the coding algorithms. As a result, RTextTools provides information on where it is having the most trouble distinguishing whether a Black-related press release or tweet is present or not. We used our sample of 5,000 press releases and tweets to predict the presence of Black-related outreach in the complete corpus of press releases and tweets, respectively. We then hand-coded press releases and tweets in which four or more of the algorithms in

TABLE A2 *Intercoder Reliability Scores for Computer-Assisted Algorithms Across Platform and Iteration of Coding. Scores are for Instances in Which 4 or More of the Coding Algorithms Agreed*

Type	Iteration	Agreement	Expected Agreement	Cohen's Kappa
Press Release	1	96.5	91.9	0.57
Twitter	1	95.9	92.15	0.48
Press Release	2	98.24	91.37	0.8
Twitter	2	98.65	91.53	0.84

RTextTools disagreed about the coding. This additional step increased the number of Black-related press releases and tweets substantially, providing the algorithms with more information about what Black-related texts included.

Following this step, we again checked the computer's ability to assess the 1,000 tweets and press releases that we used as the tester set in the first iteration of coding. In this second iteration, we combined our original coding set along with the additional set of about 4,000 press releases and 8,000 tweets, which were hand-coded and selected based on the computer's disagreement.

In the second iteration, the computer did a much better job at identifying racial outreach in both press releases and texts using the same 1,000 test sets of press releases and tweets. In this iteration, we achieved Cohen's Kappa scores greater than 0.8 for both the press releases and tweets when more than 3 of the algorithms agreed, indicating strong intercoder reliability between our own coding and that of the computer. We hand-coded the subset in which only three algorithms agreed. Table 1 presents intercoder reliability statistics for these different iterations in which more than 3 of the algorithms agreed.[12]

---

[12] In a separate analysis where we focus on differences in accuracy based on the race of the elected official, we found that RTextTools performed better in predicting racialized press releases and tweets for non-Black elected officials in comparison to Black elected officials. The reason for this is that Black elected officials tend to make more racial appeals in their press releases and tweets than non-Black elected officials. The fact that RTextTools has more difficulty classifying racial outreach when it is present than predicting the absence of racial outreach means that the group that engages in the highest levels of racial rhetorical representation will be undercounted. Consistent with this, we find that Black members of Congress have lower Cohen's Kappa scores when validating RTextTools than non-Black members. Nonetheless, for all cases, the Cohen's Kappa score was above .74, indicating at least a substantial agreement in our validity analysis of RTextTools. Given that we are more likely to undercount the levels of racial outreach among Black legislators, the

TABLE A3 *Intercoder Reliability Scores for a Random Sample of 500 Press Releases and Tweets.*

	Intercoder Reliability		
Press Release	Coder #1-Coder #2	Coder #1-Computer	Coder #2-Computer
Percent Agreement	99%	99%	99%
Cohen's Kappa		0.82	
Twitter	Coder #1-Coder #2	Coder #1-Computer	Coder #2-Computer
Percent Agreement	99%	99%	99%
Cohen's Kappa		89%	

Better assured that the computer's coding was similar to our own, we combined our initial set of 5,000 hand-coded press releases and tweets with this new set of hand-coded press releases and tweets. We then used these 9,000 press releases to code the remaining 195,806 press releases and 17,000 hand-coded tweets to code the remaining 186,303 Tweets.

Grimmer and Stewart (2013) warn that the key to automated content coding is to check and double-check that things are performing well. In addition to ensuring that the computer is coding correctly, we also took a random sample of 500 press releases and 500 tweets from the complete universe of press releases and tweets in our data set after our coding procedure was finished. We then had two researchers blindly hand-code each sample. We compared our coding with the hand-coded/computer-assisted sample's coding.

Table A3 presents the results using several intercoder reliability measures. For the Twitter data, the two reviewers and the coder agreed in 99% of cases. This includes 99% agreement for cases in which a racial appeal was absent and 92% of cases where a Black-centered statement was present.

The Cohen's Kappa score was .89, indicating near-perfect agreement. There was a little less agreement among the press releases, but overall, the overlap in coding was still strong. The hand-coders and the computer agreed in 99% of cases. This includes 100% of cases in which a Black-centered appeal was absent between coder 1 and the computer and 99%

analysis in this book likely underestimates the link between descriptive and racial rhetorical representation.

between the computer and coder 2. It also includes about 67% of cases where a racial appeal was present for all parties. This led to a Cohen's Kappa score of .82, which is just above the .80 marker for near-perfect agreement. Both demonstrate that our iterative hand-coding and computer-coding process provided reliable results.

Brief Description of Coding Algorithms Used in RTextTools

In the preceding section, we mentioned that RTextTools used six different algorithms to code the different press releases and tweets. In this section, we briefly describe how each coding algorithm classifies different documents.

Support Vector Machine: The first algorithm used in our project is SVM. SVM uses a pre-coded set of data and uses a linear plane to separate language, in our case, into two categories. For our purposes, it identifies words and frequencies of words that distinguish Black-related outreach and non-Black-related outreach and creates a cut-off line between the two types of codes. Ideally, this line maximizes the difference between Black-related and non-Black-related communication. Uncoded press releases or tweets that contain words and frequent terms similar to those we hand-coded as 1 would be coded similarly based on the SVM algorithm. All others would be coded as zero.

Scaled Linear Discriminant Analysis: The second algorithm we estimate is SLDA. SLDA begins by taking groupings of press releases that have been coded as being Black-related or not. It then uses the term frequency in each class of documents to estimate a parameter that maximizes the distance between classes and minimizes the distance within classes. By doing so, it creates a cut-off that helps predict whether an uncoded press release or tweet (based on frequent terms in the document) is Black-related or not.

Bagging: The third algorithm, Bagging, is short for bootstrap aggregation analysis. The model takes a sample of the complete data set of press releases or tweets and uses the information in the trained data set to come up with a classification model. Bagging analysis does this several times to create different models to distinguish classes of press releases or tweets. Following the creation of these models, Bagging then classifies each press release or tweet across the different models. Finally, the models aggregate the average score for each press release or tweet and assign the code that the majority of the models agreed on.

Boosting: The fourth algorithm we use is boosting. Boosting uses the complete hand-coded data set and iteratively builds a more complete model. It begins with a simple decision tree using simple weighting to determine if it can model a successful prediction of the classification of the means of press releases and tweets in the sample better than at random. Following this procedure, it updates the weights it provides to each set of predictors iteratively until it creates a strong predictive model. Once it creates this model, boosting uses it to predict the presence or absence of Black outreach in texts.

Random Forest: The fifth algorithm that we use is random forests. The random forest algorithm creates a set of decision trees to classify texts. It does this by first taking a random set of words in the hand-coded press release or tweet and creating a probability that the inclusion of the words points to a Black-related appeal to be present or absent. Random forests sequentially examine a series of present or absent tests to determine if, ultimately, the uncoded press release or tweet should be placed in the Black-related category or not. For example, let's say a particular decision tree examined whether two terms were present (or two conditions were satisfied), which meant that the press release was Black-related. The two words are "Martin" and "King." If "Martin" is present in this randomly selected tree, it stays in the "satisfied" column for being Black-related. If not, it is removed from consideration. It then goes to the "King" test, and if the word is present, it is coded as Black-related; if not, it is coded as non-Black-related. Random forest creates a large number of decision trees by randomly sampling the hand-coded data and then randomly selecting variables (the presence of words) from the dataset. It then places each uncoded press release or tweet through these different decision trees, and the ultimate classification that comes up most often is the final code for the press release or tweet. So, if fifteen decision trees lead to a press release or tweet being Black-related and five do not, the ultimate code for the uncoded document would be Black-related.

Decision Tree: The final algorithm we use is decision tree classification, which is related to the random forest algorithm. While random forest randomly selects data and variables in creating its test, decision tree uses the complete corpus of hand-coded data and identifies distinguishing features. As its name implies, it then iteratively goes through a dichotomous true or false set of decisions until it arrives at a classification. The decision tree begins with words that best distinguish classes of text. For example, let's say the presence of the word "African-American" indicates 100% of the time that a press release or tweet was Black-related. This word would serve as the root or the first test. If a press release, for example, had the word "African-American" in it, it would be coded as being Black-related, and the tree would end. If it did not, it would go on to the next test. For example, let's say "slavery" scored high on distinguishing text but needed to be in combination with the words "south." If African-American was absent, it would then see if slavery was present in the press release. If it is present, it would then go on to look for the word "south." If "south" were in the text, it would code the press release as being Black-related. However, if "south" was not present, it might look for other combinations of words that appear with slavery that indicate being a Black-related text like "Douglass," "Abolition," or "13th." The tree would repeat itself through several nodes based on a combination of words to classify each uncoded press release. If enough "True's" are present, it would be coded as Black-related, and if not, it would be coded as non-Black-related.

CLASSIFYING DIFFERENT FORMS OF RACIAL RHETORICAL OUTREACH USING KEYWORD-ASSISTED TOPIC MODELING (CHAPTER 6)

In Chapter 6, we identify which elected officials speak about a greater variety of racial topics. We also explore which topics are the most common forms of racial outreach in press releases or on Twitter. To examine these relationships, we classified each Black-oriented press release or tweet into categories using keyword-assisted topic modeling (Eshima et al. 2024). Keyword-assisted topic modeling combines keywords provided by the researcher with information about the word structure of each document to classify the various press releases or tweets into different categories. To accomplish this goal, readers provide the computer with a set of keywords for each topic that they believe is relevant to that issue. Through our review of the corpus of press releases and tweets, we identified twenty-three distinct but commonly occurring categories in our press releases and twenty-two commonly occurring categories among our Twitter data.

We then selected the words that we thought best exemplified each category and distinguished them from others. This list of topics, along with the list of keywords we selected for each topic, can be found in Table 6.1 in Chapter 6. It should be noted that we use slightly different terms for some of the same categories across press releases and Twitter because of the different time frames under examination and restrictions on the number of characters on Twitter. For example, the acronym "VRA" is more common on Twitter because of word restrictions, whereas in press releases, members of Congress have more space to write out the words "Voting Rights Act."

While we identified numerous common themes, we could not be sure that our topics covered every frequently occurring form of racial outreach. As a result, we allowed the keyword-assisted topic modeling to find up to five additional categories in both the press releases and the tweets, which were not defined by us. Keyword-assisted topic modeling identifies new topics by accounting for the correlation and frequency of words in a document that are not strongly correlated with the keyword-defined topics. If there is a distribution of related words in these non-keyword-defined topics that are tied together, the algorithm classifies them as a new category. In some cases, the algorithm is successful in finding meaningful undefined topics; in others, it is not. In press releases, there was only a single additional category that had a coherent series of words among the five we asked the computer to identify. This previously undefined topic dealt with the shooting at the Emanuel AME Church in Charleston, SC, in 2015. On Twitter, we observed two additional meaningful categories from this process. The first was discussions about public meetings, such as town halls and virtual events, and the second expressed concerns about racial biases in facial recognition software.

Following this process, the selection of keywords and some common text preprocessing steps suggested by Eshima et al. (2024), keyword assisted topic modeling explores the presence, frequency, and correlation of keywords and non-keywords in each document and provide a probability, theta, that the document belongs to any of the keyword identified topics or non-keyword identified topics. For each document, keyword-assisted topic modeling provides the probability that the document belongs in any category, which ranges from 0% to 100%.

We anticipate that elected officials of different identities and partisanship may engage in racial outreach differently (Dietrich and Hayes 2023). As a result, we do not assume an even distribution of words across all documents. Instead, our keyword-assisted topic modeling conditions the distribution of probabilities based on whether the member of Congress is Black or not, or is a Democrat or not. As is the central premise of this book, we anticipate that Black elected officials may speak about race differently than others. Thus, it makes sense not to assume the distribution of words in each topic will be the same among African Americans and others. Similarly, we would expect that Democrats may speak about race differently than their Republican counterparts. For example, Democrats may criticize Trump for his actions stoking racial divisions in their outreach around the former president and race. In contrast, Republican elected officials may speak about low unemployment for people of color when connecting Trump's presidency to Black-oriented outreach. Given these differences, it is important to provide information to the algorithm about the source of the outreach so that it can more accurately assign each document to the correct topic.

We use this information to classify each document into a single category based on the highest probability for each document. For example, if a document received an 80 percent likelihood of being in the "Court" category, we gave a score of 1 to this variable. Similarly, if a document received a 35 percent probability of being in the "Civil Rights Movement" category and this probability was the highest in the row, it was given a score of 1 for the "Civil Rights Movement" topic. This makes it so that almost every document is given a single dichotomous score of 1, indicating that it is being placed in that category, and a score of 0 for all other categories, indicating the category is not the highest probability classification. It is possible that a document fits into none of the categories. In fact, about 2 percent of press releases and tweets did not fit into any of the specified categories and were given a score of 0 (or unclassified) for all of the categories in our analysis. The spread of these scores is displayed in Tables 6.2 and 6.3 in Chapter 6.

It is important to note that our classification of a document into a single category may miss the fact that a document can fit into multiple categories simultaneously. While we acknowledge this, for the sake of validation, we place them all in a single category and compare the computer's classification of a document to a human coder's classification of the same document. With that said, if we use probability (theta) cutoffs of 20, 30, or 40 percent, which would allow documents to be in multiple categories simultaneously, we arrive at the same substantive conclusions as presented in Chapter 6. The graphs of these cutoffs can be found in the Appendix. As a result, regardless of how we categorize each document, we arrive at the results.

As is true with other forms of computer-assisted content coding, it is imperative that researchers check the validity of the analysis (Grimmer and Stewart 2013, Ying, Montgomery, and Stewart 2021). The advantage of classifying each document into a single category based on its maximum probability is that we can compare whether a human would code the document in a similar manner to the keyword-assisted topic model. To accomplish this goal, a human coder independently coded

TABLE A4 *Intercoder Reliability Scores between Human Coders' Classification of Black Related Press Releases and Tweets and the Classification of Press Releases and Tweets by the Keyword-Assisted Topic Modeling Algorithm*

Platform	Human Coder	% Agreement	% Expected Agreement	Cohen's Kappa Score
Press Release	First Choice Only	60%	6%	0.57
Press Release	Both Choices	80%	6%	0.79
Twitter	First Choice Only	58%	8%	0.54
Twitter	Both Choices	76%	9%	0.73

200 tweets and 200 press releases and placed them into 1 of 23 press release categories and 1 of 24 Twitter categories. Given that each document can have multiple topics, we asked the human coder to place the document in their first or second choice category. The coder could also only select a single category if they did not believe the document fit into more than one category. Following this, we examined agreement by whether the human coder's first choice scored well against the computer coding score and whether either the human coder's first or second choice scored well against the computer coding score.

The results of this intercoder reliability analysis are presented in Table A4. The results suggest that when we only use the first choice, the Cohen's Kappa is below acceptable standards. However, when we use the first or second choice, the Cohen's Kappa scores are in the substantial agreement category, and for press releases, they are only one decimal off from being in the almost perfect agreement category. While not perfect, it appears that the keyword-assisted content coding is classifying the documents in a meaningful way, which would not be substantially different than what a human coder would do.

Appendix

CHAPTER 1

Codebook and Dictionary for Racial Press Releases
- For each Tweet/Press Release, you are going to code for the presence of a Black-Related Appeal or Not. Black-Related Appeals will be given a score of 1, and all other appeals will be given a score of 0. The example below has all zeroes because none of these tweets included a Black-Related Appeal.
- On the next page are the topics that are considered as being Black-Related Appeals and examples of each.
- While the list is comprehensive, it may miss a few topics. If there is anything you would suspect is a Black-Related Appeal, but is not on the list, just mention it in the notes, and we will take a look. For example, the first tweet in the dataset mentions police misconduct, which would likely fit under topic 6 below, but you may not be sure. When in doubt, just type in not sure.
- Beyond the general coding scheme, please be sure to consult the dictionary below. If a term is included and it is done in a way supportive of African Americans, give the tweet/press release a score of 1.

Key Themes

1. **Any discussion of addressing/expanding/or working to collect data on racial diversity**
   - "U.S. Representative Bobby L. Rush's (D-Ill.) Allied Health Workforce Diversity Act of 2019. The legislation passed by voice vote."
   - "Reps. Judy Chu (CA-27), Marc Veasey (TX-33), and Tony Cardenas (CA-29) introduced the PPP Data Diversity and Accountability Act of 2020."
   - "Right now, our country is facing an identity crisis—and the lack of diversity and inclusion in our communications sector only exacerbates the problem."

2. **Mentions of Civil Rights or Voting Rights Related to Race (This is based on the context of the Tweet, for example, Tweets about LBGTQIA+ that mention civil rights or Disability discrimination and civil rights should not be coded as 1)**
   - "Jeff Sessions actively undermined voting rights and civil rights."
   - "Your vote is your voice, and in too many states, including Pennsylvania, voter suppression laws and tactics have been used to try to silence people of color, low-income people, young people and senior citizens."
   - Today US Rep. Ron Kind sent a letter to Wisconsin Attorney General Schimel calling for him to investigate claims that the new voter ID law was designed specifically to block voters and violate Wisconsinites' constitutional rights.
   - In her first Judiciary Committee hearing, US Rep. Debbie Mucarsel-Powell (FL-26) focused her questioning on the importance of strengthening the Voting Rights Act (VRA) following the Supreme Court's 2013 decision to gut the preclearance mechanism of the VRA and the importance of implementing Amendment 4 in Florida.

3. **Any discussion condemning Hate Crimes, Racism, Bigotry, or Racial Discrimination or White Supremacy**
   - "H.R.3545, the National Opposition to Hate, Assaults, and Threats to Equality (NO HATE) Act Aims to Improve Hate Crime Reporting and Community Engagement."
   - "The bill proposes a comprehensive approach to ensure university officials are held accountable for hate crimes and hate-based incidents that occur on their campuses."

Appendix 231

- o "Civil Justice Subcommittee Ranking Member Steve Cohen (D-TN) sent a letter to Chairman Bob Goodlatte (R-VA) calling for emergency hearings on hate crimes and domestic terrorism in the wake of recent killings by individuals with white supremacist views."
- o "Bigotry, anti-Semitism, and xenophobia should have no place in our society, and they certainly have no place in the White House.
- o "Congresswoman Barbara Lee Rips Congressman Steve King's "Perverse Worldview" Calls on Speaker to Reprimand Hateful Rhetoric Washington DC Congresswoman Barbara Lee released the following statement on Congressman Steve King's most recent racist comments."
4. **Recognition of Black People or Bills/Legislation Named After Black People (This can be tricky because not all names are of well-known people. Google the names of people you do not know).**
    - o "Historic moment makes first woman of color vice president-elect – Congressman Cohen (TN-09) is pleased to see that Joe Biden and Kamala Harris have won the required Electoral College votes to become President and Vice President, and made the following statement:"
    - o "David Price (NC-04), Alma S. Adams (NC-12), and G. K. Butterfield (NC-01) today sent a letter urging North Carolina's two U.S. Senators to support Loretta Lynch, who is a North Carolina native, in her nomination for U.S. Attorney General."
    - o On Chuck Brown's birthday, the office of Congresswoman Eleanor Holmes Norton (D-DC) today announced that Norton will introduce a resolution designating his birthday, August 22, as "Chuck Brown Dayï" in the District of Columbia and across the nation in honor of his contributions as the Godfather of Go-Go.
    - o "I am deeply saddened by the news and untimely passing of Congressman Elijah Cummings and extend my sincerest condolences to his entire family, friends and his constituents,"
    - o "Congresswoman Eleanor Holmes Norton (D-DC) introduced the Frederick Douglass Bicentennial Commission Act."
5. **Recognition of Black Holidays such as Juneteenth or MLK Day**
    - o "Congresswoman Eddie Bernice Johnson today released the following statement marking the 55th anniversary of the Rev. Dr. Martin Luther King."

- "Today, Congresswoman Doris Matsui (D-CA) and Congressman David Price (D-NC), Co-Chairs of the National Service Caucus, called on communities across the country to observe the Martin Luther King National Day of Service on Monday, January 18th by giving back through hands-on service programs."

6. **Anything Related to Black Lives Matter or Police Violence Against People of Color**
    - "Following the shooting, the Hoover Police Department mistakenly claimed EJ Bradford had fired shots at the mall, injuring two other people."
    - "Since the tragic death of George Floyd, millions of Americans have sought to exercise their First Amendment rights to protest and assemble."
    - "Speaker Nancy Pelosi participated in an interview with George Stephanopoulos for ABC's This Week to discuss the response to the killing of George Floyd, The Heroes Act…"
    - "Congresswoman Alma Adams (NC-12) released the following statement after the decision not to file charges in the shooting death of Keith Lamont Scott."
    - "Thank you, Mr. Chairman. And thank you for moving quickly to hold this necessary hearing during a time of significant pain for our nation. And I want to recognize and thank Congresswoman Bass for her leadership in healing that pain. The 'Justice in Policing Act' I"

7. **Discussions of Criminal Justice Reform**
    - "Norton has spent her career pursuing criminal justice reform."
    - "Congressman Johnson Continues His Critical Work on Criminal Justice Reform."
    - "As a lifelong civil rights advocate and a leader in the fight for criminal justice reform, I believe."

8. **Anything Issue Tied to Minorities/African Americans/Blacks/ Communities of Color/Underrepresented Groups, Etc…**
    - "Edwards Congratulates Maryland Office of Minority Health and Health Disparities on Grant Award Edwards."
    - "Co-Director of the Data Science Initiative at Harvard University to explore recent research developments and needs for further studies to understand the links between air pollution exposure and impacts of COVID-19, especially in low-income and minority communities."

- "Department of Commerce's decision to add a citizenship question to the 2020 census as simply conceding to a Department of Justice request to include the citizenship status question in order to reduce response rates from immigrant residents and Americans of color."
- The 21st Century STEM for Girls and Underrepresented Minorities Act, H.R. 2773, would eliminate barriers for girls and historically underrepresented minorities in the early stages of their education.

9. **Discussion of Reparations or Affirmative Action or Slavery (Including the 13th, 14th, and 15th Amendments and the taking down of the Confederate symbols)**
    - Congressman Charles B. Rangel released the following statement to honor the life of Middle Passage and his commitment to fighting for justice and freedom for all.
    - The US post office here in the birthplace of Thaddeus Stevens was renamed today to honor the Civil War-era congressman's pivotal role in the movement to abolish slavery.
    - Congressman Charles B. Rangel, who represents the 13th Congressional District of New York that includes upper Manhattan and parts of the Bronx, released the following statement on the removal of the Confederate Flag from the South Carolina Statehouse.
    - "In short, the Commission aims to study the impact of slavery and continuing discrimination against African-Americans, resulting directly and indirectly from slavery to segregation to the desegregation process and the present day. The commission would also make recommendations concerning any form of apology and compensation to begin the long delayed process of atonement for slavery."

10. **Recognition of People or Important Moments in the Civil Rights Movement**
    - "Today, on the 63rd anniversary of the Brown v. Board of Education decision, Congresswoman Alma Adams (NC-12) joined House Democrats in introducing the Rebuild America's Schools Act of 2017."
    - "to assist in lifting the hold placed on their bill that would expand the historic site at Little Rock Central High School, the site of integration by the Little Rock Nine 60 years ago"

- "MEMPHIS – Congressman Steve Cohen (TN-09) today celebrated the life and legacy of the Reverend Joseph Lowery, a founder of the Southern Christian Leadership Conference and longtime Civil Rights leader, who died Friday in Atlanta at the age of 98."
11. **Mentions of HBCUs or Minority Serving Institutions**
    - "Dr. Quinton T. Ross, Jr. Congresswoman Terri A. Sewell (D-AL) releases the following statement: "I'm thrilled to join the entire Alabama State University family as they induct Dr. Quinton T. Ross Jr. as the 15th president of ASU.""
    - "Hoyer Attends Morgan State University's Southern Maryland Alumni Chapter Dinner September 12, 2015 WALDORF, MD – Congressman Steny H. Hoyer (MD-5) tonight attended and delivered brief remarks at Morgan State University's Southern Maryland Alumni Chapter"
    - "Last week, 47 private partners, HBCU leaders and Members of Congress convened to discuss the importance of HBCUs using technology to create a more just and equitable society," said Congresswoman Alma Adams (NC-12), founder and Co-Chair of the Congressional Bipartisan HBCU Caucus."
12. **Racial Targeted Shootings of Blacks, Like in Buffalo or Charleston**
    - "Just days before the anniversaries of the massacres at Pulse Nightclub in Orlando and Emanuel AME Church in Charleston,"
    - "As we experienced during the massacre at Mother Emanuel AME Church in Charleston, South Carolina, these execution-style shootings are especially horrific when the gunman."
13. **Any Mentions of Black Organizations Like the NAACP or the Congressional Black Caucus**
    - "Speaker Nancy Pelosi spoke to the National Association for the Advancement of Colored People (NAACP). Below are the Speaker's remarks:"
    - "Unveiled the Mothers and Offspring Mortality & Morbidity Awareness (MOMMA) Act to Reverse America's Rising Maternal Mortality Rate Washington, DC Today, Congresswoman Robin Kelly, chair of the Congressional Black Caucus Health Braintrust."
14. **Sickle Cell Anemia**
    - "Barbara Lee and Terri Sewell lead letter to Speaker Pelosi and Minority Leader McCarthy calling for the Centers for Medicare

and Medicaid Services (CMS) to quickly develop a program for Medicare/Medicaid and Medicaid beneficiaries to improve access to comprehensive outpatient care for individuals with sickle cell disease."
15. **Black-Owned Businesses or Banks**
    o "H.R. 5315 would codify the U.S. Department of Treasury's Financial Agent Mentor-Protégé Program that helps pair minority-owned banks with financial agents to expand business and consumer products"

Black-Centered Dictionary

(All Terms in Lower Case)

diverse	james earl chaney	Bloody Sunday
diversity	andrew goodman	Fair Housing Act of 1968
african-american	michael henry schwerner	Greensboro Sit-In
african american	w.e.b. du bois	Freedom Summer
underrepresented minorities	sojourner truth	Freedom Rides
underrepresented group	marcus garvey	Executive Order 9981
black	booker t. washington	reparations
minority	jackie robinson	affirmative action
minorities	barbara jordan	fisher v. university of texas
people of color	jesse jackson	regents of the university of california v. bakke (1978)
race	ruby bridges	grutter v. bollinger (2003)
racial	a. philip randolph	Civil Rights
communities of color	james meredith	Montgomery Bus Boycott
woman of color	fred shuttlesworth	Little Rock Nine
men of color	ralph abernathy	Selma
students of color	james farmer	Freedom Riders
john lewis	bayard rustin	Sixteenth Street Baptist Church
nelson mandela	desmond tutu	Loving v. Virginia
elijah cummings	dick gregory	Jim Crow
loretta lynch	huey newton	Brown v. Board of Education
violet henderson	tarana burke	March on Washington

(continued)

(continued)

nancy wilson	shirley chisholm	I Have a Dream
aretha franklin	ida b. wells	Bloody Sunday
ej jackson	mary church terrell	Fair Housing Act of 1968
thurgood marshall	ella baker	Greensboro Sit-In
bobbie daggs jones	diane nash	Freedom Summer
russell b. sugarmon	dorothy height	Freedom Rides
frederick douglass	ezell blair jr	Executive Order 9981
martin luther king	david richmond	racism
malcolm x	franklin mccain	racist
chuck brown	joseph mcneil	discrim
harriet tubman	dred scott	systematic inequality
ron dellums	juneteenth	racial inequality
joseph lowery	black history month	bigot
peggy cooper cafritz	martin luther king jr. day	ku klux klan
rosa parks	mlk day	racist
marian spencer	reparations	neo-nazis
julian bond	affirmative action	alt-right
ralph fertig	fisher v. university of texas	confederate flag
muhammad ali	regents of the university of california v. bakke (1978)	white supremacy
prince rogers nelson	grutter v. bollinger (2003)	white nationalism
maya angelou	Civil Rights	white nationalist
bb king	Montgomery Bus Boycott	confederate monuments
gwen ifill	Little Rock Nine	Kamala Harris
chuck berry	Selma	voter id
winnie mandela	Freedom Riders	voting rights
toni morrison	Sixteenth Street Baptist Church	voter suppression
kobe bryant	Loving v. Virginia	voter disenfranchisement
little richard	Jim Crow	shelby county v. holder
chadwick boseman	Brown v. Board of Education	souls to the polls
emmett till	March on Washington	voter intimidation
medgar evers	I Have a Dream	racial gerrymandering
create a respectful and open world for natural hair	congressional black caucus	alabama a&m university
crown act	cbc	alabama state university
(crown) act	minority depository institutions	albany state university

justice in policing act	naacp	alcorn state university
police reform	sncc	allen university
police accountability	rainbow/push coalition	american baptist college
george floyd	niagara movement	arkansas at pine bluff, university of
sandra bland	national urban league	arkansas baptist college
law enforcement accountability	minority science and engineering improvement program	barber-scotia college**
trayvon martin	minority-owned	benedict college
george zimmerman	southern christian leadership conference	bennett college
James Byrd	student non-violent coordinating committee	bethune-cookman university
criminal justice	tuskegee airman	bishop state community college
eric garner	tuskegee experiment	bluefield state college
breonna taylor	minority aids initiative	bowie state university
alton sterling	minority business	carver college
philando castile	the devine nine	central state university
police reform	Alpha Phi Alpha	cheyney university of pennsylvania
choke-holds	Alpha Kappa Alpha	claflin university
de-escalation	Kappa Alpha Psi	clark atlanta university
deescalation	Omega Psi Phi	clinton college
chokeholds	Delta Sigma Theta	coahoma community college
tyre king	Phi Beta Sigma	concordia college, alabama (closed 2018)
ferguson	Zeta Phi Beta	coppin state university
michael brown	Sigma Gamma Rho	delaware state university
emanuel ame church	Iota Phi Theta	denmark technical college
patrisse cullors	middle passage	dillard university
alicia garza	slave	district of columbia, university of the
opal tometi	13th amendment	edward waters university
sayhername	14th amendment	elizabeth city state university
black lives matter	15th amendment	fayetteville state university

(continued)

(continued)

blacklivesmatter	abolition	fisk university
movement for black lives	lynching	florida a&m university
m4bl	disarm hate act	florida memorial university
dashboard camera	no hate act	fort valley state university
body camera	hate crime	gadsden state community college (valley street campus)
police killing	walter scott	grambling state university
police murder	walter wallace jr.	hampton university
police brutality	alvin cole	harris-stowe state university
racialprofiling	andrew brown jr.	hinds community college at utica
excessive use of force	andrew loku	hood theological *
aaron bailey	aura rosser	howard university
akai gurley	david jones	huston-tillotson university
alex nieto	de'von bailey	interdenominational theological center
anthony hill	ezell ford	j. f. drake state technical college
an'twan gilmore	ma'khia bryant	jackson state university
botham jean	tony robinson	jarvis christian college
carnell snell jr.	antwon rose	johnson c. smith university
casey goodson jr.	elijah mcclain	johnson c smith theological seminary
chad washington	harith augustus	kentucky state university
colby friday	patrick lyoya	knoxville college
dana fletcher	daniel prude	lane college
darell richards	deon kay	langston university
darrius stewart	rayshard brooks	lawson state community college
dravon ames	amir locke	lemoyne-owen college
sean reed	colin kaepernick	lewis college of business
isak aden	philando castile	the lincoln university
jamarion robinson	stephanie washington	lincoln university
jerame reid	terence crutcher	livingstone college
john elliott neville	ahmaud arbery	maryland eastern shore
jordan edwards	atatiana jefferson	meharry medical college

joshua beal	dontre hamilton	miles college
jérémie meli	sam dubose	miles school of law *
kendra james	sandra bland	mississippi valley state university
kevin matthews	keith lamont scott	morehouse college
kevin peterson jr.	tamir rice	morehouse school of medicine
kiwi herring	daunte wright	morgan state university
marcus golden	jamar clark	morris brown college
mario woods	jacob blake	morris college
miles jackson	freddie gray	norfolk state university
pamela turner	emanuel nine	north carolina a&t state university
redel jones	laquan mcdonald	north carolina central university
rekia boyd	anthony lamar smith	oakwood university
roshad mcintosh	stephon clark	paine college
shanita maeberry	eric garner	paul quinn college
sha'teina grady el	alton sterling	payne theological
ta'neasha chappell	breonna taylor	philander smith college
tony mcdade	michael brown	prairie view a&m university
tyre king	jonathan ferrell	rust college
zoe dowdell	markeis mcglockton	saint paul's college
z'kye husain	nia wilson	savannah state university
adriene ludd	paul o'neal	selma university
anthony mcclain	rashad cunningham	shaw university
bradley blackshire	ricky price	shelton state community college- c a fredd campus
chikesia clemons	ronald johnson	shorter college
corey mobley	thurman blevins	simmons college of kentucky
deborah danner	trayvon martin	south carolina state university
dion johnson	daniel hambrick	southern university at new orleans
earl mcneil	decynthia clements	southern university at shreveport
edson thevenin	dijon kizzee	southern university and a&m college

(continued)

(continued)

emantic fitzgerald bradford jr.	donte shannon	southwestern christian college
eric logan	john crawford iii	spelman college
jameek lowery	osaze osagie	st. augustine's university
james scurlock	virginia university of lynchburg	st. philip's college
jason walker	voorhees university	stillman college
jemel roberson	west virginia state university	talladega college
jeremy mcdole	wilberforce university	tennessee state university
h. councill trenholm state	wiley college	texas college
tuskegee university	winston-salem state university	texas southern university
virgin islands, university of the	xavier university of louisiana	tougaloo college
virginia state university	virginia union university	national urban league
underrepresented group		

CHAPTER 3

TABLE 3.1A *OLS Regression Predicting Percent of Black-Centered Press Releases and Tweet for Members of Congress*

	Black Outreach Press Releases	Black Outreach Twitter
Black Rep	0.0784***	0.0218***
	(0.0107)	(0.00788)
Latino/a Rep	0.00618**	0.00272
	(0.00288)	(0.00407)
Asian Am Rep	0.000479	0.00494
	(0.00524)	(0.00954)
Female Rep	0.00929**	0.00645*
	(0.00360)	(0.00328)
Democrat Rep	0.00974***	0.0275***
	(0.00211)	(0.00226)
Age of Rep	0.000163	3.61e-05
	(0.000107)	(0.000116)
HBCU	0.0121	0.0207*
	(0.0216)	(0.0117)
Ivy	0.00357	0.00139
	(0.00442)	(0.00544)

	Black Outreach Press Releases	Black Outreach Twitter
Public College	-0.00129	-0.00138
	(0.00198)	(0.00231)
Percent Black in District	0.000892***	0.000211
	(0.000178)	(0.000156)
Cook's PVI	0.000264***	0.000712***
	(9.41e-05)	(0.000184)
115th Congress	-0.00706***	
	(0.00179)	
116th Congress	0.00481*	
	(0.00264)	
Constant	-0.0104	-0.00333
	(0.00667)	(0.00655)
Number of Congress Members	1,201	421
R-squared	0.636	0.567

*** $p<0.01$, ** $p<0.05$, * $p<0.1$. Standard Errors Clustered for Member of Congress

CHAPTER 4

TABLE 4.1A *OLS Regression Predicting the Proportion of High-Profile Racial Outreach of All Racial Outreach by Race of Elected Official*

	Proportion of High-Profile Racial Outreach	
	Press Release	Twitter
Black	-0.15***	-0.08**
	(0.05)	(0.04)
Latino	-0.11**	-0.01
	(0.04)	(0.03)
Asian American	-0.03	-0.01
	(0.07)	(0.05)
Female	-0.02	-0.02
	(0.03)	(0.02)
Democrat	0.01	-0.04*
	(0.03)	(0.02)
Age	0.00	0.00*
	(0.00)	(0.00)
Percent Black in District	0.00	-0.00
	(0.00)	(0.00)
Cook's PVI	-0.00	-0.00
	(0.00)	(0.00)
115th Congress	0.00	
	(0.03)	

(continued)

TABLE 4.1A (*continued*)

	Proportion of High-Profile Racial Outreach	
	Press Release	Twitter
116th Congress	0.06* (0.03)	
Constant	0.66*** (0.07)	0.48*** (0.05)
Observations	736	389
R-squared	0.04	0.07

*** $p<0.01$, ** $p<0.05$, * $p<0.1$ Clustered Standard Errors in Parenthesis

TABLE 4.2A *Black Lives Matter Dictionary*

Justice Act	Philando Castile	Body Camera	Colby Friday
Justice In Policing Act	Deescalation	Police Killing	Dan Fletcher
Police Reform	Chokeholds	Police Murder	Darell Richards
Police Accountability	Tyre King	Police Brutality	Darrius Stewart
George Floyd	Ferguson	Racial profiling	Dravon Ames
Sandra Bland	Michael Brown	Excessive Use Of Force	Sean Reed
Law Enforcement Accountability	Emanuel Ame Church	Aaron Bailey	Isak Aden
Trayvon Martin	Patrisse Cullors	Akai Gurley	Jamarion Robinson
George Zimmerman	Alicia Garza	Alex Nieto	Jerame Reid
James Byrd	Opal Tometi	Anthony Hill	John Elliott Neville
Criminal Justice	Sayhername	An'Twan Gilmore	Jordan Edwards
Eric Garner	Black Lives Matter	Botham Jean	Joshua Beal
Breonna Taylor	Blacklivesmatter	Carnell Snell Jr.	Jérémie Meli
Alton Sterling	Movement For Black Lives	Casey Goodson Jr.	Kendra James
M4Bl	Dashboard Camera	Chad Washington	Kevin Matthews
Daniel Prude	Stephanie Washington	Keith Lamont Scott	Freddie Gray
Deon Kay	Terence Crutcher	Tamir Rice	Emanuel Nine
Rayshard Brooks	Ahmaud Arbery	Daunte Wright	Laquan Mcdonald
Amir Locke	Atatiana Jefferson	Jamar Clark	Anthony Smith
Colin Kaepernick	Dontre Hamilton	Jacob Blake	Stephon Clark
Sam Dubose	Adriene Ludd	Jeremy Mcdole	Walter Scott
Kevin Peterson Jr.	Anthony Mcclain	Jonathan Ferrell	Walter Wallace Jr.

Kiwi Herring	Bradley Blackshire	Markeis Mcglockton	Alvin Cole
Marcus Golden	Chikesia Clemons	Nia Wilson	Andrew Brown Jr.
Mario Woods	Corey Mobley	Paul O'Neal	Andrew Loku
Miles Jackson	Deborah Danner	Rashad Cunningham	Aura Rosser
Pamela Turner	Dion Johnson	Ricky Price	David Jones
Redel Jones	Earl Mcneil	Ronald Johnson	De'Von Bailey
Rekia Boyd	Edson Thevenin	Thurman Blevins	Ezell Ford
Roshad Mcintosh	Emantic Bradford Jr.	Daniel Hambrick	Ma'Khia Bryant
Shanita Maeberry	Eric Logan	Decynthia Clements	Tony Robinson
Sha'Teina Grady El	Jameek Lowery	Dijon Kizzee	Antwon Rose
Ta'Neasha Chappell	James Scurlock	Donte Shannon	Elijah Mcclain
Tony Mcdade	Jason Walker	John Crawford Iii	Harith Augustus
Zoe Dowdell	Jemel Roberson	Osaze Osagie	Patrick Lyoya
Z'Kye Husain			

CHAPTER 5

TABLE 5.1A *OLS Regression Predicting the Percent of Press Releases from the 114th, 115th, and 116th Congress Which Include Mentions of Uncrystallized Black Issues.*

	% Uncrystallized
Black Rep	0.0138***
	(0.00157)
Latino Rep	0.00170
	(0.00141)
AAPI Rep	-0.00110
	(0.00208)
Female	0.00215**
	(0.000916)
Democrat	0.00145
	(0.00101)
Age	-2.15e-05

(continued)

TABLE 5.1A *(continued)*

	% Uncrystallized
Percent Black in District	0.000106***
	(3.62e-05)
Cook's PVI	1.03e-05
	(3.72e-05)
115th Congress	0.00107
	(3.92e-05)
116th Congress	0.00692***
	(0.00103)
Constant	-0.00196
	(0.000999)
	(0.00233)
Observations	734
R-squared	0.350

*** $p<0.01$, ** $p<0.05$, * $p<0.1$. Standard Errors Clustered for Member of Congress

TABLE 5.2A *OLS Regression Predicting the Percent of Black-Centered Appeals Among COVID-19 Related Press Releases in the First Six Months of the Pandemic*

	Press Releases	Twitter
Black Rep	0.0267***	0.0334***
	(0.00810)	(0.00658)
Latino Rep	-0.00380	0.00516
	(0.00695)	(0.00577)
AAPI Rep	-0.0171	0.0121
	(0.0106)	(0.00867)
Female	-0.00201	0.00978***
	(0.00483)	(0.00376)
Democrat	0.0185***	-0.00808
	(0.00460)	(0.00509)
Age	-0.000191	6.35e-05
	(0.000174)	(0.000134)
Percent Black in District	0.000467**	2.89e-05
	(0.000192)	(0.000154)
Cook's PVI	0.000620***	-0.001000***
	(0.000238)	(0.000173)
Constant	0.000387	0.0129
	(0.00974)	(0.00897)

	Press Releases	Twitter
Observations	386	398
R-squared	0.239	0.379

*** p<0.01, ** p<0.05, * p<0.1. Standard Errors Clustered for Member of Congress

CHAPTER 6

TABLE 6.1A *Negative Binomial Regression Predicting the Number of Black-Centered Topics Members of Congress Put Out via Press Releases and Twitter*

	Number of Black Focused Topics	
	Press Releases	Twitter
Black Rep	0.606***	0.0741
	(0.0689)	(0.0650)
Latino Rep	-0.0563	0.0457
	(0.0806)	(0.0586)
Asian Am Rep	-0.107	0.107
	(0.116)	(0.0827)
Female Rep	0.155***	0.109***
	(0.0493)	(0.0384)
Democrat Rep	0.402***	0.701***
	(0.0847)	(0.0636)
Age of Rep	0.00179	-0.000999
	(0.00206)	(0.00148)
Percent Black in District	0.00323*	0.00288*
	(0.00189)	(0.00161)
Cook's PVI	0.0151***	0.00794***
	(0.00251)	(0.00200)
115th Congress	-0.237***	
	(0.0736)	
116th Congress	0.162**	
	(0.0650)	
LN Alpha	-2.617***	-4.459***
	(0.226)	(0.700)
Constant	0.448***	1.791***
	(0.142)	(0.0985)
Observations	741	390

*** p<0.01, ** p<0.05, * p<0.1 Clustered Standard Errors in Parenthesis

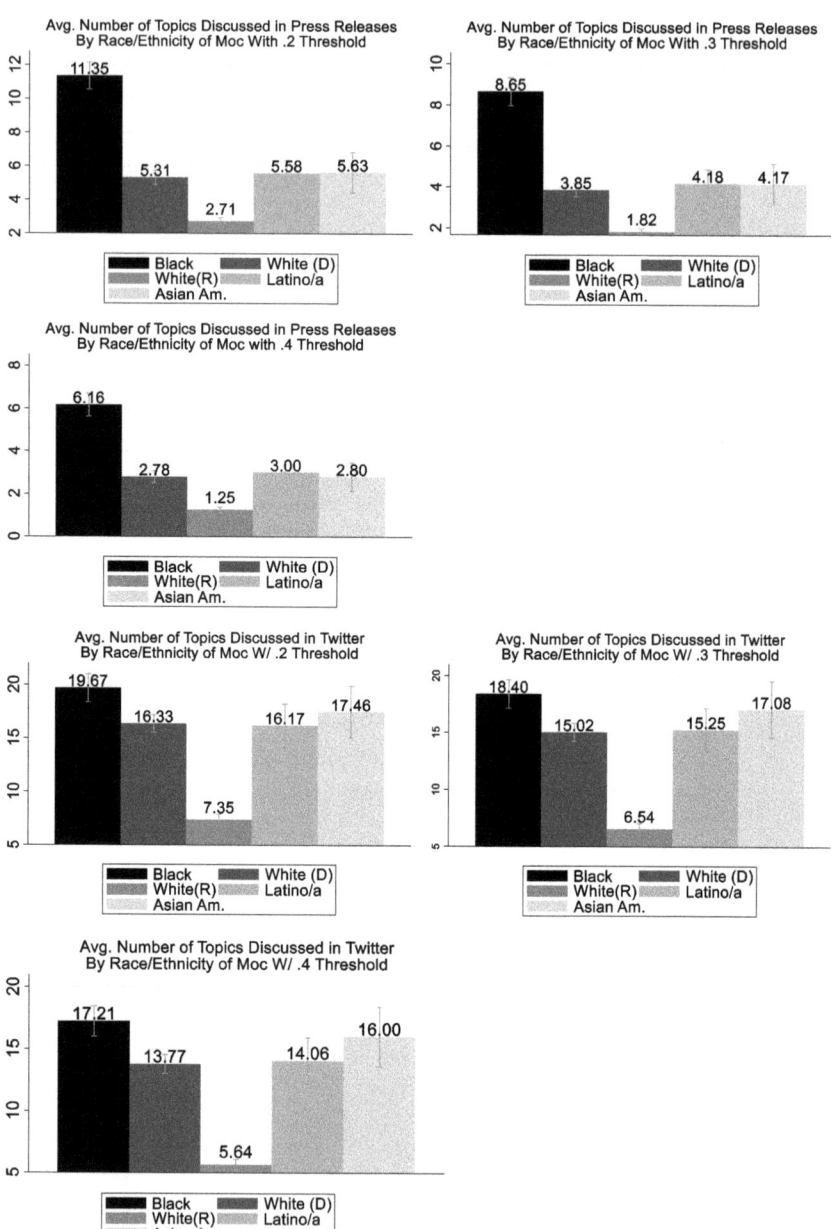

FIGURE 6.1A Replication of the Results in Chapter 6 Using Different Theta Thresholds Rather than Classifying Texts into a Singly Category

Appendix 247

CHAPTER 7

TABLE 7.1A *OLS Regression Predicting Primary Sponsorship of Black-Centered Legislation, Co-Sponsorship of Black-Centered Legislation, Black-Centered Hearing Statements and LCCR Scores by the Percent of All Black Appeals in Press Releases*

	Primary Spons	Co-Spons.	Hearing Statements	LCCR Score
% Black Appeal	0.00106**	0.000601***	0.000954***	0.00696***
	(0.000455)	(8.13e-05)	(0.000143)	(0.00194)
Black Rep	0.0703***	0.0424***	0.00738*	0.169***
	(0.0128)	(0.00282)	(0.00429)	(0.0575)
Latino Rep	0.00550	0.0104***	0.00642*	0.214***
	(0.00516)	(0.00229)	(0.00345)	(0.0476)
AAPI Rep	0.0147**	0.0155***	0.00160	0.358***
	(0.00723)	(0.00371)	(0.00532)	(0.0484)
Female Rep	0.00195	0.00661***	0.00276	0.177***
	(0.00454)	(0.00152)	(0.00214)	(0.0354)
Age	0.000392***	0.000135**	-9.15e-06	0.00293**
	(0.000146)	(5.49e-05)	(7.78e-05)	(0.00127)
Percent Black in District	0.00108***	0.000456***	5.71e-05	-0.00179
	(0.000231)	(6.00e-05)	(8.42e-05)	(0.00133)
Cook's PVI	7.15e-05	0.000390***	5.72e-05	0.0130***
	(0.000119)	(4.56e-05)	(6.78e-05)	(0.000888)
Constant	-0.0220***	0.0150***	0.00121	0.163**
	(0.00845)	(0.00323)	(0.00473)	(0.0758)
Observations	1,247	1,247	431	1,246
R-squared	0.394	0.631	0.283	0.455

*** $p<0.01$, ** $p<0.05$, * $p<0.1$ Clustered Standard Errors in Parenthesis

TABLE 7.2A *OLS Regression Predicting Primary Sponsorship of Black-Centered Legislation, Co-Sponsorship of Black-Centered Legislation, Black-Centered Hearing Statements and LCCR Scores by the Percent of High-Profile Black Appeals in Press Releases*

	Primary Spons.	Co-Spons.	Hearing Statements	LCCR Score
% High Profile Black Appeal	0.331**	0.230***	0.105***	1.229***
	(0.152)	(0.0826)	(0.0313)	(0.443)

(continued)

TABLE 7.2A (continued)

	Primary Spons.	Co-Spons.	Hearing Statements	LCCR Score
Black Rep	0.0686***	0.0399***	0.00990**	0.191***
	(0.0126)	(0.00418)	(0.00457)	(0.0606)
Latino Rep	0.00560	0.0104***	0.00715**	0.216***
	(0.00518)	(0.00240)	(0.00358)	(0.0477)
AAPI Rep	0.0140**	0.0150***	0.00245	0.356***
	(0.00711)	(0.00306)	(0.00552)	(0.0493)
Female Rep	0.00387	0.00751***	0.00463**	0.194***
	(0.00485)	(0.00171)	(0.00220)	(0.0352)
Age	0.000405***	0.000139**	2.15e-05	0.00308**
	(0.000149)	(6.67e-05)	(8.06e-05)	(0.00127)
Percent Black in District	0.00103***	0.000413***	9.56e-05	-0.00172
	(0.000226)	(8.00e-05)	(8.72e-05)	(0.00134)
Cook's PVI	0.000101	0.000395***	0.000131*	0.0135***
	(0.000113)	(5.12e-05)	(6.91e-05)	(0.000896)
Constant	-0.0224***	0.0149***	-0.000107	0.158**
	(0.00862)	(0.00410)	(0.00490)	(0.0760)
Observations	1,247	1,247	431	1,246
R-squared	0.394	0.638	0.228	0.447

*** p<0.01, ** p<0.05, * p<0.1 Clustered Standard Errors in Parenthesis

TABLE 7.3A *OLS Regression Predicting Primary Sponsorship of Black-Centered Legislation, Co-Sponsorship of Black-Centered Legislation, Black-Centered Hearing Statements and LCCR Scores by the Percent of Low-Profile Black Appeals in Press Releases*

	Primary Spons.	Co-Spons.	Hearing Statements	LCCR Score
% Low Profile Black Appeal	0.743***	0.259***	0.244***	2.114***
	(0.180)	(0.0551)	(0.0480)	(0.561)
Black Rep	0.0484***	0.0370***	0.00599	0.144**
	(0.0121)	(0.00423)	(0.00459)	(0.0630)
Latino Rep	0.00369	0.00994***	0.00676*	0.211***
	(0.00487)	(0.00225)	(0.00352)	(0.0472)
AAPI Rep	0.0144**	0.0153***	0.00164	0.358***
	(0.00649)	(0.00283)	(0.00543)	(0.0478)
Female Rep	0.00153	0.00720***	0.00432**	0.189***
	(0.00452)	(0.00175)	(0.00216)	(0.0354)
Age	0.000386***	0.000140**	-5.90e-06	0.00305**
	(0.000145)	(6.86e-05)	(7.94e-05)	(0.00127)

	Primary Spons.	Co-Spons.	Hearing Statements	LCCR Score
Percent Black in District	0.000940***	0.000427***	5.26e-05	-0.00187
	(0.000212)	(8.17e-05)	(8.66e-05)	(0.00133)
Cook's PVI	7.20e-06	0.000394***	9.10e-05	0.0133***
	(0.000101)	(4.66e-05)	(6.87e-05)	(0.000891)
Constant	-0.0211***	0.0151***	0.00138	0.161**
	(0.00812)	(0.00422)	(0.00483)	(0.0758)
Observations	1,247	1,247	431	1,246
R-squared	0.426	0.636	0.253	0.452

*** p<0.01, ** p<0.05, * p<0.1 Clustered Standard Errors in Parenthesis

TABLE 7.4A *OLS Regression Predicting Primary Sponsorship of Black-Centered Legislation, Co-Sponsorship of Black-Centered Legislation, Black-Centered Hearing Statements and LCCR Scores by the Percent of All Black Appeals in Tweets*

	Primary Spons.	Co-Spons.	LCCR Score
% Black Appeal	0.230**	0.449***	7.585***
	(0.105)	(0.0377)	(0.668)
Black Rep	0.0509***	0.0369***	0.172**
	(0.0116)	(0.00415)	(0.0737)
Latino Rep	-0.000442	0.0142***	0.291***
	(0.00919)	(0.00330)	(0.0586)
AAPI Rep	-0.00307	0.0137***	0.335***
	(0.0147)	(0.00528)	(0.0937)
Female Rep	0.00553	0.00977***	0.206***
	(0.00641)	(0.00230)	(0.0408)
Age	0.000197	0.000249***	0.00364**
	(0.000234)	(8.40e-05)	(0.00149)
Percent Black in District	0.00106***	0.000472***	-0.000675
	(0.000260)	(9.36e-05)	(0.00166)
Cook's PVI	6.40e-05	-0.000275**	-0.0133***
	(0.000318)	(0.000114)	(0.00203)
Constant	-0.0112	0.00821*	0.208**
	(0.0131)	(0.00471)	(0.0834)
Observations	422	422	422
R-squared	0.313	0.715	0.486

*** p<0.01, ** p<0.05, * p<0.1 Clustered Standard Errors in Parenthesis

TABLE 7.5A *OLS Regression Predicting Primary Sponsorship of Black-Centered Legislation, Co-Sponsorship of Black-Centered Legislation, Black-Centered Hearing Statements and LCCR Scores by the Percent of High-Profile Black Appeals in Tweets*

	Primary Spons.	Co-Spons.	LCCR Score
% High Profile Black Appeal	0.428**	0.849***	14.94***
	(0.215)	(0.0790)	(1.382)
Black Rep	0.0544***	0.0436***	0.277***
	(0.0112)	(0.00411)	(0.0719)
Latino Rep	0.000574	0.0161***	0.320***
	(0.00915)	(0.00337)	(0.0589)
AAPI Rep	−0.00255	0.0146***	0.345***
	(0.0147)	(0.00541)	(0.0947)
Female Rep	0.00643	0.0114***	0.231***
	(0.00635)	(0.00233)	(0.0409)
Age	0.000188	0.000228***	0.00319**
	(0.000235)	(8.64e-05)	(0.00151)
Percent Black in District	0.00107***	0.000501***	−0.000272
	(0.000260)	(9.57e-05)	(0.00168)
Cook's PVI	0.000106	−0.000194*	−0.0120***
	(0.000317)	(0.000116)	(0.00204)
Constant	−0.0113	0.00818*	0.208**
	(0.0131)	(0.00482)	(0.0844)
Observations	422	422	422
R-squared	0.312	0.700	0.474

*** $p<0.01$, ** $p<0.05$, * $p<0.1$ Clustered Standard Errors in Parenthesis

TABLE 7.6A *OLS Regression Predicting Primary Sponsorship of Black-Centered Legislation, Co-Sponsorship of Black-Centered Legislation, Black-Centered Hearing Statements and LCCR Scores by the Percent of Low-Profile Black Appeals in Tweets*

	Primary Spons.	Co-Spons.	LCCR Score
% Low Profile Black Appeal	0.357**	0.687***	11.22***
	(0.175)	(0.0646)	(1.153)
Black Rep	0.0505***	0.0364***	0.174**
	(0.0118)	(0.00434)	(0.0774)
Latino Rep	−0.000351	0.0144***	0.299***
	(0.00921)	(0.00340)	(0.0606)
AAPI Rep	−0.00226	0.0154***	0.368***
	(0.0147)	(0.00541)	(0.0966)
Female Rep	0.00576	0.0103***	0.219***
	(0.00641)	(0.00237)	(0.0422)

	Primary Spons.	Co-Spons.	LCCR Score
Age	0.000222	0.000297***	0.00449***
	(0.000233)	(8.60e-05)	(0.00153)
Percent Black in District	0.00107***	0.000492***	-0.000261
	(0.000260)	(9.61e-05)	(0.00171)
Cook's PVI	5.18e-05	-0.000297**	-0.0136***
	(0.000319)	(0.000118)	(0.00210)
Constant	-0.0114	0.00786	0.201**
	(0.0131)	(0.00483)	(0.0862)
Observations	422	422	422
R-squared	0.312	0.699	0.451

*** $p<0.01$, ** $p<0.05$, * $p<0.1$ Clustered Standard Errors in Parenthesis

Bibliography

Abramowitz, Alan I. 2006. "National Conditions, Strategic Politicians, and U.S. Congressional Elections: Using the Generic Vote to Forecast the 2006 House and Senate Elections." *PS: Political Science & Politics*, 39(4): 863–66.
Adler, E. Scott, and John D. Wilkerson. 2013. *Congress and the Politics of Problem Solving*. Cambridge University Press.
Ajrouch, Kristine J., Toni C. Antonucci, and Mary R. Janevic. 2001. "Social Networks Among Blacks and Whites: The Interaction Between Race and Age." *The Journals of Gerontology: Series B*, 56(2): 112–18.
Alemán, Eduardo, Juan Pablo Micozzi, and Sebastián Vallejo Vera. 2023. "Congressional Committees, Electoral Connections, and Legislative Speech." *Political Research Quarterly*, 76(2): 994–1011.
Alexander-Floyd, Nikol G. 2012. "Disappearing Acts: Reclaiming Intersectionality in the Social Sciences in a Post-Black Feminist Era." *Feminist Formations*, 24(1): 1–25.
Allen, Robert L., Jared A. Ball, Cynthia McKinney, Thabiti Asukile, Linda Burnham, and David Covin. "'A Black Scholar Readers' Forum on President Obama' Barack Obama and the Children of Globalization." *The Black Scholar*, 38(4): 32–49.
Alvarez, R. Michael. 2016. *Computational Social Science*. Cambridge University Press.
Anderson, Sarah E., Daniel M. Butler, and Laurel Harbridge-Yong. 2020. *Rejecting Compromise: Legislators' Fear of Primary Voters*. Cambridge University Press.
Anglin, Roland V. 2004. *Building the Organizations That Build Communities*. Washington, DC: US Department of Housing and Urban Development.
Ansolabehere, Stephen, and Philip Edward Jones. 2010. "Constituents' Responses to Congressional Roll-Call Voting." *American Journal of Political Science*, 54(3): 583–97.
Arora, Maneesh. 2019. *Which Race Card? Understanding Racial Appeals in US politics*. Irvine: University of California.

Arora, Maneesh, and Hannah J. Kim. 2020. "Stopping the hate: Political Condemnations of Anti-Asian Rhetoric During the COVID-19 Crisis." *Journal of Asian American Studies,* 23(3): 387–405.

et al., 2025. "How Crises Shape Interest in Elected Officials of Color: Social Media Activity, Race and Responsiveness to Members of Congress on Twitter." *Political Communication,* 42 (2): 268–285.

Asher, Herbert B. 1974. "Committees and the Norm of Specialization." *The ANNALS of the American Academy of Political and Social Science,* 411(1): 63–74.

Assari, Shervin, Ehsan Moazen-Zadeh, Cleopatra Howard Caldwell, and Marc A. Zimmerman. 2017. "Racial Discrimination during Adolescence Predicts Mental Health Deterioration in Adulthood: Gender Differences among Blacks." *Frontiers in Public Health,* 5: 104

Austin, Sarah D.W., and Richard T. Middleton IV. 2004. "The Limitations of the Deracialization Concept in the 2001 Los Angeles Mayoral Election." *Political Research Quarterly,* 57(2): 283–93.

Bai, Matt. 2008. "Is Obama the End of Black Politics?" New York Times Magazine.

Ban, Pamela, Ju Yeon Park, and Hye Young You. 2023. "How Are Politicians Informed? Witnesses and Information Provision in Congress." *American Political Science Review,* 117(1): 122–39.

Bane, Kaitlin C. 2019. "Tweeting the Agenda." *Journalism Practice,* 13(2): 191–205.

Barber, Michael J., and Nolan McCarty. 2015. "Causes and Consequences of Polarization." *Solutions to Political Polarization in America* 15: 50.

Barbera, P., Boydstun A., S. Linn, R. McMahon, and J. Nagler, 2016. "Methodological Challenges in Estimating Tone: Application to News Coverage of the US Economy." In *Meeting of the Midwest Political Science Association,* Chicago, IL.

Barbu, Oana. 2014. "Advertising, Microtargeting and Social Media." *Procedia - Social and Behavioral Sciences,* 163: 44–49.

Barnes, Tiffany D., and Erin Cassesse. 2017. "American Party Women: A Look at the Gender Gap within Parties." *Political Research Quarterly,* 70(1): 127–41.

Barreto, Matt A. 2007. "¡Sí Se Puede! Latino Candidates and the Mobilization of Latino Voters." *American Political Science Review,* 101(3): 425–41.

Barreto, Matt A., and Loren Collingwood. 2015. "Group-Based Appeals and the Latino Vote in 2012: How Immigration Became a Mobilizing Issue." *Electoral Studies,* 40: 490–99.

Bejarano, Christina., Nadia E. Brown, Sarah A. Gershon, and Celeste Montoya. 2021. "Shared identities: Intersectionality, Linked Fate, and Perceptions of Political Candidates." *Political Research Quarterly,* 74(4): 970–85.

Bennett, Lance W. 1990. "Toward a Theory of Press-State Relations in the United States." *Journal of Communications,* 40(2): 103–25.

2006. "Toward a Theory of Press–State Relations in the US." *Journal of Communication,* 40: 103–27.

Benveniste, Luis, Martin Carnoy, and Richard Rothstein. 2013. *All Else Equal: Are Public and Private Schools Different?* Routledge.

Block Jr., Ray. 2011. "Backing Barack Because He's Black: Racially Motivated Voting in the 2008 Election*." *Social Science Quarterly*, 92(2): 423–46.

Blum, Rachel, Lindsey Cormack, and Kelsey Shoub. 2023. "Conditional Congressional Communication: How Elite Speech Varies Across Medium." *Political Science Research and Methods*, 11(2): 394–401.

Bobo, Lawrence, and James R. Kluegel. 1993. "Opposition to Race-Targeting: Self-Interest, Stratification Ideology, or Racial Attitudes?" *American Sociological Review*, 58(4): 443–64.

Bonilla, Tabitha. 2022. *The Importance of Campaign Promises*. Cambridge University Press.

Bonilla, Tabitha, and Alvin B. Tillery. 2020. "Which Identity Frames Boost Support for and Mobilization in the #BlackLivesMatter Movement? An Experimental Test." *American Political Science Review*, 114(4): 947–62.

Boulianne, Shelley, and Anders Olof Larsson. 2023. "Engagement with Candidate Posts on Twitter, Instagram, and Facebook during the 2019 Election." *New Media & Society*, 25(1): 119–40.

Boutyline, Andrei, and Robb Willer. 2017. "The Social Structure of Political Echo Chambers: Variation in Ideological Homophily in Online Networks." *Political Psychology*, 38(3): 551–69.

Bratton, Kathleen A., and Kerry L. Haynie. 1999. "Agenda Setting and Legislative Success in State Legislatures: The Effects of Gender and Race." *Journal of Politics*, 61: 658–79.

Bratton, Kathleen A., Kerry L. Haynie, and Beth Reingold. 2006. "Agenda Setting and African American Women in State Legislatures." *Journal of Women, Politics & Policy*, 28: 71–96.

Bräuninger, Thomas, and Nathalie Giger. 2018. "Strategic Ambiguity of Party Positions in Multi-Party Competition." *Political Science Research and Methods*, 6(3): 527–48.

Broersma, Marcel, and Todd Graham. 2013. "Twitter as a News Source: How Dutch and British Newspapers Used Tweets in Their News Coverage, 2007–2011." *Journalism Practice*, 7(4): 446–64.

Broockman, David E. 2013. "Black Politicians Are More Intrinsically Motivated to Advance Blacks' Interests: A Field Experiment Manipulating Political Incentives." *American Journal of Political Science*, 57(3): 521–36.

Broockman, David., and Joshua Kalla. 2016. Durably reducing transphobia: A Field Experiment on Door-To-Door Canvassing. *Science*, 352(6282): 220–24.

Brown, Nadia E. 2014. *Sisters in the Statehouse: Black Women and Legislative Decision Making*. Oxford University Press.

Brown, Nadia E., and Sarah Allen Gershon. 2016. "Intersectional Presentations: An Exploratory Study of Minority Congresswomen's Websites' Biographies." *Du Bois Review: Social Science Research on Race*, 13(1): 85–108.

2017. "Examining Intersectionality and Symbolic Representation." *Politics, Groups, and Identities*, 5(3): 500–05.

Bunyasi, Tehama Lopez, and Candis Watts Smith. 2019. "Do All Black Lives Matter Equally to Black People? Respectability Politics and the Limitations of Linked Fate." *Journal of Race, Ethnicity, and Politics*, 4(1): 180–215.

Burden, Barry C. 2007. *Personal Roots of Representation*. Princeton University Press.
    2011. "Polarization, Obstruction, and Governing in the Senate." *The Forum*, 9(4). https://www.degruyter.com/document/doi/10.2202/1540-8884.1480/html (November 29, 2023).
Burge, Camille D., Julian J. Wamble, and Rachel R. Cuomo. 2020. "A Certain Type of Descriptive Representative? Understanding How the Skin Tone and Gender of Candidates Influences Black Politics." *The Journal of Politics*, 82(4): 1596–1601.
Butler, Daniel M., and David E. Broockman. 2011. "Do Politicians Racially Discriminate Against Constituents? A Field Experiment on State Legislators." *American Journal of Political Science*, 55(3): 463–77.
Butler, Daniel M., Adam G. Hughes, Craig Volden, and Alan E. Wiseman. 2023. "Do Constituents Know (or Care) about the Lawmaking Effectiveness of Their Representatives?" *Political Science Research and Methods*, 11(2): 419–28.
Callahan, Shannon P., and Alison Ledgerwood. 2016. "On the Psychological Function of Flags and Logos: Group Identity Symbols Increase Perceived Entitativity." *Journal of Personality and Social Psychology*, 100(4): 528.
Canon, David T. 1999. "Electoral Systems and the Representation of Minority Interests in Legislatures." *Legislative Studies Quarterly*, 24(3): 331–85.
Carmines, Edward G., and James A. Stimson. 1980. "The Two Faces of Issue Voting." *American Political Science Review*, 74(1): 78–91.
Carter, Niambi M., and Pearl Ford Dowe. 2015. "The Racial Exceptionalism of Barack Obama." *Journal of African American Studies*, 19(2): 105–19.
Chen, Sijing, Lu Xiao, and Akit Kumar. 2023. "Spread of Misinformation on Social Media: What Contributes to It and How to Combat It." *Computers in Human Behavior*, 141: 107643.
Childs, Sarah. 2002. "Concepts of Representation and the Passage of the Sex Discrimination (Election Candidates) Bill." *The Journal of Legislative Studies*, 8(3): 90–108.
Christensen, Donna M. 2005. "On Being a Physician and a Member of Congress." *AMA Journal of Ethics*, 7(12): 823–25.
Chykina, Volha, and Charles Crabtree. 2018. "Using Google Trends to Measure Issue Salience for Hard to Survey Populations." *Socius*, 4.
Clark, Christopher J. 2019. *Gaining Voice: The Causes and Consequences of Black Representation in the American States*. Oxford University Press.
Cobb, Michael D., and James H. Kuklinski. 1997. "Changing Minds: Political Arguments and Political Persuasion." *American Journal of Political Science*, 41(1): 88–121.
Cohen, Cathy J. 1999. *The Boundaries of Blackness: AIDS and the Breakdown of Black Politics*. University of Chicago Press.
Colleoni, Elanor, Alessandro Rozza, and Adam Arvidsson. 2014. "Echo Chamber or Public Sphere? Predicting Political Orientation and Measuring Political Homophily in Twitter Using Big Data." *Journal of Communication*, 64(2): 317–32.

Collingwood, Loren. 2020. *Campaigning in a Racially Diversifying America: When and How Cross-Racial Electoral Mobilization Works*. Oxford University Press.
Collingwood, Loren, and John Wilkerson. 2012. "Tradeoffs in Accuracy and Efficiency in Supervised Learning Methods." *Journal of Information Technology & Politics* 9(3): 298–318.
Condon, Meghan, and Amber Wichowsky. 2017. "Same Blueprint, Different Bricks: Reexamining the Sources of the Gender Gap in Political Ideology." *Gender and Political Psychology*. Routledge, 16–32.
Conway, Bethany A., Kate Kenski, and Di Wang. 2013. "Twitter Use by Presidential Primary Candidates during the 2012 Campaign." *American Behavioral Scientist*, 57(11): 1596–610.
Cormack, Lindsey. 2018. *Congress and U.S. Veterans: From the GI Bill to the VA Crisis*. Bloomsbury Publishing USA.
Costa, Mia. 2021. "Ideology, Not Affect: What Americans Want from Political Representation." *American Journal of Political Science*, 65(2): 342–58.
Crawford, Nyron N. 2021. "We'd Go Well Together: A Critical Race Analysis of Marijuana Legalization and Expungement in the United States." *Public Integrity*, 23(5): 459–83.
Crenshaw, Kimberlé. 1989. "Demarginalizing the Intersection of Race and Sex: A Black Feminist Critique of Antidiscrimination Doctrine, Feminist Theory and Antiracist Politics." University of Chicago Legal Forum 1, Article 8.
  et al. 2015. "Say Her Name: Resisting Police Brutality Against Black Women." *Faculty Scholarship*. https://scholarship.law.columbia.edu/faculty_scholarship/3226.
Crowder, Chaya. 2023. "When #BlackLivesMatter at the Women's March: A Study of the Emotional Influence of Racial Appeals on Instagram." *Politics, Groups, and Identities*, 11(1): 55–73.
Currinder, Marian. 2010. "Campaign Finance: Fundraising and Spending in the 2008 Elections." *The Elections of (2008)*: 163–186.
Damore, David F. 2022. *Presidential Swing States*. Rowman & Littlefield.
Dancey, Logan, and Geoffrey Sheagley. 2013. "Heuristics Behaving Badly: Party Cues and Voter Knowledge." *American Journal of Political Science*, 57(2): 312–25.
Dancey, Logan, and Jasmine Masand. 2019. "Race and Representation on Twitter: Members of Congress' Responses to the Deaths of Michael Brown and Eric Garner." *Politics, Groups, and Identities*, 7(2): 267–86.
Davidson, Roger H., Walter J. Oleszek, Frances E. Lee, and Eric Schickler. 2019. *Congress and Its Members*. CQ Press.
Dawson, Michael C. 1995. *Behind the Mule: Race and Class in African-American Politics*. Princeton University Press.
  2001. *Black Visions: The Roots of Contemporary African-American Political Ideologies*. University of Chicago Press.
  2011. "The Color Line Reconsidered: Du Bois in the Twenty-First Century." *Du Bois Review: Social Science Research on Race*, 8(2): 309–313. Web.
  2019. *Not in Our Lifetimes: The Future of Black Politics*. University of Chicago Press.

Deering, Christopher J., and Steven S. Smith. 1997. *Committees in Congress*. CQ Press.

DeSante, Christopher D., and Candis Watts Smith. 2020. "Less Is More: A Cross-Generational Analysis of the Nature and Role of Racial Attitudes in the Twenty-First Century." *The Journal of Politics*, 82(3): 967–80.

"Descriptive and Substantive Representation in Congress: Evidence from 80,000 Congressional Inquiries – Lowande – 2019 – American Journal of Political Science – Wiley Online Library." https://onlinelibrary.wiley.com/doi/abs/10.1111/ajps.12443 (November 30, 2023).

Devine, Patricia G., Margo J. Monteith, Julia R. Zuwerink, and Andrew J. Elliot. 1991. "Prejudice With and Without Compunction." *Journal of Personality and Social Psychology*, 60(6): 817–30.

Dietrich, Bryce J., and Matthew Hayes. 2023. "Symbols of the Struggle: Descriptive Representation and Issue-Based Symbolism in US House Speeches." *The Journal of Politics*, 85(4): 1368–84.

Dietrich, Bryce J., Matthew Hayes, and Diana Z. O'Brien. 2019. "Pitch Perfect: Vocal Pitch and the Emotional Intensity of Congressional Speech." *American Political Science Review*, 113(4): 941–62.

Dittmar, Kelly, et al. 2017. "Representation Matters: Women in the US Congress." New Brunswick, NJ: Center for American Women and Politics, Eagleton Institute of Politics, Rutgers, The State University of New Jersey.

Dittmar, Kelly, Kira Sanbonmatsu, and Susan J. Carroll. 2018. *A Seat at the Table: Congresswomen's Perspectives on Why Their Presence Matters*. Oxford University Press.

Dolan, Julie, and Jonathan S. Kropf. 2004. "Credit Claiming from the U.S. House: Gendered Communication Styles?" *Harvard International Journal of Press/Politics*, 9(1): 41–59.

Dolan, Mark K., John H. Sonnett, and Kirk A. Johnson. 2009. "Katrina Coverage in Black Newspapers Critical of Government, Mainstream Media." *Newspaper Research Journal*, 30(1): 34–42.

Dovi, Suzanne. 2002. "Preferable Descriptive Representatives: Will Just Any Woman, Black, or Latino Do?" *American Political Science Review*, 96(4): 729–43.

Dowe, Pearl K. Ford, and Pearl K. Ford. 2023. *The Radical Imagination of Black Women: Ambition, Politics, and Power*. Oxford University Press.

Draper, B.S., 2020. *Crossing the Divine Line: Exploring Perceptions of Trans Membership and Retention of Membership within African-American Sororities* (Doctoral dissertation, East Stroudsburg University).

Edelman, Murray J. 1964. *The Symbolic Uses of Politics*. Urbana: University of Illinois Press.

Endres, Kyle, and Kristin J. Kelly. 2018. "Does Microtargeting Matter? Campaign Contact Strategies and Young Voters." *Journal of Elections, Public Opinion and Parties*, 28(1): 1–18.

Engelhardt, Andrew M. 2021. "Racial Attitudes Through a Partisan Lens." *British Journal of Political Science*, 51(3): 1062–79.

2023. "Observational Equivalence in Explaining Attitude Change: Have White Racial Attitudes Genuinely Changed?" *American Journal of Political Science*, 67(2): 411–425.

Epstein, Lee, and Jeffrey A. Segal. 2000. "Measuring Issue Salience." *American Journal of Political Science*, 44(1) 66–83.

Eshima, Shusei, Kosuke Imai, and Tomoya Sasaki. 2024. "Keyword-Assisted Topic Models." *American Journal of Political Science*, 68(2): 730–50.

Esterling, Kevin M. 2007. "Buying Expertise: Campaign Contributions and Attention to Policy Analysis in Congressional Committees." *American Political Science Review*, 101(1): 93–109.

Eulau, Heinz, and Paul D. Karps. 1977. "The Puzzle of Representation: Specifying Components of Responsiveness." *Legislative Studies Quarterly*, 2(3): 233–54.

Evans, Diana. 2011. "Pork Barrel Politics." In *The Oxford Handbook of the American Congress*. Oxford University Press.

Evans, Heather K., and Jennifer H. Clark. 2016. "'You Tweet Like a Girl!' How Female Candidates Campaign on Twitter." *American Politics Research*, 44(2): 326–52.

Fenno, Richard F. 1977. "US House Members in Their Constituencies: An Exploration." *American Political Science Review*, 71(3): 883–917.

1978. *Home Style: House Members in Their Districts*. Boston: Little, Brown.

2003. *Going Home: Black Representatives and Their Constituents*. University of Chicago Press.

Filindra, Alexandra, and Noah Kaplan. 2017. "Testing Theories of Gun Policy Preferences Among Blacks, Latinos, and Whites in America*." *Social Science Quarterly*, 98(2): 413–28.

Fraga, Bernard L. 2016. "Candidates or Districts? Reevaluating the Role of Race in Voter Turnout." *American Journal of Political Science*, 60(1): 97–122.

Francis, Katherine, and Brittany Bramlett. 2017. "Precongressional Careers and Committees: The Impact of Congruence." *American Politics Research*, 45(5): 755–89.

Freelon, Deen, Charlton D. McIlwain, and Meredith Clark. 2016. "Beyond the Hashtags: #Ferguson, #Blacklivesmatter, and the Online Struggle for Offline Justice." https://papers.ssrn.com/abstract=2747066 (November 29, 2023).

Frymer, Paul. 2011. *Uneasy Alliances: Race and Party Competition in America*. Princeton University Press.

2014. "'A Rush and a Push and the Land is ours': Territorial Expansion, Land Policy, and US State Formation." *Perspectives on Politics*, 12(1): 119–44.

Gamble, Katrina. 2011. "Black Voice: Deliberation in the United States Congress." *Polity*, 43(3), 291–312.

Garcia, Jennifer, and Christopher Stout. 2022. "The Empowering Effects of Racial Messaging: The Link between Racial Outreach, Descriptive Representation and Black Political Mobilization." *Political Communication*, 39(5): 589–606.

Gause, LaGina. 2022. *The Advantage of Disadvantage*. Cambridge University Press.

Gay, Claudine, and Katherine Tate. 1998. "Doubly Bound: The Impact of Gender and Race on the Politics of Black Women." *Political Psychology*, 19(1): 169–84.

Gerber, Alan S., Eric M. Patashnik, and Patrick D. Tucker. 2022. "How Voters Use Contextual Information to Reward and Punish: Credit Claiming, Legislative Performance, and Democratic Accountability." *The Journal of Politics*, 84(3): 1839–43.

Gershon, Sarah Allen. 2008. "Communicating Female and Minority Interests Online: A Study of Web Site Issue Discussion Among Female, Latino, and African American Members of Congress." *The International Journal of Press/Politics*, 13(2): 120–40.

Gervais, Bryan, and Walter Wilson. 2018. "New Media for the New Electorate? US Representatives Use of Spanish in Tweets." *Politics, Groups, and Identities*, 7(2): 205–323.

Gilens, Martin. 2001. "Political Ignorance and Collective Policy Preferences." *American Political Science Review*, 95(2): 379–396.

2009. *Why Americans Hate Welfare: Race, Media, and the Politics of Antipoverty Policy*. University of Chicago Press.

Gillespie, Andra. 2010. *Whose Black Politics?: Cases in Post-Racial Black Leadership*. Routledge.

2012. "The New Black Politician: Cory Booker, Newark, and Post-Racial America." In *The New Black Politician*, New York University Press.

2020. "Race and the Obama Administration: Substance, Symbols, and Hope." In *Race and the Obama Administration*, Manchester University Press.

Gillion, Daniel Q. 2016. *Governing with Words: The Political Dialogue on Race, Public Policy, and Inequality in America*. Cambridge University Press.

Gleason, Shane A., and Christopher T. Stout. 2014. "Who Is Empowering Who: Exploring the Causal Relationship Between Descriptive Representation and Black Empowerment." *Journal of Black Studies*, 45(7): 635–59.

Graham, Roderick, and Shawn Smith. 2016. "The Content of Our# Characters: Black Twitter as a Counterpublic." *Sociology of Race and Ethnicity*, 2(4): 433–49.

Greer, Christina M. 2013. *Black Ethnics: Race, Immigration, and the Pursuit of the American Dream*. Oxford University Press.

Gregory, Anne, Dewey Cornell, and Xitao Fan. 2011. "The Relationship of School Structure and Support to Suspension Rates for Black and White High School Students." *American Educational Research Journal*, 48(4): 904–934.

Griffin, John D., and Michael Keane. 2011. "Are African Americans Effectively Represented in Congress?" *Political Research Quarterly*, 64(1): 145–56.

Griffin, John D., and Patrick Flavin. 2011. "How Citizens and Their Legislators Prioritize Spheres of Representation." *Political Research Quarterly*, 64(3): 520–33.

Grimmer, Justin. 2013. *Representational Style in Congress: What Legislators Say and Why It Matters*. Cambridge University Press.

Grimmer, Justin, and Brandon M. Stewart. 2013. "Text as Data: The Promise and Pitfalls of Automatic Content Analysis Methods for Political Texts." *Political Analysis*, 21(3): 267–97.

Grimmer, Justin, Sean J. Westwood, and Solomon Messing. 2014. "The Impression of Influence: Legislator Communication, Representation, and

Democratic Accountability." In *The Impression of Influence*, Princeton University Press.
Grose, Christian R. 2005. "Disentangling Constituency and Legislator Effects in Legislative Representation: Black Legislators or Black Districts?*." *Social Science Quarterly*, 86(2): 427–43.
    2011. *Congress in Black and White: Race and Representation in Washington and at Home*. Cambridge University Press.
    2013. "Risk and Roll Calls: How Legislators' Personal Finances Shape Congressional Decisions." https://papers.ssrn.com/abstract=2220524 (December 3, 2023).
Grossmann, Matt, and David A. Hopkins. 2016. *Asymmetric Politics: Ideological Republicans and Group Interest Democrats*. Oxford University Press.
Grumbach, Jacob. 2022. *Laboratories Against Democracy: How National Parties Transformed State Politics*. Princeton University Press.
Gurin, Patricia. 1985. "Women's Gender Consciousness." *Public Opinion Quarterly*, 49(2): 143–63.
Hager, Lisa. 2018. "Are Members of Congress Simply 'Single-Minded Seekers of Reelection'? An Examination of Legislative Behavior in the 114th Congress." *PS: Political Science & Politics*, 51(1): 115–18.
Hagerman, Margaret A. 2020. "Racial Ideology and White Youth: From Middle Childhood to Adolescence." *Sociology of Race and Ethnicity*, 6(3): 319–32.
Hajnal, Zoltan L. 2009. *America's Uneven Democracy: Race, Turnout, and Representation in City Politics*. Cambridge University Press.
Haider-Markel, Donald P. 2007. "Representation and Backlash: The Positive and Negative Influence of Descriptive Representation." *Legislative Studies Quarterly*, 32(1): 107–33.
Haines, Pavielle E., Tali Mendelberg, and Bennett Butler. 2019. "'I'm Not the President of Black America': Rhetorical versus Policy Representation." *Perspectives on Politics*, 17(4): 1038–58.
Hamilton, Charles. 1977. "Deracialization: Examination of a Political Strategy." *First World* Mar/Apr.
Hamm, Keith E., Ronald D. Hedlund, and Stephanie Shirley Post. 2011. "Committee Specialization in U.S. State Legislatures during the 20th Century: Do Legislatures Tap the Talents of Their Members?" *State Politics & Policy Quarterly*, 11(3): 299–324.
Hansen, Eric R., Nicholas Carnes, and Virginia Gray. 2019. "What Happens When Insurers Make Insurance Laws? State Legislative Agendas and the Occupational Makeup of Government." *State Politics & Policy Quarterly*, 19(2): 155–79.
Hargrave, Lotte, and Jack Blumenau. 2022. "No Longer Conforming to Stereotypes? Gender, Political Style and Parliamentary Debate in the UK." *British Journal of Political Science*, 52(4): 1584–1601.
Hargrave, Lotte, and Jessica C. Smith. 2023. "Working Hard or Hardly Working? Gender and Voter Evaluations of Legislator Productivity." *Political Behavior*, 46(2), 909–930. https://doi.org/10.1007/s11109-022-09853-8 (November 30, 2023).

Hargrave, Lotte, and Tone Langengen. 2021. "The Gendered Debate: Do Men and Women Communicate Differently in the House of Commons?" *Politics & Gender*, 17(4): 580–606.

Harris, Fredrick. 2012. *The Price of the Ticket: Barack Obama and Rise and Decline* Harris-Lacewell, Melissa Victoria. 2010. *Barbershops, Bibles, and BET: Everyday Talk and Black Political Thought*. Princeton University Press.

Hasen, Richard L. 2020. "Three Pathologies of American Voting Rights Illuminated by the COVID-19 Pandemic, and How to Treat and Cure Them." *Election Law Journal: Rules, Politics, and Policy*, 19(3): 263–88.

Hassell, Hans J. G., and J. Quin Monson. 2014. "Campaign Targets and Messages in Direct Mail Fundraising." *Political Behavior*, 36(2): 359–76.

Hawkesworth, Mary. 2003a. "Congressional Enactments of Race–Gender: Toward a Theory of Raced–Gendered Institutions." *American Political Science Review*, 97(4): 529–50.

Hayes, Matthew, and Matthew V. Hibbing. 2017. "The Symbolic Benefits of Descriptive and Substantive Representation." *Political Behavior* 39: 31–50.

2003b. "Congressional Enactments of Race–Gender: Toward a Theory of Raced–Gendered Institutions." *American Political Science Review*, 97(4): 529–50.

Hemphill, Libby, and Andrew J. Roback. 2014. "Tweet Acts: How Constituents Lobby Congress via Twitter." In *Proceedings of the 17th ACM Conference on Computer Supported Cooperative Work & Social Computing*, CSCW'14, New York, NY, USA: Association for Computing Machinery, 1200–10. https://dl.acm.org/doi/10.1145/2531602.2531735 (November 30, 2023).

Hero, Rodney E., and Robert R. Preuhs. 2013. *Black–Latino Relations in U.S. National Politics: Beyond Conflict or Cooperation*. Cambridge University Press.

Herrnson, Paul S., Michael J. Hanmer, and Ho Youn Koh. 2019. "Mobilization Around New Convenience Voting Methods: A Field Experiment to Encourage Voting by Mail with a Downloadable Ballot and Early Voting." *Political Behavior*, 41(4): 871–95.

Hersh, Eitan D., and Brian F. Schaffner. 2013. "Targeted Campaign Appeals and the Value of Ambiguity." *The Journal of Politics*, 75(2): 520–34.

Hickey, Daniel, Matheus Schmitz, Daniel Fessler, Paule E. Smaldino, Goran Muric, and Keith Burghardt. 2023. "Auditing Elon Musk's Impact on Hate Speech and Bots." In *Proceedings of the International AAAI Conference on Web and Social Media*, 17: 1133–37.

Highton, B., 2008. "Job Approval and Senate Election Outcomes in the United States." *Legislative Studies Quarterly*, 33(2): 245–61.

Higginbotham Jr., A. Leon. 1998. *Shades of freedom: Racial politics and presumptions of the American legal process*. Oxford University Press.

Hill, Kim Quaile, and Patricia A. Hurley. 2002. "Symbolic Speeches in the U.S. Senate and Their Representational Implications." *Journal of Politics*, 64(1): 219–31.

Hillygus, D. Sunshine, and Todd G. Shields. 2008. *The Persuadable Voter: Wedge Issues in Presidential Campaigns*. Princeton University Press.

Hinojosa, Magda, Jill Carle, and Gina Serignese Woodall. 2018. "Speaking as a Woman: Descriptive Presentation and Representation in Costa Rica's Legislative Assembly." *Journal of Women, Politics & Policy*. 39(4): 407–429.

Holman, Mirya R., Monica C. Schneider, and Kristin Pondel., 2015. "Gender Targeting in Political Advertisements." *Political Research Quarterly*, 68(4): 816–29.

Hope, E.C., V.V. Volpe, A.S. Briggs, and G.P. Benson. 2022. "Anti-Racism Activism Among Black Adolescents and Emerging Adults: Understanding the Roles of Racism and Anticipatory Racism-Related Stress." *Child Development*, 93(3): 717–31.

Howell, Junia, and Elizabeth Korver-Glenn. 2018. "Neighborhoods, Race, and the Twenty-First-Century Housing Appraisal Industry." *Sociology of Race and Ethnicity*, 4(4): 473–90.

Hutchings, Vincent L., Vanessa Cruz Nichols, LaGina Gause, and Spencer Piston. 2021. "Whitewashing: How Obama Used Implicit Racial Cues as a Defense against Political Rumors." *Political Behavior*, 43(3): 1337–60.

Jackson, John E., and John W. Kingdon. 1992. "Ideology, Interest Group Scores, and Legislative Votes." *American Journal of Political Science*, 36(3): 805–23.

Jacobs, Lawrence R., and Robert Y. Shapiro. 2000. *Politicians Don't Pander: Political Manipulation and the Loss of Democratic Responsiveness*. University of Chicago Press.

Jacobs, Walt. "Post-Race – Is Obama the End of Black Politics? – NYTimes.Com."

Jacobson, Gary C. 2021. "The Presidential and Congressional Elections of 2020: A National Referendum on the Trump Presidency." *Political Science Quarterly*. 136(1): 11–45.

Jennings, James. 2000. *The Politics of Black Empowerment: The Transformation of Black Activism in Urban America*. Wayne State University Press.

Jennings, M. Kent. 1987. "Residues of a Movement: The Aging of the American Protest Generation." *American Political Science Review*, 81(2): 367–82.

Johnson, Richard. 2017. "HAMILTON'S DERACIALIZATION: Barack Obama's Racial Politics in Context." *Du Bois Review: Social Science Research on Race*, 14(2): 621–38.

Johnston, Christopher D., and Julie Wronski. 2015. "Personality Dispositions and Political Preferences Across Hard and Easy Issues." *Political Psychology*, 36(1): 35–53.

Jones, Bryan D. 2001. *Politics and the Architecture of Choice: Bounded Rationality and Governance*. University of Chicago Press.

Jones, Philip Edward. 2011. "Which Buck Stops Here? Accountability for Policy Positions and Policy Outcomes in Congress." *The Journal of Politics*, 73(3): 764–82.

  2016. "Constituents' Responses to Descriptive and Substantive Representation in Congress." *Social Science Quarterly*, 97(3): 682–98.

Jungherr, Andreas. 2016. "Twitter Use in Election Campaigns: A Systematic Literature Review." *Journal of Information Technology & Politics*, 13(1): 72–91.

Junn, Jane, et al. 2008. "What Revolution? Incorporating Intersectionality in Women and Politics." *Political Women and American Democracy*: 64–78.

Jurka, Timothy P., et al. 2013. "RTextTools: A Supervised Learning Package for Text Classification." *The R Journal*, 5(1): 6.

Kahn, Kim Fridkin, and Patrick J. Kenney. 1999. "Do Negative Campaigns Mobilize or Suppress Turnout? Clarifying the Relationship between Negativity and Participation." *American Political Science Review*, 93(4): 877–89.

Kamin, Debra. 2020. "Black Homeowners Face Discrimination in Appraisals." *New York Times* 25.

Kartik, Navin, and Richard Van Weelden. 2019. "Informative Cheap Talk in Elections." *The Review of Economic Studies*, 86(2): 755–84.

Kaufmann, Karen M. 2003. "Cracks in the Rainbow: Group Commonality as a Basis for Latino and African-American Political Coalitions." *Political Research Quarterly*, 56(2): 199–210.

King, Desmond S., and Rogers M. Smith. 2005. "Racial Orders in American Political Development." *American Political Science Review*, 99(1): 75–92.

Kiousis, Spiro. 2004. "Explicating Media Salience: A Factor Analysis of New York Times Issue Coverage During the 2000 US Presidential Election." *Journal of Communications*, 54(1): 71–87.

Krutz, Glen S. 2005. "Issues and Institutions: 'Winnowing' in the U.S. Congress." *American Journal of Political Science*, 49(2): 313–26.

Langehennig, Stefani, Joseph Zamadics, and Jennifer Wolak. 2019. "State Policy Outcomes and State Legislative Approval." *Political Research Quarterly*, 72(4): 929–43.

Laniyonu, Ayobami. 2019. "The Political Consequences of Policing: Evidence from New York City." *Political Behavior*, 41(2): 527–58.

Lapinski, John., Matt, Levendusky., Ken, Winneg. and KathleenH Jamieson., 2016. "What Do Citizens Want From Their Member of Congress?," *Political Research Quarterly*, 69(3): 535–45.

Lebron, Christopher J. 2023. *The Making of Black Lives Matter: A Brief History of an Idea, Updated Edition*. Oxford University Press.

Lee, ByungGu, Jinha Kim, and Dietram A. Scheufele. 2016. "Agenda Setting in the Internet Age: The Reciprocity Between Online Searches and Issue Salience." *International Journal of Public Opinion Research*, 28(3): 440–55.

Lee, Frances. 2016. *Insecure Majorities: Congress and the Perpetual Campaign*. University of Chicago Press.

Legewie, Joscha. 2016. "Racial Profiling and Use of Force in Police Stops: How Local Events Trigger Periods of Increased Discrimination." *American Journal of Sociology*, 122(2): 379–424.

Leighley, Jan E., and Jonathan Nagler. 2013. *Who Votes Now?: Demographics, Issues, Inequality, and Turnout in the United States*. Princeton University Press.

Levendusky, Matthew. 2009. *The Partisan Sort: How Liberals Became Democrats and Conservatives Became Republicans*. University of Chicago Press.

Lewis, Angela K., Pearl K. Ford Dowe, and Sekou M. Franklin. 2013. "African Americans and Obama's Domestic Policy Agenda: A Closer Look at Deracialization, the Federal Stimulus Bill, and the Affordable Care Act." *Polity*, 45(1): 127–52.

Loper, Edward, and Steven Bird. 2002. "NLTK: The Natural Language Toolkit." http://arxiv.org/abs/cs/0205028 (November 30, 2023).
Lorenz-Spreen, Philipp, Bjarke Mørch Mønsted, Philipp Hövel, and Sune Lehmann. 2019. "Accelerating Dynamics of Collective Attention." *Nature Communications* 10(1): 1759.
Lowande, Kenneth, Melinda Ritchie, and Erinn Lauterbach. 2019. "Descriptive and Substantive Representation in Congress: Evidence from 80,000 Congressional Inquiries." *American Journal of Political Science*, 63(3): 644–59.
Lublin, David. 1999. "Racial Redistricting and African-American Representation: A Critique of 'Do Majority-Minority Districts Maximize Substantive Black Representation in Congress?'" *American Political Science Review*, 93(1): 183–86.
Lyons, Benjamin A., and Aaron S. Veenstra. 2016. "How (Not) to Talk on Twitter: Effects of Politicians' Tweets on Perceptions of the Twitter Environment." *Cyberpsychology, Behavior, and Social Networking*, 19(1): 8–15.
Maeda, Kaede, and Hirofumi Hashimoto. 2020. "Time Pressure and In-Group Favoritism in a Minimal Group Paradigm." *Frontiers in Psychology*, 11. https://www.frontiersin.org/articles/10.3389/fpsyg.2020.603117 (December 3, 2023).
Mangum, Maurice. 2003. "Psychological Involvement and Black Voter Turnout." *Political Research Quarterly*, 56(1): 41–48.
Manjoo, Farhad. 2013. "You won't finish this article." Why people online don't read to the end: Slate (2013).
Mansbridge, Jane. 1999. "Should Blacks Represent Blacks and Women Represent Women? A Contingent 'Yes.'" *The Journal of Politics*, 61(3): 628–57.
Mansbridge, Jane, and Cathie Jo Martin. 2015. *Political Negotiation: A Handbook*. Brookings Institution Press.
Mansbridge, Jane, and Katherine Tate. 1992. "Race Trumps Gender: The Thomas Nomination in the Black Community." *PS: Political Science & Politics*, 25(3): 488–492.
Marable, Manning. 2000. *Dispatches from the Ebony Tower: Intellectuals Confront the African American Experience*. Columbia University Press.
Mastin, Teresa, Shelly Campo, and M. Somjen Frazer. 2005. "In Black and White: Coverage of U.S. Slave Reparations by the Mainstream and Black Press." *Howard Journal of Communications*, 16(3): 201–23.
Mayhew, David R. 1974. *Congress: The Electoral Connection*, 2nd ed. Yale University Press.
McAdam, Doug, 2017. "Social Movement Theory and the Prospects for Climate Change Activism in the United States." *Annual Review of Political Science*, 20: 189–208.
McClain, Paula D., et al. 2006. "Racial Distancing in a Southern City: Latino Immigrants' Views of Black Americans." *The Journal of Politics*, 68(3): 571–84.
McCowan, Carla J., and Reginald J. Alston. 1998. "Racial Identity, African Self-Consciousness, and Career Decision Making in African American College

Women." *Journal of Multicultural Counseling and Development*, 26(1): 28–38.

McDonald, Jared. 2021. "Who Cares? Explaining Perceptions of Compassion in Candidates for Office." *Political Behavior*, 43(4): 1371–94.

McDonald, Jared, Sarah E. Croco, and Candace Turitto. 2019. "Teflon Don or Politics as Usual? An Examination of Foreign Policy Flip-Flops in the Age of Trump." *The Journal of Politics*, 81(2): 757–66.

McIlwain, Charlton, and Stephen M. Caliendo. 2011. *Race Appeal: How Candidates Invoke Race in U.S. Political Campaigns*. Temple University Press.

Mckenzie, Brian D. 2004. "Religious Social Networks, Indirect Mobilization, and African-American Political Participation." *Political Research Quarterly*, 57(4): 621–32.

McKinney, Cynthia. 2013. *Ain't Nothing Like Freedom*. SCB Distributors.

Mctague, John, and Shanna Pearson-Merkowitz. 2015. "Thou Shalt Not Flip Flop: Senators' Religious Affiliations and Issue Position Consistency." *Legislative Studies Quarterly*, 40(3): 417–40.

Meier, Florian, David Elsweiler, and Max Wilson. 2014. "More than Liking and Bookmarking? Towards Understanding Twitter Favouriting Behaviour." *Proceedings of the International AAAI Conference on Web and Social Media*, 8(1): 346–55.

Meier, K.J, P.D. McClain, J.L. Polinard, and R.D. Wrinkle 2004. "Divided or Together? Conflict and Cooperation Between African Americans and Latinos. *Political Research Quarterly*, 57: 399–409.

Meinke, Scott R. 2019. "The Resilience of Electoral Responsiveness in a Polarized Congress." e17–e22.

Mellon, Jonathan. 2013. "Where and When Can We Use Google Trends to Measure Issue Salience?" *PS: Political Science & Politics*, 46(2): 280–90.

   2014. "Internet Search Data and Issue Salience: The Properties of Google Trends as a Measure of Issue Salience." *Journal of Elections, Public Opinion & Parties*, 24(1): 45–72.

Mendelberg, Tali. 2001. "The Race Card: Campaign Strategy, Implicit Messages, and the Norm of Equality." In *The Race Card*, Princeton University Press.

Metz, David Haywood, and Katherine Tate. 1995. "The Color of Urban Campaigns." *Classifying by Race*: 262–77.

Miller, Warren E., and Donald E. Stokes. 1963. "Constituency Influence in Congress." *American Political Science Review*, 57(1): 45–56.

Milita, K., J. B. Ryan, and E. N. Simas, 2014. "Nothing to Hide, Nowhere to Run, or Nothing to Lose: Candidate Position-Taking in Congressional Elections." *Political Behavior*, 36(2): 427–49.

Minta, Michael D. 2011. *Oversight: Representing the Interests of Blacks and Latinos in Congress*. Princeton University Press.

   2020. "Diversity and Minority Interest Group Advocacy in Congress." *Political Research Quarterly*, 73(1): 208–20.

   2021. *No Longer Outsiders: Black and Latino Interest Group Advocacy on Capitol Hill*. University of Chicago Press.

Monteith, Margo J. 1993. "Self-Regulation of Prejudiced Responses: Implications for Progress in Prejudice-Reduction Efforts." *Journal of Personality and Social Psychology*, 65(3): 469–85.

Nelson, Sherice J. 2022 *The Congressional Black Caucus: Fifty Years of Fighting for Equality*. Archway Publishing.

Niven, David, and Jeremy Zilber. 2001. "Do Women and Men in Congress Cultivate Different Images? Evidence from Congressional Web Sites." *Political Communication*, 18(4): 395–405.

Nteta, Tatishe M. and Douglas Rice. 2021. "Driving a Wedge? Republicans, Immigration, and the Impact of Substantive Appeals on African American Vote Choice." *Political Research Quarterly*, 74(1): 228–42.

Nteta, Tatishe M., and Jill S. Greenlee. 2013. "A Change Is Gonna Come: Generational Membership and White Racial Attitudes in the 21st Century." *Political Psychology*, 34(6): 877–97.

Nunnally, Shayla C. 2011. "(Dis) Counting on Democracy to Work: Perceptions of Electoral Fairness in the 2008 Presidential Election." *Journal of Black Studies*, 42(6): 923–942.

Nunnally, Shayla C. 2012. "Trust in Black America: Race, Discrimination, and Politics." In *Trust in Black America*, New York University Press.

Nyhan, Brendan, Jaime Settle, Emily Thorson, Magdalena Wojcieszak, Pablo Barbera, Annie Y. Chen, Hunt Allcott et al. 2023. "Like-Minded Sources on Facebook are Prevalent But Not Polarizing." *Nature*, 620(7972): 137–44.

Orey, B.D.A., 2000. Black Legislative Politics in Mississippi. *Journal of Black Studies*, 30(6): 791–814.

Paluck, Elizabeth Levy. 2011. "Peer Pressure against Prejudice: A High School Field Experiment Examining Social Network Change." *Journal of Experimental Social Psychology*, 47(2): 350–58.

Park, Ju Yeon. 2021. "When do politicians grandstand? Measuring message politics in committee hearings." *The Journal of Politics*, 83(1): 214–228.

Parker, Christopher S., and Matt Barreto. 2013 *"Change They Can't Believe In: The Tea Party and Reactionary Politics in America."* Princeton University Press.

Parkinson, Joe., and Hinshaw, Drew. 2021. "Twitter Activism Turned the Fight Against Boko Haram Upside Down." *The Washington Post*, pp.NA–NA.

Peay, Periloux C. 2021. "Incorporation Is Not Enough: The Agenda Influence of Black Lawmakers in Congressional Committees." *Journal of Race, Ethnicity, and Politics*, 6(2): 402–38.

Peay, Periloux C., and Alexander Leasure. 2023. "Information Infrastructures for Black-Interest Advocacy in Congress." *Congress & the Presidency*, 50(2): 220–48.

Peer, Eyal, et al. 2020. "Erratum to Peer et al. (2021) Data Quality of Platforms and Panels for Online Behavioral Research." *Behavior Research Methods* 54(5): 2618–2620.

Peffley, Mark, and Jon Hurwitz. 2007. "Persuasion and Resistance: Race and the Death Penalty in America." *American Journal of Political Science*, 51(4): 996–1012.

Pérez, Efrén, Crystal Robertson, and Bianca Vicuña. 2023. "Prejudiced When Climbing Up or When Falling Down? Why Some People of Color Express Anti-Black Racism." *American Political Science Review*, 117(1): 168–83.

Perry, Melissa Harris. 2004. *Barbershops, Bibles and BET: Everyday Talk and Black Political Thought.*

"Personality Dispositions and Political Preferences Across Hard and Easy Issues – Johnston – 2015 – Political Psychology – Wiley Online Library."

Pew Research Center. *Public's Support for Protests and Protesters Amid COVID-19.* 12 June 2020. www.pewresearch.org/wp-content/uploads/sites/20/2020/06/PSDT_06.12.20_protest_fullreport.pdf

Philpot, Tasha S., and Hanes Walton Jr. 2007. "One of our Own: Black Female Candidates and the Voters Who Support Them." *American Journal of Political Science*, 51(1): 49–62.

Piscopo, Jennifer M. 2011. "Rethinking Descriptive Representation: Rendering Women in Legislative Debates." *Parliamentary Affairs*, 64(3): 448–472.

Piston, Spencer. 2010. "How Explicit Racial Prejudice Hurt Obama in the 2008 Election." *Political Behavior*, 32(4): 431–51.

Piston, Spencer, Yanna Krupnikov, Kerri Milita, and John Barry Ryan. 2018. "Clear as Black and White: The Effects of Ambiguous Rhetoric Depend on Candidate Race." *The Journal of Politics*, 80(2): 662–74.

Pitkin, Hanna Fenichel. 1967. *The Concept of Representation.* Berkeley: University of California Press.

2016. "27. The Concept of Representation." In *27. The Concept of Representation*, Columbia University Press, 155–58.

Polsby, Nelson W. "The Institutionalization of the US House of Representatives." *American Political Science Review*, 61(1): 144–68.

Pope, Devin G., Joseph Price, and Justin Wolfers. 2018. "Awareness Reduces Racial Bias." *Management Science*, 64(11): 4988–95.

Pressman, Jeremy, et al. 2022. "PROTESTS UNDER TRUMP, 2017–2021*." *Mobilization: An International Quarterly*, 27(1): 13–26.

Preuhs, Robert R. 2005. "Descriptive Representation, Legislative Leadership, and Direct Democracy: Latino Influence on English Only Laws in the States, 1984–2002." *State Politics & Policy Quarterly*, 5(3): 203–24.

Preuhs, R.R., and Hero, R.E., 2011. "A Different Kind of Representation: Black and Latino Descriptive Representation and the Role of Ideological Cuing." *Political Research Quarterly*, 64(1): 157–71.

Price, Melanye T. 2016. *The Race Whisperer: Barack Obama and the Political Uses of Race.* NYU Press.

Purdie-Vaughns, Valerie, and Richard P. Eibach. 2008. "Intersectional Invisibility: The Distinctive Advantages and Disadvantages of Multiple Subordinate-Group Identities." *Sex Roles*, 59(5): 377–91.

Ray, Rashawn. 2021. "The Case for a Civil Rights Exception to the Filibuster." https://policycommons.net/artifacts/4144797/the-case-for-a-civil-rights-exception-to-the-filibuster/4953335/ (December 3, 2023).

Reed Jr, Adolph. 2013. "Marx, Race, and Neoliberalism." In *New Labor Forum*, 22(1): 49–57

Reeves, Keith. 1997. *Voting Hopes or Fears?: White Voters, Black Candidates & Racial Politics in America*. Oxford University Press.

Reingold, Beth. 1992. "Concepts of Representation Among Female and Male State Legislators." *Legislative Studies Quarterly*, 17(4): 509–37.

Reny, Tyler. T, Ali A. Valenzuela, and Loren Collingwood. 2020. "'No, You're Olaying the Race Card': Testing the Effects of Anti-Black, Anti-Latino, and Anti-Immigrant Appeals in the Post-Obama Era." *Political Psychology*, 41(2):.283–302.

Reny, Tyler T., and Benjamin J. Newman. 2021. "The Opinion-Mobilizing Effect of Social Protest Against Police Violence: Evidence From the 2020 George Floyd Protests." *American Political Science Review*, 115(4): 1499–507.

Rich, Wilbur. 2007. *African American Perspectives on Political Science*. Temple University Press.

Ricks, Byron D'Andra Orey, and Boris E. 2007. "A Systematic Analysis of the Deracialization Concept." In *The Expanding Boundaries of Black Politics*, Routledge.

Roberts, Margaret E., et al. 2014. "Structural Topic Models for Open-Ended Survey Responses." *American Journal of Political Science*, 58(4): 1064–82.

Robnett, Belinda. 1997. "Commentary and Debate: Formal Titles and Bridge Leaders: Reply to Keys." *American Journal of Sociology*, 102(6): 1698–1701.

2000. *How Long? How Long?: African American Women in the Struggle for Civil Rights*. Oxford University Press.

Robnett, Belinda, and Katherine Tate. 2023 *Gendered Pluralism*. University of Michigan Press.

Rocca, Michael S., Gabriel R. Sanchez, and Jason L. Morin. 2011. "The Institutional Mobility of Minority Members of Congress." *Political Research Quarterly*, 64(4): 897–909.

Rosenberg, Howard, and Charles S. Feldman. 2008. *No Time to Think: The Menace of Media Speed and the 24-Hour News Cycle*. A&C Black.

Russell, Annelise. 2021. *Tweeting Is Leading: How Senators Communicate and Represent in the Age of Twitter*. Oxford University Press.

Schaffner, Brian F. 2006. "Local News Coverage and the Incumbency Advantage in the U.S. House." *Legislative Studies Quarterly*, 31(4): 491–511.

Schulze, Corina. 2013. "Women, Earmarks, and Substnative Representation." *Journal of Women, Politics & Policy*, 34(2): 138–58.

Schwindt-Bayer, Leslie A., and William Mishler. 2005. "An Integrated Model of Women's Representation." *The Journal of Politics*, 67(2): 407–28.

Seamster, Louise, and Raphaël Charron-Chénier. 2017. "Predatory Inclusion and Education Debt: Rethinking the Racial Wealth Gap." *Social Currents*, 4(3): 199–207.

Sekimoto, Kenshin, Yoshifumi Seki, Mitsuo Yoshida, and Kyoji Umemura. 2020. "The Metrics of Keywords to Understand the Difference between Retweet and Like in Each Category." In *2020 IEEE/WIC/ACM International Joint Conference on Web Intelligence and Intelligent Agent Technology (WI-IAT)*, 560–67.

Serra, George, and David Moon. 1994. "Casework, Issue Positions, and Voting in Congressional Elections: A District Analysis." *The Journal of Politics*, 56(1): 200–13.
"Local News Coverage and the Incumbency Advantage in the US House." *Legislative Studies Quarterly*, 31(4): 491–511.
Shah, Paru, and Robert S. Smith. 2021. "Legacies of Segregation and Disenfranchisement: The Road from Plessy to Frank and Voter ID Laws in the United States." *RSF: The Russell Sage Foundation Journal of the Social Sciences*, 7(1): 134–46.
Sharma, Sanjay. 2013. "Black Twitter? Racial Hashtags, Networks and Contagion." *New Formations* 78(78): 46–64.
Shogan, Colleen J. 2001. "Speaking Out: An Analysis of Democratic and Republican Woman Invoked Rhetoric of the 105th Congress." *Women & Politics* 23 (1/2):129–146. doi:10.1300/J014v23n01_08.
Shorette, Kristen, Megan Thiele, and Catherine Bolzendahl. 2021. "Degrees of Support: State Spending on Higher Education and Public Postsecondary Degrees across State Legislatures, 2005 and 2014." *Socius*, 7: 23780231211009992.
Simas, Elizabeth N. 2018. "Perceptions of the Heterogeneity of Party Elites in the United States." *Party Politics*, 24(4): 444–54.
Simas, Elizabeth N., Kerri Milita, and John Barry Ryan. 2021. "Ambiguous Rhetoric and Legislative Accountability." *The Journal of Politics*, 83(4): 1695–1705.
Simien, Evelyn M. 2005. "Race, Gender, and Linked Fate." *Journal of Black Studies* 35(5): 529–50.
Sinclair, Barbara. 2016. *Unorthodox Lawmaking: New Legislative Processes in the U.S. Congress*. CQ Press.
Sinclair-Chapman, Valeria N. 2018. "(De)Constructing Symbols: Charlottesville, the Confederate Flag, and a Case for Disrupting Symbolic Meaning." *Politics, Groups, and Identities*, 6(2): 316–23.
   2002. *Symbols and Substance: How Black Constituents Are Collectively Represented in the United States Congress through Roll-Call Voting and Bill Sponsorship*. The Ohio State University.
Slakoff, Danielle C. 2013. *Newsworthiness and the "Missing White Woman Syndrome."* California State University, Long Beach.
Smith, Robert C. 1996. "We Have No Leaders: African Americans in the Post-Civil Rights Era." State University of New York Press.
Smith, Robert C., Cedric Johnson, and Robert G. Newby. 2014. *What Has This Got to Do with the Liberation of Black People?: The Impact of Ronald W. Walters on African American Thought and Leadership*. SUNY Press.
Smooth, Wendy G. 2013. "Intersectionality from Theoretical Framework to Policy Intervention." In *Situating Intersectionality: Politics, Policy, and Power*, The Politics of Intersectionality, ed. Angelia R. Wilson. New York: Palgrave Macmillan US, 11–41.
Sobolewska, Maria, Rebecca McKee, and Rosie Campbell. 2018. "Explaining Motivation to Represent: How Does Descriptive Representation Lead to Substantive Representation of Racial and Ethnic Minorities?" *West European Politics*, 41(6): 1237–61.

Stephens-Dougan, LaFleur. 2020. *Race to the Bottom: How Racial Appeals Work in American Politics*. University of Chicago Press.
   2021. "The Persistence of Racial Cues and Appeals in American Elections." *Annual Review of Political Science*, 24: 301–20.
Stout, Christopher T. 2015. *Bringing Race Back In: Black Politicians, Deracialization, and Voting Behavior in the Age of Obama*. University of Virginia Press.
   2020. *The Case for Identity Politics: Polarization, Demographic Change, and Racial Appeals*. University of Virginia Press.
Stout, Christopher T., Kristine Coulter, and Bree Edwards. 2017. "Black Representation, Intersectionality, and Politicians' Responses to Black Social Movements on Twitter." *Mobilization*, 22(4): 493–509.
Stout, C.T., Katherine Tate, and Meghan Wilson, 2021. "Does Black Representation Matter? A Review of Descriptive Representation for African Americans in Legislative Offices." *National Review of Black Politics*, 2(1): 2–21.
Stout, C.T., and Keith Baker. 2018. "How Increasing Party Diversity May Lead to Worsening Reported Racial Attitudes." *Social Science Quarterly*, 99(5): 1765–75.
Strolovitch, D.Z. 2008. *Affirmative Advocacy: Race, Class, and Gender in Interest Group Politics*. University of Chicago Press.
Sulkin, Tracy. 2009. "Campaign Appeals and Legislative Action." *The Journal of Politics*, 71(3): 1093–1108.
   2011. *The Legislative Legacy of Congressional Campaigns*. Cambridge University Press.
Sulkin, Tracy., Paul Testa, and Kaye Usry. 2015. "What Gets Rewarded? Legislative Activity and Constituency Approval." *Political Research Quarterly*, 68(4): 690–702.
Svolik, Milan W. 2013. "Learning to Love Democracy: Electoral Accountability and the Success of Democracy." *American Journal of Political Science*, 57(3): 685–702.
Swain, Carol M. 1995. "The Future of Black Representation." *American Prospect* 2: 1–5.
   (Carol Miller). "Black Faces, Black Interests: The Representation of African Americans in Congress." *(No Title)*. https://cir.nii.ac.jp/crid/1130000796060648832 (December 3, 2023).
Swers, Michele L. 2002. *The Difference Women Make: The Policy Impact of Women in Congress*. University of Chicago Press.
Tajfel, Henri, and John C. Turner. 1982 "The Social Identity Theory of Intergroup Behavior." In *Political Psychology*, eds. John T. Jost and Jim Sidanius. Psychology Press, 276–93. https://www.taylorfrancis.com/books/9781135151355/chapters/10.4324/9780203505984-16 (December 3, 2023).
Tate, Katherine. 1994. *From Protest to Politics: The New Black Voters in American Elections*. Harvard University Press.
   2003. "Black Opinion on the Legitimacy of Racial Redistricting and Minority-Majority Districts." *American Political Science Review*, 97(1): 45–56.
   2004. *Black Faces in the Mirror: African Americans and Their Representatives in the U.S. Congress*. Princeton University Press.

2010. *What's Going On?: Political Incorporation and the Transformation of Black Public Opinion.* Georgetown University Press.

2014. *Concordance: Black Lawmaking in the US Congress from Carter to Obama.* University of Michigan Press.

Teague, Greyson. 2024. "Oscar DePriest and Black Agency in American Politics, 1928–1934." *Journal of Policy History*, 36(1): 134–60.

Tesler, Michael. 2016. "Post-Racial or Most-Racial?: Race and Politics in the Obama Era." In *Post-Racial or Most-Racial?*, University of Chicago Press. https://www.degruyter.com/document/doi/10.7208/9780226353159/html (December 3, 2023).

Tesler, Michael, and David O. Sears. 2010. *Obama's Race: The 2008 Election and the Dream of a Post-Racial America.* University of Chicago Press.

Thomas, Scott, and Bernard, Grofman. 1993. "The Effects of Congressional Rules About Bill Cosponsorship on Duplicate Bills: Changing Incentives for Credit Claiming." *Public Choice*, 75(1): 93–98.

Thomsen, Danielle M. 2020. "Ideology and Gender in US House Elections." *Political Behavior*, 42: 415–42.

Tillery, Alvin B. 2019. "What Kind of Movement Is Black Lives Matter? The View from Twitter." *Journal of Race, Ethnicity, and Politics*, 4(2): 297–323.

Tomz, Michael, and Robert P. Van Houweling. 2009. "The Electoral Implications of Candidate Ambiguity." *American Political Science Review*, 103(1): 83–98.

Towler, Christopher C., Nyron N. Crawford, and Robert A. Bennett. 2020. "Shut Up and Play: Black Athletes, Protest Politics, and Black Political Action." *Perspectives on Politics*, 18(10): 111–27.

Towner, Terri L., and David A. Dulio. 2013. "New Media and Political Marketing in the United States: 2012 and Beyond." In *Political Marketing in Retrospective and Prospective*, Routledge.

Treul, Sarah, Danielle M. Thomsen, Craig Volden, and Alan E. Wiseman. 2022. "The Primary Path for Turning Legislative Effectiveness into Electoral Success." *The Journal of Politics*, 84(3): 1714–26.

Trilling, Damian, Petro Tolochko, and Björn Burscher. 2017. "From Newsworthiness to Shareworthiness: How to Predict News Sharing Based on Article Characteristics." *Journalism & Mass Communication Quarterly*, 94(1): 38–60.

Tyson, Vanessa. 2016. *Twist of Fate: Multiracial Coalitions and Minority Representation in the US House of Representatives.* Oxford University Press.

Valentino, Nicholas A., Fabian G. Neuner, and L. Matthew Vandenbroek. 2018. "The Changing Norms of Racial Political Rhetoric and the End of Racial Priming." *The Journal of Politics*, 80(3): 757–71.

Vishwanath, Arjun. 2025. "Race, Legislative Speech, and Symbolic Representation in Congress." *American Journal of Political Science*, 69(2): 578–93.

Volden, Craig, and Alan E. Wiseman. 2018. "Legislative Effectiveness in the United States Senate." *The Journal of Politics*, 80(2): 731–35.

Wäckerle, Jens, and Bruno Castanho Silva. 2023. "Distinctive Voices: Political Speech, Rhetoric, and the Substantive Representation of Women in European Parliaments." *Legislative Studies Quarterly*, 48(4): 797–831.

Wallace, Sophia J. 2014. "Representing Latinos: Examining Descriptive and Substantive Representation in Congress." *Political Research Quarterly*, 67(4): 917–29.
Walton Jr., Hanes, 1985. *Invisible Politics: Black Political Behavior*. State University of New York Press.
Walton Jr., Hanes, Robert C. Smith, and Sherri L. Wallace. 2017. *American Politics and the African American Quest for Universal Freedom*, 8th ed. Routledge.
  2020. *American Quest for Universal Freedom*, 9th ed. New York: Routledge.
Wamble, Julian. 2018. "Show Us That You Care: How Community Commitment Signals Affect Black Political Consideration." http://hdl.handle.net/1903/20965 (December 3, 2023).
Weitzer, Ronald, and Steven A. Tuch. 2002. "Perceptions of Racial Profiling: Race, Class, and Personal Experience*." *Criminology*, 40(2): 435–56.
Wetts, Rachel, and Robb Willer. 2022. "Antiracism and Its Discontents: The Prevalence and Political Influence of Opposition to Antiracism among White Americans." https://doi.org/10.31235/osf.io/xvcf2.
Whitby, Kenny J. 1997. *The Color of Representation*. University of Michigan Press.
  2000. *The Color of Representation: Congressional Behavior and Black Interests*. University of Michigan Press.
White, Ismail K., and Chryl N. Laird. 2020. "Steadfast Democrats: How Social Forces Shape Black Political Behavior." In *Steadfast Democrats*, Princeton University Press. https://www.degruyter.com/document/doi/10.1515/9780691201962/html (December 3, 2023).
Wilkinson, Betina Cutaia. 2014. "Perceptions of Commonality and Latino–Black, Latino–White Relations in a Multiethnic United States." *Political Research Quarterly*, 67(4): 905–16.
Wilson, William J. 1987. *The Truly Disadvantaged: The Inner City, the Underclass, and Public Policy*. University of Chicago Press.
  2011. "The Declining Significance of Race: Revisited & Revised." *Daedalus*, 140(2): 55–69.
  2015. *Partners or Rivals?: Power and Latino, Black, and White Relations in the Twenty-First Century*. University of Virginia Press.
Williams, Linda F. 1990. "White/Black Perceptions of the Electability of Black Political Candidates." *Black Electoral Politics*. Routledge: 45–64.
Williams, Melissa S. 2000. *Voice, Trust, and Memory: Marginalized Groups and the Failings of Liberal Representation*. Princeton University Press.
Wilson, William Julius. 2012. *The Truly Disadvantaged: The Inner City, the Underclass, and Public Policy*. University of Chicago Press.
Wright Austin, Sharon D. 2023. *Political Black Girl Magic: The Elections and Governance of Black Female Mayors*. Philadelphia: Temple University Press.
  2018. "The Declining Significance of Race: Blacks and Changing American Institutions." In *Inequality in the 21st Century*, Routledge.
Zarate, Marques G. "How Voting History and Issue Type Shape Perceptions of Political Pandering."
  2022. "Perceptions of Pandering and Political Trust."

Index

Abolitionist movement, 215
abortion, 73, 125
Adams, Alma, 8, 22, 114, 215
Adams, John, 96
African Americans
  assimilation of, 58
  and gerrymandering, 194
  and law enforcement, 53
AIDS, 122, 125
Ali, Muhammed, 121
Amendments to the US Constitution, 200
American Civil Liberties Union (ACLU), 136
anti-DEI, 214
approval ratings, 149, 151
  Black respondents, 161, 165–67, 178–79, 182, 184
  and legislative performance, 173, 175–76
  and racial outreach, 152
  White liberal respondents, 161–63
  White moderate/conservative respondents, 163–64
  White respondents, 167–68, 179–80
Arbery, Ahmaud, 75, 77, 86, 105, 211
Asian Americans
  assimilation of, 54, 58
  and Black-related issues, 63
  competition with, 54
  cooperation with, 56
  and gender, 57
Austin, Sharon Wright, 64, 152

Babin, Brian, 126
Bai, Matt, 191
Barragan, Nannette, 122
Bass, Karen, 199
Beatty, Joyce, 93, 97
Biden, Joe, 205
Black Americans. *See* African Americans
Black History Month, 11, 74, 121, 215
Black Lives Matter, 21–22, 25, 72, 77, 84–90, 118, 122–23, 125, 129, 135, 153, 155, 187, 201, 211, 214
Blacks. *See* African Americans
Blige, Mary J., 9
Boko Haram, 9–10
Bond, Julian, 121
Booker, Cory, 199
Boycott, Divestment and Sanctions (BDS) Movement, 44–48
brand, 28, 30, 36–39, 41
Braun, Carol Moseley, 112
Brewer, Roz, 114
#Bringbackourgirls, 9
Broockman, David E., 53
Brooks, Mo, 83
Brown, Anthony G., 99
Brown, LaTosha, 131
Brown, Michael, 84, 90, 211
Brown, Nadia E., 57, 64
brutality, police. *See* violence, police
Buck, Ken, 216
Bush, Cori, 15, 204
business owners, 73

Butler, Daniel M., 175
Byrne, Bradley, 81

Cardenas, Tony, 125
Castile, Philando, 211
Centers for Disease Control (CDC), 204
Chauvin, Derek, 155
childcare centers, safety in, 121
Chisholm, Shirley, 51, 217
Chu, Judy, 103
Civil Rights Act, 140, 200
Civil Rights Movement, 7, 58, 66, 74, 215
Clardy, Brittany, 188, 206
Clarke, Yvette, 83
Clyburn, James, 83
Cohen, Steve, 71, 88
Cole, Tom, 88
Coleman, Bonnie Watson, 189
Collaborative Multiracial Post-Election Survey, 174
Collingwood, Loren, 152
Commission to Study and Develop Reparation Proposals for African Americans Act, 137
committees, 35–36, 39
communications directors, 18, 24, 28, 76
  on committee assignments, 35–36
  constituent outreach, 31–33
  and legislators' backgrounds, 33
  and proactive rhetorical representation, 30–31, 36–39
  and reactive rhetorical representation, 40–42
  sample, 29
communities
  Black, 47
  Latino, 47
  LGBTQIA+, 47, 73
Congressional Asian Pacific American Caucus (CAPAC), 123
Congressional Black Caucus (CBC), 14, 50, 123, 157, 174, 215
Congressional Caucus on Black Women and Girls, 188
Congressional Hispanic Caucus (CHC), 123
Congressional Tri-Caucus, 123
constituents, 38
  trust of, 10, 31, 131, 173
Conyers, John Jr., 116
Costa, Mia, 152
countlove.org, 21

COVID-19, 15, 92, 100–1, 116, 122–23, 125, 204, 213
  and financial strain, 92
  and race, 193
  as uncrystallized policy issue, 104–6
Crane, Eli, 14
Crow, Jason, 88
Cummings, Elijah, 45, 116, 121, 130

Daughters of the Confederacy, 112, 115
Davis, Danny, 93
Dellums, Ron, 83
Democratic Party, 14, 191
Democratic Policy and Communications Committee (DPCC), 42
Democratic Women's Caucus, 157
DePriest, Oscar, 50
diabetes, 122, 125
Dietrich, Bryce J., 6, 17, 159, 219
disasters, natural, 40
discrimination, racial, 9
  employment, 26, 176, 178, 180, 184, 186
  polling about, 55
districts, legislative, 60, 67
diversity in media, 121
Dowe, Pearl K. Ford, 57, 64

Edelman, Murray J., 6
Ellison, Keith, 103
Emancipation Proclamation, 70
Emanuel AME church shooting, 74, 116, 211, 226
employment discrimination, 159
enslavement, 9, 70, 200
environmentalism, 28
ephrame.com, 21
Equitable Data Collection and Disclosure on COVID-19 Act, 105
Eulau, Heinz, 5
Evangelicals, 73

Facebook, 13, 28, 34
filibusters, 196
flag, Confederate, 72, 112, 212
Floyd, George, 3, 17, 22, 29, 74–75, 77, 85–86, 101–5, 118, 125, 130, 135, 155, 187–88, 196, 202, 211, 216
FUTURE Act, 140

Gallego, Ruben, 122
Garcia, Jennifer, 154

Gay, Claudine, 64
George Floyd Justice in Policing Act, 121, 197, 216
Gerber, Alan S., 175
gerrymandering, 195
Gillespie, Andra, 58
Gillion, Daniel Q., 133–35
Goodson, Casey Jr., 75
Google Trends, 85
Gosar, Paul, 126
Grimmer, Justin, 175, 222
Grose, Christian R., 12
gun control, 22
gun owners, 73

Haines, Pavielle E., 133–34
hair care, 9
Hamilton, Dontre, 89
Hargrave, Lotte, 175
Harris, Andrea, 114
Harris, Mark (hypothetical person), 156, 165, 177, 181, 194
Hatch, Orrin, 14
Hathaway, Anne, 9
Hawkesworth, Mary, 15
Hayes, Dennisha, 131
Hayes, Matthew, 6, 17, 159, 219
Helms, Jesse, 14
Hero, Rodney E., 55
HEROES Act, 105
Hill, Andre, 75
Hill, French, 120
Historically Black Colleges and Universities (HBCUs), 21, 34, 120, 140, 214
Hogan, Larry, 99
Hope, E.C., 112
Horsford, Steven, 97
Hoyer, Steny, 99

identity, 2, 12, 29–30, 44, 46, 48
  legislative, 28, 34–35, 39, 49, 137
  racial, 30, 52, 201
Ifill, Gwen, 121, 188
Imai, Kosuke, 226
immigration, 32, 34, 40
inequality, 8–9
  and crime, 22
  and education, 110, 121
  and health care, 15–16, 22, 92, 98, 100, 121, 125
  and welfare, 22
  employment, 92
  political, 16, 194
  wealth, 16
Internal Revenue Service (IRS), 100
intersectionality, 56, 129, 192

Jackson, Mary W., 83
Jenkins, Andrea, 1
John R. Lewis Voting Rights Advancement Act of 2021, 137
Johnson, Derrick, 197, 199
Johnson, Dion, 85
Johnson, Kira, 22, 215
Juneteenth, 70–71, 121, 202, 215
Just and Unifying Solutions to Invigorate Communities Everywhere (JUSTICE) Act, 85, 88, 197
JUSTICE Act, 120, 125
Justice in Policing Act, 85, 88, 157

Kaiser Family Foundation, 109
Karps, Paul D., 5
Kavanaugh, Brett, 194
Kelly, Robin, 83, 114, 188
Kennedy, Joe III, 93
Khanna, Ro, 83
King, Martin Luther Jr., 45, 72, 74, 79, 116, 191, 193, 217
Kira Johnson Act, 215
Kirkpatrick, Ann, 125

Laird, Chryl, 13
Latino/a Americans
  assimilation of, 54, 58
  and Black-related issues, 63
  competition with, 54
  cooperation with, 56
  and gender, 57
Leadership Conference on Civil and Human Rights (LCCR), 132
Lee, Barbara, 14, 71, 83, 90, 93, 98, 105, 125
Lee, Sheila Jackson, 70–71
Legal Assistance to Prevent Evictions Act of 2020, 83
legislation, Congressional, 38, 76, 79, 133
  correlation with rhetorical representation, 147, 180–85
  co-sponsorship of, 3, 138, 141–42
  sponsorship of, 3, 137
Lewis, John, 29, 81, 116, 123, 130

Lieu, Ted, 88
linked fate, 13
Lorenz-Spreen, Philipp, 200
Lowenthal, Alan, 126
Lowery, Jameek, 85
Luper, Clara, 74
Luria, Elaine, 105

Manney, Christopher, 89
Mansbridge, Jane, 25, 94–98, 106–8, 193
marginalization, 33
   in Congress, 15
   and gender, 57
Martin Luther King Jr. Day, 215
Martin, Trayvon, 85
mass shootings, 40
maternal health, 122, 125, 212, 215
McAtee, David, 75
McCarthy, Kevin, 93
McCormick, Sheila Cherfilus, 2
McDonald, Laquan, 88
McKinney, Cynthia, 53
Meier, K.J., 55
microtargeting, 72
Middleton, Richard T. IV, 152
Minta, Michael D., 112
Mishler, William, 4
Moody, Anne, 121
Moon, David, 152
Moore, Gwen, 71, 89
Moseley-Braun, Carol, 14
Murry, George, 121
Musk, Elon, 202

NAACP, 55, 140, 197, 199, 215
National Hispanic Leadership Agenda, 55
National Rifle Association (NRA), 136
newspapers, Black-focused, 76
Nichols, Tyre, 43

Obama, Barack, 2, 134, 154, 190–91, 196, 211
Obama, Michelle, 9
outreach
   high-profile, 77–81, 155
   low-profile, 77–78, 81, 139, 147, 150, 155–56

Pallone, Frank, 106
Palmer, Alberto, 188

pandering, perceptions of, 135, 137, 144, 147, 151, 154–55, 170–71
Paycheck Protection Program (PPP), 93, 97
Peay, Periloux, 15
Pelosi, Nancy, 93, 205
Pitkin, Hanna, 4–5
Planned Parenthood, 136
Pocan, Mark, 88
polarization, growth of, 196
police reform, 53, 118, 123, 125, 129, 155, 159, 161–64, 168, 176, 196, 215
policy issues, uncrystallized, 94–96, 99–104
Pope, Devin G., 113
power, post-racial, 2
press releases, 18–19, 61, 63, 71, 75, 78–81, 210
   Black-centered outreach, 115–16
   and Black Lives Matter, 85
   and COVID-19, 94, 104
   and race-based outreach, 111, 143
   and uncrystallized policy issues, 94, 99, 101
Pressley, Ayanna, 8
Preuhs, Robert R., 55
process, legislative
   aggregative stage, 95
   deliberative stage, 95
Psaki, Jen, 205

race
   and gender, 56–58
   and legislative identity, 7, 34, 44
   and partisanship, 59–60
   and public discourse, 8
racism, 13–14, 22, 33, 66, 73, 111–15, 134, 168, 187, 215
   movements against, 190, See also Black Lives Matter
reelection, 28, 54, 60, 72, 149, 151, 174
reparations, 9, 73
representation, political
   descriptive, 4, 52–53, 190, 192, 205
   formal, 4–5
   substantive, 4–5, 52
   symbolic, 4
representation, rhetorical, 2
   advantages of, 199
   and age, 58–59, 66
   breadth of, 115
   and communication, 17
   constituent response to, 149
   and district populations, 60

    and gender, 57, 64
    and silence, 42–43
  legislation, 179
    and partisanship, 66
    proactive, 3, 8, 12, 25–26, 30, 44–48, 71, 78, 94, 110, 133, 139, 150, 159, 206
    proactive racial, 191–93
    racial, 21, 29, 51, 63, 110, 118–23, 126–29, 171, 175, 189
    reactive, 3, 8, 29, 40–42, 139–40, 150
    risks of, 28
  representation, surrogate, 46
  representatives, Asian American, 64, 81, 122, 126
    and age, 66
  representatives, Black, 6, 81, 126
    Black identity of, 50–51
    and partisanship, 66
    personal background of, 33
    racial rhetorical representation, 189
    social media, 38
    social networks of, 34, 45, 115
    specialties of, 33–35, 139
    and uncrystallized policy issues, 94
  representatives, Latino/a, 64, 81, 111, 122, 126
    and age, 66
  representatives, White, 81, 111, 118
    and age, 66
    Democrats, 126
    and partisanship, 59
    and racial discrimination, 58
    and racial outreach, 155
    Republicans, 126
  responsiveness
    allocation, 5
    policy, 5
    service, 5
    symbolic, 5–6, 26
  Robinson, Tony, 88
  Rodgers, Cathy McMorris, 120
  Rush, Bobby, 100, 103, 188

  Salaam, Yussef, 1
  Sasaki, Tomoya, 226
  Schakowsky, Jan, 81
  Schiff, Adam, 157
  Schumer, Chuck, 205
  Schwindt-Bayer, Leslie, 4
  Scott, Tim, 14, 53
  Scottsboro boys, 50

Sennsenbrenner, Jim, 120
Serra, George, 152
Sewell, Terri, 93
Shenker-Osorio, Anat, 205
sickle cell anemia, 215
sickle cell disease (SCD), 93
Simas, Elizabeth N., 173
Simien, Evelyn M., 57, 64
Smith, Jessica C., 175
Smith, Robert C., 190
social media, 44, 201–2
STARZ, 104
Stephanopoulos, George, 211
Sterling, Alton, 211
Stewart, Brandon M., 222
Stokes, Louis, 13, 50, 121
Stout, Christopher, 152, 154
Strength in Diversity Act, 120
Sulkin, Tracy, 133
Supreme Court of the United States, 194

Taliaferro, Ray, 121
Tate, Katherine, 58, 64, 191
Taylor, Breonna, 75, 77, 85–86, 105, 211
Tester, Jon, 4
Thevenin, Edson, 85
Treul, Sarah, 173
Trone, David, 157
Trump, Donald J., 11, 92, 116, 125, 211–12
Twitter, 18–21, 28, 61, 63, 71, 75, 78–81, 83, 200–1, 210, 215
  Black, 201
  and Black Lives Matter, 85
  and Black-centered outreach, 115–16, 123, 130
  change to X, 202–4
  and COVID-19, 94, 104
  and race-based outreach, 111, 143
Tyson, Vanessa, 55

Underwood, Lauren, 8
Unite the Right Rally, 11, 120

Veasey, Marc, 105
violence, gun, 121
violence, police, 16–17, 40, 75, 116, 187, 200
violence, racial, 74
Volden, Craig, 175
voters, Black, 7
  and empathy, 152
  and racial issues, 154

voters, White
   and discrimination, 153
voting rights, 11, 29, 109–10, 116, 123, 125, 129, 135, 155, 174
Voting Rights Act, 75, 81, 120, 194, 200

Walker-Peddakotla, Arti, 205
Wamble, Julian, 152
Waters, Maxine, 83, 103

Wheeler, Tom, 103
White supremacy, 11, 29, 72, 120, 123
White, Ismail K., 13
Wilson, Frederica, 10, 89
Wiseman, Alan E., 175
woke political agenda, 3
women, 47, 56–58, 64

Zeldin, Lee, 125

For EU product safety concerns, contact us at Calle de José Abascal, 56–1°, 28003 Madrid, Spain or eugpsr@cambridge.org.

www.ingramcontent.com/pod-product-compliance
Ingram Content Group UK Ltd.
Pitfield, Milton Keynes, MK11 3LW, UK
UKHW022004250126
467190UK00019B/358